Reading STREET

Grade **4**

Scott Foresman

Reader's and Writer's Notebook

Glenview, Illinois • Boston, Massachusetts • Chandler, Arizona •
Upper Saddle River, New Jersey

Copyright © by Pearson Education, Inc., or its affiliates. All Rights Reserved. Printed in the United States of America. This publication is protected by copyright, and permission should be obtained from the publisher prior to any prohibited reproduction, storage in a retrieval system, or transmission in any form or by any means, electronic, mechanical, photocopying, recording, or likewise. The publisher hereby grants permission to reproduce these pages, in part or in whole, for classroom use only, the number not to exceed the number of students in each class. Notice of copyright must appear on all pages. For information regarding permissions, write to Pearson Curriculum Group Rights & Permissions, One Lake Street, Upper Saddle River, New Jersey 07458.

Pearson, Scott Foresman, and Pearson Scott Foresman are trademarks, in the U.S. and/or other countries, of Pearson Education, Inc., or its affiliates.

ISBN-13: 978-0-328-47673-2
ISBN-10:   0-328-47673-0

11 12 13 14 V011 18 17 16 15 14 13

CC1

Unit 1: Turning Points

Unit 2: Teamwork

Unit 3: Patterns in Nature

Unit 4: Puzzles and Mysteries

Unit 5: Adventures by Land, Air, and Water

Unit 6: Reaching for Goals

Name _____

Unit 1 Independent Reading Log

© Pearson Education, Inc., 4

Reading Time	Title and Author	What is it about?	How would you rate it?	Explain your rating.
From ___ to ___			Great 5 4 3 2 1 Awful	
From ___ to ___			Great 5 4 3 2 1 Awful	
From ___ to ___			Great 5 4 3 2 1 Awful	
From ___ to ___			Great 5 4 3 2 1 Awful	
From ___ to ___			Great 5 4 3 2 1 Awful	

Name _____

Unit 2 Independent Reading Log

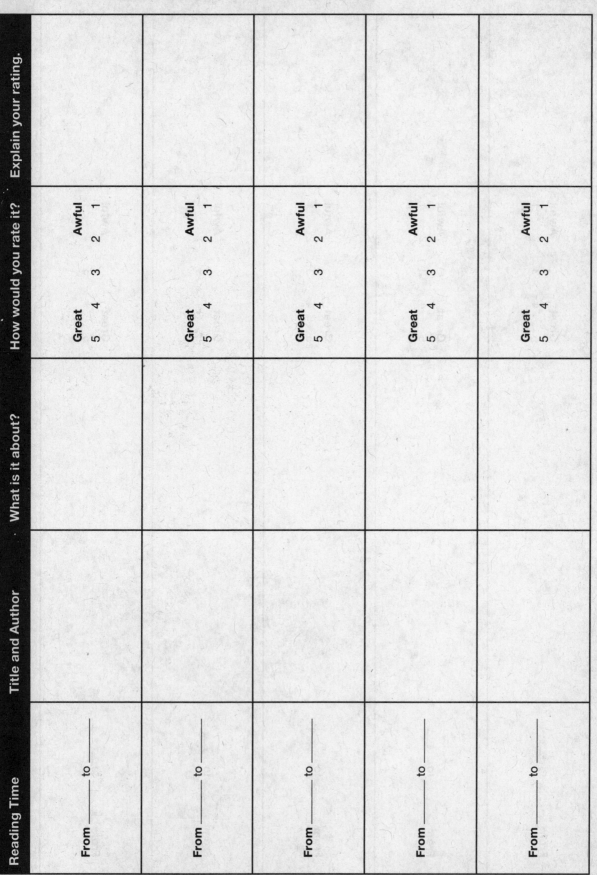

Reading Time	Title and Author	What is it about?	How would you rate it?	Explain your rating.
From ____ to ____			Great 5 4 3 2 1 Awful	
From ____ to ____			Great 5 4 3 2 1 Awful	
From ____ to ____			Great 5 4 3 2 1 Awful	
From ____ to ____			Great 5 4 3 2 1 Awful	
From ____ to ____			Great 5 4 3 2 1 Awful	

© Pearson Education, Inc., 4

Name _____

Unit 3 Independent Reading Log

Reading Time	Title and Author	What is it about?	How would you rate it?	Explain your rating.
From ____ to ____			Great 5 4 3 2 1 Awful	
From ____ to ____			Great 5 4 3 2 1 Awful	
From ____ to ____			Great 5 4 3 2 1 Awful	
From ____ to ____			Great 5 4 3 2 1 Awful	
From ____ to ____			Great 5 4 3 2 1 Awful	

© Pearson Education, Inc., 4

Name _____

Unit 4 Independent Reading Log

Reading Time	Title and Author	What is it about?	How would you rate it?	Explain your rating.
From ____ to ____			**Great** 5 4 3 2 1 **Awful**	
From ____ to ____			**Great** 5 4 3 2 1 **Awful**	
From ____ to ____			**Great** 5 4 3 2 1 **Awful**	
From ____ to ____			**Great** 5 4 3 2 1 **Awful**	
From ____ to ____			**Great** 5 4 3 2 1 **Awful**	

© Pearson Education, Inc., 4

Name _____

Unit 5 Independent Reading Log

© Pearson Education, Inc., 4

Reading Time	Title and Author	What is it about?	How would you rate it?	Explain your rating.
From ____ to ____			**Great** 5 4 3 2 1 **Awful**	
From ____ to ____			**Great** 5 4 3 2 1 **Awful**	
From ____ to ____			**Great** 5 4 3 2 1 **Awful**	
From ____ to ____			**Great** 5 4 3 2 1 **Awful**	
From ____ to ____			**Great** 5 4 3 2 1 **Awful**	

Name _____

Unit 6 Independent Reading Log

Reading Time	Title and Author	What is it about?	How would you rate it?	Explain your rating.
From ____ to ____			Great 5 4 3 2 1 Awful	
From ____ to ____			Great 5 4 3 2 1 Awful	
From ____ to ____			Great 5 4 3 2 1 Awful	
From ____ to ____			Great 5 4 3 2 1 Awful	
From ____ to ____			Great 5 4 3 2 1 Awful	

© Pearson Education, Inc., 4

Selection Title _____ **Author** _____

Realistic fiction tells the story of imaginary people and events. Characteristics of realistic fiction include the following.

- The characters seem like real people that you might know.
- The setting is realistic, such as a city or town, a school, or other places you might know.
- The plot is possible and could happen in real life.

Directions As you read *Because of Winn-Dixie,* look for examples of character, setting, and plot that make this story realistic fiction. Write those examples below.

Character _____

_____

_____

Setting _____

_____

_____

Plot _____

_____

_____

Explore the Genre

Think about the characters, setting, and plot in another story you've read that's realistic fiction. What similarities and differences do you find between that story and *Because of Winn-Dixie?* Write about it. Use a separate sheet of paper if you need more space.

_____

_____

_____

© Pearson Education, Inc., 4

Name _____

Selection Title _____ **Author** _____

Good readers ask questions as they read. **Questioning** helps us monitor our comprehension and clarify anything that's confusing. Questioning also helps to make inferences, interpret the texts we read, and promote discussion. As you read, use the following questioning strategy.

- Preview the selection and think about any questions you have about the topic.

- Read with a question in mind and make notes when you find information that addresses the question.

- Write down other questions that come up as you read and look for answers in the text.

- Remember that not all questions are answered in the text. Sometimes we have to make inferences or interpretations based on the information the author provides.

Directions As you read the selection, use the chart below to write down any questions that you have about the text in the column on the left. Write down any answers you find or inferences you make in the right hand column.

Questions	Answers, Inferences, Interpretations

© Pearson Education, Inc., 4

Name _____

Selection Title _____ **Author** _____

Background knowledge is what we already know about a topic. Using background knowledge can help us better understand what we're reading. Activate your background knowledge by doing the following.

- Preview the selection to find out what it's about.

- Think about what you already know about the topic.

- Connect the selection to your own world—to people, places, and events you already know.

Directions Use the KWL chart below to chart your background knowledge about the selection. List what you already know in the K column. Then list what you want to learn in the W column. After reading, list what you learned in the L column. Write a brief summary of the selection on a separate sheet of paper.

K	W	L

© Pearson Education, Inc., 4

Selection Title _____ Author _____

Trickster tales tell a story about an animal who outsmarts bigger, stronger characters in the story. Characteristics of a trickster tale include the following.

- The trickster character is usually mischievous and clever.
- The trickster is usually trying to gain something or escape a dangerous situation.
- The characters in the story usually learn a lesson.

Directions As you read *The Horned Toad Prince,* look for examples of a trickster character, what the trickster character gains or escapes, and what lesson is learned by the characters in the story. Write those examples below.

Trickster Character _____

_____

_____

What Is Gained or Escaped _____

_____

_____

Lesson _____

_____

_____

Explore the Genre

Think about another trickster tale that you've read. What similarities and differences do you find between that story and *The Horned Toad Prince?* Write about it. Use a separate sheet of paper if you need more space.

_____

_____

© Pearson Education, Inc., 4

Name _____

Selection Title _____ **Author** _____

Text structure refers to the way an author organizes a text. Cause and effect and compare and contrast are two types of text structure. Knowing how a text is structured can improve our comprehension. Here are ways to identify text structure.

• Before you read, preview the text. Make predictions, ask questions, and use titles, headings, and illustrations to try to identify the structure.

• As you read, look for language that gives clues to the organization.

• After reading, recall the organization and summarize the text

Directions As you preview and read the selection, write down features of the text that help you identify the text structure. Remember to ask questions, use text features, and look for language clues to identify the text structure. After reading, write the name of the text structure and a brief summary of the selection.

Before Reading _____

_____

_____

_____

During Reading _____

_____

_____

_____

Text Structure/Summary _____

_____

_____

_____

© Pearson Education, Inc., 4

Name _____

Selection Title _____ **Author** _____

Background knowledge is what we already know about a topic. Using background knowledge can help us better understand what we're reading. Activate your background knowledge by doing the following.

- Preview the selection to find out what it's about.
- Think about what you already know about the topic.
- Connect the selection to your own world—to people, places, and events you already know.

Directions Use the KWL chart below to chart your background knowledge about the selection. List what you already know in the K column. Then list what you want to learn in the W column. After reading, list what you learned in the L column. Write a brief summary of the selection on a separate sheet of paper.

K	W	L

© Pearson Education, Inc., 4

Selection Title _____ Author _____

Historical fiction, like realistic fiction, is a made-up story that may include both real and imaginary characters and events. Characteristics of historical fiction include the following.

- The story takes place in the past.
- The setting is a place that still exists or existed in the past.
- Authentic details about the characters and setting help the reader understand what it was like to live in that place at that time.

Directions As you read *Coyote School News,* look for examples of the time and place in which the story is set and the authentic details that make this story historical fiction. Write those examples below.

Time _____

_____

Place _____

_____

Authentic Details _____

_____

Explore the Genre

Think about the time, place, and authentic details in another story you've read that's historical fiction. What similarities and differences do you find between that story and *Coyote School News*? Write about it. Use a separate sheet of paper if you need more space.

_____

_____

_____

© Pearson Education, Inc., 4

Name _____

Selection Title _____ Author _____

Dramas, or plays, are stories that are to be acted out for an audience. Dramas are divided into acts and scenes. Dramas have the same story elements as other types of fiction. Story elements of dramas include the following.

- Character and setting
- Plot
- Theme

Directions As you read *Scene Two,* look for examples of the story elements of drama. Write those examples below.

Character and Setting _____

_____

_____

Plot _____

_____

_____

Theme _____

_____

_____

Explore the Genre

Think about character, setting, plot, and theme in another drama that you've read. What similarities and differences do you find between that drama and *Scene Two*? Write about it. Use a separate sheet of paper if you need more space.

_____

_____

© Pearson Education, Inc., 4

Selection Title _____ **Author** _____

Strategic readers **monitor** their understanding of what they've read and use fix-up strategies to **clarify** understanding. Ways to monitor and clarify include the following.

- Ask questions during and after reading and summarize to check your understanding.
- Adjust your reading rate, read on, or reread the section that caused confusion.
- Visualize what you are reading.
- Use text features and illustrations to help clarify the text.

Directions As you read, write down the page numbers of places that you had trouble understanding. Then describe the fix-up strategy you used to clarify the meaning.

Where in the text I had trouble: _____ _____ _____

_____ _____ _____ _____ _____

Fix-Up Strategies I Used

_____

_____

_____

_____

_____

Selection Summary

Write a two- or three-sentence summary of the selection. Use a separate sheet of paper if you need more space.

_____

_____

_____

_____

© Pearson Education, Inc., 4

Name _____

Selection Title _____ **Author** _____

When we **infer**, we use our background knowledge with information from the text to come up with our own ideas about what we're reading. To infer, or make inferences, try the following steps.

- Think about what you already know about the topics.
- Combine what you know with information from the text to make inferences.
- Based on your inferences, think about ideas, morals, lessons, or themes in the text.

Directions As you read the selection, use your background knowledge and clues from the text to make inferences. Use the chart below to show how you made your inferences. Then write a statement that summarizes the theme, moral, or lesson from the selection.

What I Know	Information from the Text	What I Infer

Statement that summarizes the theme, moral, or lesson _____

_____

_____

_____

© Pearson Education, Inc., 4

Name _____

Selection Title _____ **Author** _____

Important ideas in nonfiction texts are the main ideas and details about a topic that the author wants the reader to understand. You can do the following to help identify important ideas and details as you read.

• Preview the selection and read the title, headings, and captions.

• Look for words in special type such as italics, boldface, and bulleted lists.

• Watch for signal words and phrases such as *for example* and *most important*.

• Use text features including photographs and illustrations, diagrams, charts, and maps.

Directions As you read the selection, use the chart below to write down any important ideas and details that you find. List any text features or signal words you used to locate these ideas. Use the important ideas and details to write a short summary of the selection.

Important Ideas	Details

Write a Summary _____

_____

_____

_____

_____

© Pearson Education, Inc., 4

Selection Title _____ **Author** _____

Text structure refers to the way an author organizes a text. Cause and effect and compare and contrast are two types of text structure. Knowing how a text is structured can improve our comprehension. Here are ways to identify text structure.

- Before you read, preview the text. Make predictions, ask questions, and use titles, headings, and illustrations to try to identify the structure.

- As you read, look for language that gives clues to the organization.

- After reading, recall the organization and summarize the text

---

Directions As you preview and read the selection, write down features of the text that help you identify the text structure. Remember to ask questions, use text features, and look for language clues to identify the text structure. After reading, write the name of the text structure and a brief summary of the selection.

Before Reading _____

_____

_____

_____

_____

During Reading _____

_____

_____

_____

_____

Text Structure/Summary _____

_____

_____

_____

_____

© Pearson Education, Inc., 4

Name _____

Selection Title _____ Author _____

Myths are old stories that have been passed down through word of mouth for hundreds of years. Some myths have many different versions depending on the culture. Characteristics of myths include the following.

- The beliefs of a particular culture are reflected in the story.
- Characters are usually gods, goddesses, and humans interacting with natural forces.
- The plot often centers around events that try to explain a force of nature.

Directions As you read *How Night Came from the Sea,* look for examples of a particular culture, characters such as gods, goddesses, and humans, and events that try to explain nature. These elements make this story a myth. Write those examples below.

Culture _____

_____

_____

Characters _____

_____

_____

Events _____

_____

_____

Explore the Genre

Think about the culture, characters, and events in another story you've read that's a myth. What similarities and differences do you find between that story and *How Night Came from the Sea*? Write about it. Use a separate sheet of paper if you need more space.

_____

© Pearson Education, Inc., 4

Selection Title _____ **Author** _____

When we **predict,** we tell what we think might happen in a selection. Predictions are based on our preview or what we've already read. We **set a purpose** to guide our reading. We can do the following to predict and set a purpose.

- Read the title and the author's name. Look at the illustrations and other text features.
- Think about why you're reading and set a purpose.
- Use your prior knowledge—what you already know—to make a prediction.
- As you read, check and change your prediction based on new information.

Directions Preview the selection. Make a prediction and set a purpose for reading the selection. As you read, check your predictions and set a new purpose as necessary. When you finish reading, write a summary of the selection.

Before Reading
Make a Prediction _____

_____

Purpose for Reading _____

_____

During Reading
Check and Change Prediction _____

_____

Set a New Purpose _____

_____

After Reading
Write a Summary _____

_____

_____

© Pearson Education, Inc., 4

Name _____

Selection Title _____ Author _____

A **tall tale** is a humorous story that uses realistic details to tell a story about characters and events that are impossible. Characteristics of a tall tale include the following.

- Many details are from everyday life.
- Characters are greatly exaggerated.
- The events described could not really happen.

Directions As you read *Paul Bunyan,* look for examples of realistic details, exaggerated characters, and impossible events that make the story a tall tale. Write those examples below.

Realistic Details _____

_____

_____

Exaggerated Characters _____

_____

_____

Impossible Events _____

_____

_____

Explore the Genre

Think about the realistic details, exaggerated characters, and impossible events in another story you've read that's a tall tale. What similarities and differences do you find between that story and *Paul Bunyan*? Write about it. Use a separate sheet of paper if you need more space.

_____

_____

© Pearson Education, Inc., 4

Selection Title _____ **Author** _____

We **visualize** to create pictures in our minds as we read. Creating pictures can help us better understand what we're reading. To visualize, try the following.

- Combine what you already know with details from the text to make a mental image.
- Think about the events of the story or selection. Use your five senses to create pictures and to try to put yourself in the story or selection.

Directions As you read the selection, use your senses to help you visualize what's happening or the information the author provides. Write down what you can see, hear, taste, smell, and touch.

See _____

_____

_____

Hear _____

_____

_____

Taste _____

_____

_____

Smell _____

_____

_____

Touch _____

_____

_____

© Pearson Education, Inc., 4

Selection Title _____ **Author** _____

Expository text tells about real people and events. Expository text is a type of expository nonfiction. Characteristics of expository text include the following.

- The topic provides information about the real world and people.
- The information in the text is factual.
- Selections often include text features such as diagrams, maps, charts, and graphs.

Directions As you read *Encantado: Pink Dolphin of the Amazon,* look for examples of expository text. Write those examples below.

Selection Topic _____

_____

_____

Facts _____

_____

_____

_____

Text Features _____

_____

_____

_____

Explore the Genre

Think about another selection you've read that is expository text. What similarities and differences do you find between that selection and *Encantado: Pink Dolphin of the Amazon*? Write about it. Use a separate sheet of paper if you need more space.

_____

_____

_____

© Pearson Education, Inc., 4

Selection Title _____ **Author** _____

Important ideas in nonfiction texts are the main ideas and details about a topic that the author wants the reader to understand. You can do the following to help identify important ideas and details as you read.

- Preview the selection and read the title, headings, and captions.
- Look for words in special type such as italics, boldface, and bulleted lists.
- Watch for signal words and phrases such as *for example* and *most important.*
- Use text features including photographs and illustrations, diagrams, charts, and maps.

Directions As you read the selection, use the chart below to write down any important ideas and details that you find. List any text features or signal words you used to locate these ideas. Use the important ideas and details to write a short summary of the selection.

Important Ideas	Details

Write a Summary _____

_____

_____

_____

© Pearson Education, Inc., 4

Selection Title _____ Author _____

A **biography** tells the story of all or part of a real person's life. Events in the person's life are generally told in the order that they happen. Characteristics of a biography include the following.

- The subject is part or all of the life of a real person.
- The events in the person's life are told in the order that they happened.
- Events are told in a third-person narration, using *he, she, him,* or *her* when referring to the person.

Directions As you read *Seeker of Knowledge,* look for elements that make this selection a biography: the subject is a person, events are in sequential order, and they are narrated by third person. Write examples of those elements below.

Subject _____

_____

_____

Events _____

_____

_____

Third-person Narration _____

_____

_____

Explore the Genre

Think about another selection you've read that is a biography. What similarities and differences do you find between that biography and *Seeker of Knowledge*? Write about it. Use a separate sheet of paper if you need more space.

_____

© Pearson Education, Inc., 4

Name _____

Selection Title _____ Author _____

Strategic readers **monitor** their understanding of what they've read and use fix-up strategies to **clarify** understanding. Ways to monitor and clarify include the following.

- Ask questions during and after reading, and summarize to check your understanding.
- Adjust your reading rate, read on, or reread the section that caused confusion.
- Visualize what you are reading.
- Use text features and illustrations to help clarify the text.

Directions As you read, write down the page numbers of places that you had trouble understanding. Then describe the fix-up strategy you used to clarify the meaning.

Where in the text I had trouble: _____ _____ _____

_____

Fix-up Strategies I Used

_____

_____

_____

_____

_____

Selection Summary

Write a two- or three-sentence summary of the selection. Use a separate sheet of paper if you need more space.

_____

_____

_____

_____

© Pearson Education, Inc., 4

Name _____

Selection Title _____ Author _____

Important ideas in expository texts are the main ideas and details about a topic that the author wants the reader to understand. You can do the following to help identify important ideas and details as you read.

- Preview the selection and read the title, headings, and captions.
- Look for words in special type such as italics, boldface, and bulleted lists.
- Watch for signal words and phrases such as *for example* and *most important*.
- Use text features including photographs and illustrations, diagrams, charts, and maps.

Directions As you read the selection, use the chart below to write down any important ideas and details that you find. List any text features or signal words you used to locate these ideas. Use the important ideas and details to write a short summary of the selection.

Important Ideas	Details

Write a Summary _____

_____

_____

_____

_____

© Pearson Education, Inc., 4

Selection Title _____ **Author** _____

We **visualize** to create pictures in our minds as we read. Creating pictures can help us better understand what we're reading. To visualize, try the following.

- Combine what you already know with details from the text to make a mental image.
- Think about the events of the story or selection. Use your five senses to create pictures and to try to put yourself in the story or selection.

Directions As you read the selection, use your senses to help you visualize what's happening or the information the author provides. Write down what you can see, hear, taste, smell, and touch.

See _____

_____

_____

Hear _____

_____

_____

Taste _____

_____

_____

Smell _____

_____

_____

Touch _____

_____

_____

© Pearson Education, Inc., 4

Name _____

Selection Title _____ Author _____

Story structure is the arrangement of the important parts of the story into a beginning, middle, and end. To identify story structure, strategic readers do the following.

- Look for the conflict, or problem, at the beginning of the story.
- Track the action as conflict builds.
- Recognize the climax when the characters face conflict.
- Identify how the conflict gets resolved.

Directions As you read the story, chart the story structure using the plot map below. When you are finished, briefly retell the story on a separate sheet of paper.

Plot Structure

Title _____

Characters

Setting

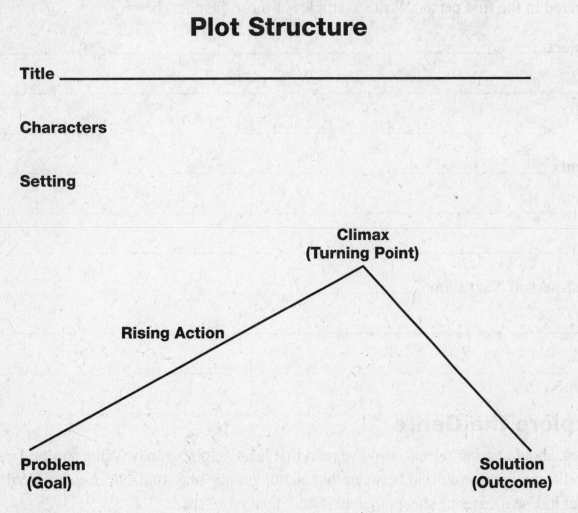

© Pearson Education, Inc., 4

Selection Title _____ **Author** _____

An **autobiography** is a form of literary nonfiction. Like a biography, it tells the story of all or part of a real person's life. But with an autobiography, a person tells his or her own story. Characteristics of an autobiography include the following.

- The subject is part or all of the life of a real person.
- The events in the person's life are usually told in the order that they happened.
- Events are told in the first-person point of view.

Directions As you read *Antarctic Journal,* look for elements that make this selection an autobiography: the subject is a person, events are in sequential order, and they are narrated in the first person. Write examples of those elements below.

Subject _____

_____

_____

Events _____

_____

_____

First-person Narration _____

_____

_____

Explore the Genre

Think about another selection you've read that is an autobiography. What similarities and differences do you find between that autobiography and *Antarctic Journal?* Write about it. Use a separate sheet of paper if you need more space.

_____

_____

© Pearson Education, Inc., 4

Name _____

Selection Title _____ Author _____

Science fiction is a made-up story that usually tells about life in the future or in another world. Characteristics of science fiction include the following.

- Events and plot may be based on real laws, theories, and beliefs of science.
- Some characters and events may be fantastic and not based on scientific fact.
- Descriptions of the setting may include details about what the future or another world might be like.

Directions As you read *Moonwalk,* look for examples of real laws of science, fantastic elements such as characters and events, and details about the future or another world that make this story science fiction. Write those examples below.

Real Science _____

_____

_____

Fantastic Elements _____

_____

_____

Details of Future or Other World _____

_____

_____

Explore the Genre

Think about another story you've read that is science fiction. What similarities and differences do you find between that story and *Moonwalk?* Write about it. Use a separate sheet of paper if you need more space.

_____

_____

© Pearson Education, Inc., 4

Name _____

Selection Title _____ Author _____

Good readers ask questions as they read. **Questioning** helps us monitor our comprehension and clarify anything that's confusing. Questioning also helps to make inferences, interpret the texts we read, and promote discussion. As you read, use the following questioning strategy.

- Preview the selection and think about any questions you have about the topic.

- Read with a question in mind and make notes when you find information that addresses the question.

- Write down other questions that come up as you read and look for answers in the text.

- Remember that not all questions are answered in the text. Sometimes we have to make inferences or interpretations based on the information the author provides.

Directions As you read the selection, use the chart below to write down any questions that you have about the text in the column on the left. Write down any answers you find or inferences you make in the right hand column.

Questions	Answers, Inferences, Interpretations

© Pearson Education, Inc., 4

Name _____

Selection Title _____ Author _____

When we **summarize** and **paraphrase,** we capture the important ideas or events of a selection in a few sentences. Paraphrasing is putting what we've read into our own words. Good readers summarize and paraphrase what they've read to check understanding and improve comprehension. Keeping important ideas and events in a logical order also improves comprehension. To summarize or paraphrase, do the following.

- In fiction, look for the important events of the plot, including the climax.

- In nonfiction, look for the important ideas that the author presents.

- Jot notes as you read to help you summarize or paraphrase, keeping events in a logical order.

- Restate important pieces of information in your own words.

Directions As you read the selection, use the chart below to write down any important ideas or plot events. Remember to record events in a logical order. When you're finished reading, use your notes to summarize or paraphrase the selection.

Important Ideas or Events

_____

_____

_____

_____

_____

Summary

_____

_____

_____

_____

_____

© Pearson Education, Inc., 4

Selection Title _____ **Author** _____

When we **infer,** we use our background knowledge with information from the text to come up with our own ideas about what we're reading. To infer, or make inferences, try the following steps.

- Think about what you already know about the topics.
- Combine what you know with information from the text to make inferences.
- Based on your inferences, think about ideas, morals, lessons, or themes in the text.

Directions As you read the selection, use your background knowledge and clues from the text to make inferences. Use the chart below to show how you made your inferences. Then write a statement that summarizes the theme, moral, or lesson from the selection.

What I Know	Information from the Text	What I Infer

Statement that summarizes the theme, moral, or lesson _____

_____

_____

_____

© Pearson Education, Inc., 4

Name _____

Selection Title _____ Author _____

When we **predict,** we tell what we think might happen in a selection. Predictions are based on our preview or what we've already read. We **set a purpose** to guide our reading. We can do the following to predict and set a purpose.

• Read the title and the author's name. Look at the illustrations and other text features.

• Think about why you're reading and set a purpose.

• Use your prior knowledge—what you already know—to make a prediction.

• As you read, check and change your prediction based on new information.

Directions Preview the selection. Make a prediction and set a purpose for reading the selection. As you read, check your predictions and set a new purpose as necessary. When you finish reading, write a summary of the selection.

Before Reading
Make a Prediction _____

_____

Purpose for Reading _____

_____

During Reading
Check and Change Prediction _____

_____

Set a New Purpose

_____

_____

After Reading
Write a Summary _____

_____

_____

© Pearson Education, Inc., 4

Selection Title _____ **Author** _____

Background knowledge is what we already know about a topic. Using background knowledge can help us better understand what we're reading. Activate your background knowledge by doing the following.

- Preview the selection to find out what it's about.

- Think about what you already know about the topic.

- Connect the selection to your own world—to people, places, and events you already know.

Directions Use the KWL chart below to chart your background knowledge about the selection. List what you already know in the K column. Then list what you want to learn in the W column. After reading, list what you learned in the L column. Write a brief summary of the selection on a separate sheet of paper.

K	W	L

© Pearson Education, Inc., 4

Name _____

Book Talk Tips
- Speak clearly.
- Make eye contact.
- Talk about a book YOU liked reading.
- Don't give away the ending.
- Talk for 2–4 minutes, sharing amusing or important information from the book.

Directions Use the talking points below to help organize your book talk.

1. What is the title of the book?

2. Who is the author?

3. What is the genre?

4. What other book has the author written?

If your book is fiction…

5. What is the most exciting part of this book? The plot, characters, theme? Explain why.

6. Briefly describe a setting, scene, or character from this book.

If your book is nonfiction…

7. What important information did you learn from this book?

8. Briefly describe an interesting part of the book.

9. Do you have a personal connection with the story or topic? Explain.

10. Explain why your listeners should read this book.

© Pearson Education, Inc., 4

Before writing

- Help your partner brainstorm ideas for writing.

- Discuss the writing topic with your partner. Does he or she need to narrow the topic or expand it?

After the first draft

- Before you exchange papers, tell your partner what you would like him or her to look for when they read your writing.

- Using sticky notes or a piece of notebook paper, note any questions or comments you have about your partner's writing.

- Point out the information or ideas that are well written.

- Discuss any information that seems unneeded or confusing, but make sure your comments are helpful and considerate.

Revision

- Read your partner's paper out loud to listen for strengths as well as places for improvement.

- Always tell your partner what you think works well in his or her paper.

- Start with a compliment, or strength, and then offer suggestions for improvement. For example, "I liked how you _____. What if you also _____?"

- Remember also to look for correct spelling and grammar.

Other areas you might comment on:

- Title

- Introduction

- Conclusion

- Descriptions

- Examples

- Use of verbs, nouns, adjectives, or adverbs

© Pearson Education, Inc., 4

Name _____

Name of Writing Product _____

Directions Review your final draft. Rate yourself on a scale from 4 to 1 (4 is a top score) on each writing trait. After you fill out the chart, answer the questions below.

Writing Traits	4	3	2	1
Focus/Ideas				
Organization				
Voice				
Word Choice				
Sentences				
Conventions				

1. What is the best part of this piece of writing? Why do you think so?

   _____

   _____

   _____

2. Write one thing you would change about this piece of writing if you had the chance to write it again.

   _____

   _____

   _____

   _____

© Pearson Education, Inc., 4

Sequence

- Events in a story occur in a certain order, or **sequence**. The sequence of events can be important to understanding a story.

Directions Read the following passage. Then complete the time line below by putting events in the order in which they happen.

When Anna first met Lexi, they were waiting to audition for the school play. Anna's family had just moved to America from Uruguay a month before, and Anna was still learning English. Her mother, a well-known actor in her country, encouraged Anna to try out for the play. Anna wanted to do a good job and please her mother.

While the drama coach listened to each student perform, Anna and Lexi quietly practiced their lines. Lexi turned to Anna and asked, "Do you want to practice together?" Anna nodded her head, but inside she was afraid Lexi would laugh at the way she said some of the words.

But Lexi didn't laugh. Instead, Lexi whispered Anna's lines to her, which helped Anna pronounce them correctly. This helped Anna relax and not feel worried. Soon, the girls were giggling like best friends. In fact, they were best friends for the rest of the year.

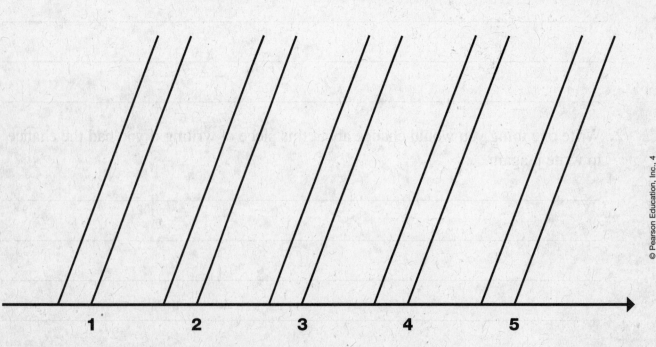

1   2   3   4   5

© Pearson Education, Inc., 4

School + Home **Home Activity** Your child completed a time line with the order of events from a short passage. Talk together about the main events of a typical day. Ask your child to put those events in sequential order using a simple time line.

Writing • Realistic Fiction

Key Features of Realistic Fiction

- has made-up people and events
- has events that could happen in real life
- happens in a setting that seems real
- discusses problems that people in real life could have

The Most Important Moment

This year Travis was determined to make the basketball team. Try-outs were the next day. Travis practiced shooting and dribbling until dark that night. He didn't even study for his math test.

The next day Travis did not do very well on his math test.

"Oh well. Right now basketball is more important," he thought.

When the bell rang Travis ran to the gym.

"One, two, three . . ." Travis counted how many others were trying out. "Twelve. I have to just be better than seven other boys to make the team."

By the end Travis felt pretty good about how he did.

The next morning Travis got to school and ran to the gym. The list of the new basketball team would be posted. Travis thought this was the most important moment of his life. He read it once. It couldn't be. He read it again. Travis did all he could to keep from crying. He would have to wait until next year to try again.

Then over the loudspeaker he heard his name, "Travis Sorenson, please come to the office."

"Why would they want me in the office?" Travis thought as he walked down the hall. When he went into the office, Coach Roberts was there with Principal Stevens.

"Sit down, Travis," Mr. Stevens said. "Coach Roberts has something to say to you."

"It's about the try-outs," Coach Roberts said. "You probably found out that you weren't selected."

"Yes, Coach," Travis was embarrassed and a little confused. Why was Coach Roberts talking to him about this?

"I just want you to know why I didn't pick you. It's not because I didn't want to pick you. I couldn't pick you. You've got to get your math grade up before I can let you on the team. If you work harder during the year, you can try out again mid-winter."

Suddenly Travis grinned from ear to ear. Working harder in math would be like working harder to get on the basketball team.

"I get it, Coach," Travis said. "And I know I can do it."

1. What was the main problem in this story?

_____

2. Underline the turning point for the main character.

© Pearson Education, Inc., 4

Vocabulary

Directions Choose the word from the box that best matches each definition. Write the word on the line shown to the left.

_____ **1.** remembers

_____ **2.** without doubt

_____ **3.** excellent

_____ **4.** strange

_____ **5.** picking out

Check the Words You Know

___grand
___memorial
___peculiar
___positive
___prideful
___recalls
___selecting

Directions Choose the word from the box that best matches the meaning of the underlined words. Write the word on the line shown to the left.

_____ **6.** She needed help <u>choosing</u> a book.

_____ **7.** We had a <u>great</u> time in Florida.

_____ **8.** Greg saw a <u>statue that helps people remember</u> the town's early settlers.

_____ **9.** I was <u>certain</u> that I had my keys with me.

_____ **10.** She is a person who <u>thinks a lot of herself</u>.

Write a Story

On a separate sheet of paper, write a story about becoming friends with someone new. Use as many vocabulary words as you can.

Home Activity Your child identified and used vocabulary words from *Because of Winn-Dixie*. With your child, create original sentences using the vocabulary words.

© Pearson Education, Inc., 4

Declarative and Interrogative Sentences

A **sentence** is a group of words that expresses a complete thought. A sentence begins with a capital letter. A sentence that tells something is a **declarative sentence.** A declarative sentence ends with a period. A sentence that asks a question is an **interrogative sentence.** An interrogative sentence ends with a question mark.

Declarative Sentence	There was a dog in the library.
Interrogative Sentence	May I have this book?

Directions Read each sentence and add the correct punctuation. Then write whether each sentence is declarative or interrogative.

1. The old woman told her a story

_____

2. She was glad to have a new friend

_____

3. How many books did you read

_____

Directions Change each sentence to the kind named in ( ). Write the new sentence.

4. Sasha wants a very large dog. (interrogative)

_____

5. Is she new in town? (declarative)

_____

Home Activity Your child learned about declarative and interrogative sentences. Have your child write two declarative and two interrogative sentences about something he or she did today.

© Pearson Education, Inc., 4

Short Vowels VCCV

Spelling Words				
admire	magnet	contest	method	custom
rally	soccer	engine	sudden	finger
accident	mitten	intend	fabric	flatten
rascal	gutter	mammal	happen	cannon

Classifying Write the list word that fits each group.

1. rules, game, winner, _____
2. wheels, trunk, hood, _____
3. foot, toe, hand, _____
4. mistake, error, mishap, _____
5. cotton, wool, silk, _____
6. baseball, football, basketball, _____
7. pancake, road, dough, _____
8. otter, wolf, horse, _____
9. mean, plan, aim, _____
10. iron, attract, pole, _____
11. meeting, gathering, assembly, _____
12. habit, ritual, routine, _____
13. hat, scarf, earmuffs, _____

1. _____
2. _____
3. _____
4. _____
5. _____
6. _____
7. _____
8. _____
9. _____
10. _____
11. _____
12. _____
13. _____

Context Clues Choose a list word to complete each sentence of the script. Write the word.

14. Bowler 1: Hooray! I got a strike! Did you see it __?
15. Bowler 2: I __ your skill.
16. Bowler 3: The ball looked as if it had been shot from a __.
17. Bowler 1: My bowling __ is perfect!
18. Bowler 2: Then how come your ball just rolled into the __?
19. Bowler 1: All of a __ I just lost control of the ball.
20. Bowler 1: You __! I think you enjoyed my mistake.

14. _____
15. _____
16. _____
17. _____
18. _____
19. _____
20. _____

© Pearson Education, Inc., 4

School + Home

Home Activity Your child spelled words with short vowels in VCCV pattern. Read the script aloud with your child. Have your child spell the list words with closed eyes.

Name _____

Story Sequence A

Title _____

Beginning

Middle

End

© Pearson Education, Inc., 4

Vocabulary • Suffixes

- A **suffix** is a syllable added to the end of a base word to change its meaning or the way it is used in a sentence.

- The suffix *–ful* means "full of _____," as in *careful.* The suffix *–al* means "from, of, or like _____," as in *fictional.* You can use suffixes to help you figure out the meanings of words.

Directions Read the following story about a trip to the library. Then answer the questions below.

> When I went to King Memorial School, there was a contest for telling a story about our town's original settlers. My friends and I formed a team and went to the local library. I was doubtful that our team would win until we talked to the town historian in the library. She told us the wonderful story of one brave pioneer family. To us, the story was a logical choice. I was really prideful when my team won the prize for telling our town's most colorful story.

1. What does the word *prideful* mean in the story?

_____

2. What does the word *original* mean in the story?

_____

3. What is the suffix in the word *wonderful*? What does *wonderful* mean?

_____

4. What does the suffix mean in the word *logical*? What does *logical* mean?

_____

5. Think of another word that ends with either *–ful* or *–al*. Tell the meaning of the word. Then use it in an original sentence.

_____

_____

© Pearson Education, Inc., 4

Home Activity Your child identified suffixes in words to understand their meanings. With your child, read a short selection. Ask your child to point out words that use suffixes and what those words mean.

Map/Globe/Atlas

- A **map** is a drawing of a place that shows where something is or where something happened.
- A map's **legend** has a **compass rose** to show direction, a **scale** to show distance, and a **key** to symbols.
- A **globe** is a sphere with a map of the world, and an **atlas** is a book of maps.

Directions Use this map of Texas to answer the questions below.

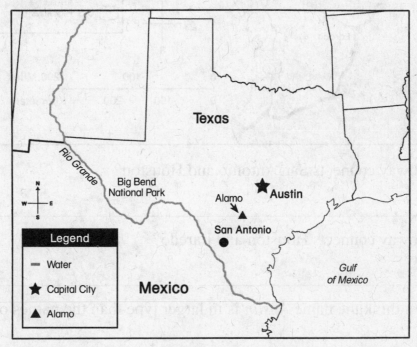

1. What large body of water lies just to the east of Texas?

_____

2. What natural landform forms the border between Mexico and Texas?

_____

3. What does the star on the map tell you?

_____

4. How do you think Big Bend National Park got its name?

_____

5. What important Texas landmark could a tourist visit in San Antonio?

_____

© Pearson Education, Inc., 4

Directions Use this road map of Texas to answer the questions below.

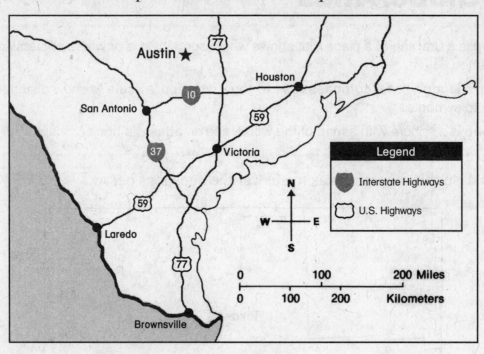

6. Which highway connects San Antonio and Houston?

_____

7. Which highway connects Houston and Laredo?

_____

8. Why do you think the name *Austin* is in larger type than the names of the other cities?

_____

9. What is the southernmost city on this map?

_____

10. A road atlas of the United States provides road maps for all the states. When would you use a road atlas?

_____

_____

© Pearson Education, Inc., 4

Home Activity Your child learned about using maps, atlases, and globes. Together, look at a map of your state. Examine the legend and locate significant cities or features with which your child is familiar.

Short Vowels VCCV

Proofread a Newspaper Column Circle five misspelled words in the newspaper column. Write the words correctly. Then write the sentence that has a punctuation mistake correctly.

Roof Rally

By Dan Green

Most days I idmire that little rascle, the squirrel. That furry little mummal is always busy. Its usual costum is to keep busy burying food all day long. On one recent day a squirrel decided to take a break. He brought twenty of his cusins and held a rally on my roof. The noise was terrible! How could this happen? Stop it, I shouted. They scampered over the gutter and ran away. It was good to have peace and quiet again.

Spelling Words
admire
magnet
contest
method
custom
rally
soccer
engine
sudden
finger
accident
mitten
intend
fabric
flatten
rascal
gutter
mammal
happen
cannon

1. _____   2. _____

3. _____   4. _____

5. _____   6. _____

Frequently Misspelled Words
with
cousin

Proofread Words Circle the correctly spelled word. Write the word.

7. cannon   cannen   kannon   7. _____

8. mignet   magnet   manget   8. _____

9. accident   ecident   eccident   9. _____

10. ingune   engine   ingine   10. _____

11. soccor   socor   soccer   11. _____

12. fabrik   fibrak   fabric   12. _____

Home Activity Your child identified misspelled words with short vowels in VCCV pattern. Say each spelling word. Ask your child to name the short vowel in the first syllable.

© Pearson Education, Inc., 4

Declarative and Interrogative Sentences

Directions Read the selection. Then read each question. Circle the letter of the correct answer.

At the Library

(1) You can borrow books from a Library. (2) Do you need another book.
(3) one dog at a time is allowed in the library. (4) You can find books on dogs and other animals. (5) You can read the book to the dog if you want?

1 What change, if any, should be made in sentence 1?

  A   Change *Library* to **library.**

  B   Change *borrow* to **loan.**

  C   Change *You* to **I.**

  D   Make no change.

2 What change, if any, should be made in sentence 2?

  A   Change *Do* to **do.**

  B   Change *another book* to **other books.**

  C   Change the period to a question mark.

  D   Make no change.

3 What change, if any, should be made in sentence 3?

  A   Change *one dog* to **One Dog.**

  B   Change *one dog* to **One dog.**

  C   Change *is allowed* to **isn't allowed.**

  D   Make no change.

4 What change, if any, should be made in sentence 4?

  A   Change *find* to **read.**

  B   Change *dogs and other animals* to **animals.**

  C   Change the period to a question mark.

  D   Make no change.

5 What change, if any, should be made in sentence 5?

  A   Change *You* to **I.**

  B   Change *read* to **show.**

  C   Change the question mark to a period.

  D   Make no change.

© Pearson Education, Inc., 4

Home Activity Your child prepared for taking tests on declarative and interrogative sentences. Say *declarative* or *interrogative* and have your child say a sentence of the correct kind.

Author's Purpose

- The **author's purpose** is the reason or reasons the author has for writing.
- An author may write to persuade, to inform, to entertain, or to express ideas and feelings.

Directions Read the passage below. Use the graphic organizer to keep track of the author's purpose before and during reading, and then answer the last question.

> **Stagecoach Mary, Tough as Iron**
>
> In 1885, Mary Fields headed west, looking for adventure. She was 53 years old and a former slave. She had no education, but she stood over six feet tall and weighed over two hundred pounds. She wasn't shy about defending herself. In fact, she was said to have knocked down dangerous men with one punch. Mary took jobs delivering mail by mule, and then driving a stagecoach. Armed with six-shooters and rifles, she did her job, despite the challenges of the "Wild West." She braved the weather during heat and blizzards. Outlaws and wild animals learned to leave "Stagecoach Mary" alone.

	Author's Purpose	**Why do you think so?**
Before you read: What do you think it will be?	1.	2.
As you read: What do you think it is?	3.	4.

5. Do you think the author met his or her purpose? Why or why not?

_____

_____

© Pearson Education, Inc., 4

Home Activity Your child identified the author's purpose in a passage. Work with your child to identify the author's purpose in an editorial in the newspaper.

Writing • Expository Composition

Key Features of an Expository Composition

- tells of real people and events
- presents factual information
- includes a topic sentence, a body, and a closing sentence
- may include text features such as photos, captions, and subheads

Homesteading: A Great Opportunity

On May 20, 1862, the Homestead Act, which made owning land possible for people who could not afford to purchase land, was passed.

What was the Homestead Act?

The Homestead Act promised ownership of 160 acres of public land to any citizen over the age of 21. To become homesteaders, settlers had to do several things. First, they had to move to the West. Next, they had to settle the land by building a house that was at least 12 feet x 14 feet in size. Finally, they had to successfully make a living on it. If settlers occupied the land for five years, the person in charge then owned the land.

The first landowner

January 1, 1863, was the first day settlers could make a claim to land under the new act. On this day, Daniel Feeman became the first person to take advantage of the opportunity. His homestead in Beatrice, Nebraska, is now a monument to the memory of all homesteaders.

The impact of the Homestead Act

More than a half million people followed in Freeman's footsteps. Brave families left behind a life they had always known to head for the Great Plains and become farmers on their own land. Life was tough on the Great Plains, but the promise for free land was stronger than any fears. For most people, successful farms became a reality along with owning property.

Homesteading was truly a great opportunity.

© Pearson Education, Inc., 4

1. Choose a paragraph. Write the heading. Then write the main idea for that paragraph.

_____

_____

2. Circle two details that support the main idea for the paragraph you chose.

Vocabulary

Directions Choose the word from the box that best matches each definition. Write the word on the line.

_____ 1. platforms built on the shore or out from it; piers

_____ 2. to look over hastily

_____ 3. a smell

_____ 4. moving from one place to settle in another

_____ 5. another word for dock

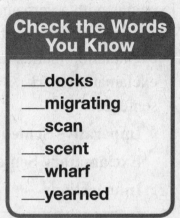

Check the Words You Know

___docks
___migrating
___scan
___scent
___wharf
___yearned

Directions Choose the word from the box that best completes each statement. Write the word on the line shown to the left.

_____ 6. Josh _____ for home while he was on a long journey.

_____ 7. Tanya could smell the _____ of the ocean in the air.

_____ 8. Like the wharf in our hometown, these _____ are filled with sailors.

_____ 9. The people _____ to the West had to bring enough supplies to last the whole trip.

_____ 10. I had to _____ the pages of the manual to find the diagram.

Write a Journal Entry

On a separate sheet of paper write a journal entry you might make after discovering a new part of the world. Use as many vocabulary words as you can.

© Pearson Education, Inc., 4

Home Activity Your child identified and used vocabulary words from *Lewis and Clark and Me*. With your child, imagine you are walking along a busy waterfront. Write a short story together about your imaginary walk. Use as many vocabulary words as you can.

Imperative and Exclamatory Sentences

An **imperative sentence** gives a command or makes a request. It usually begins with a verb and ends with a period. The subject (you) is not shown. An **exclamatory sentence** shows strong feeling or surprise. It ends with an exclamation mark. An **interjection** also shows strong feeling and ends with an exclamation mark. An interjection is a word or group of words, not a complete sentence.

Imperative Sentence	Look for elk in the woods.
Exclamatory Sentences	The squirrels were all swimming!
Interjections	Wow! Ouch! Oh no! Hurray!

Directions Read each sentence. Write *C* if the end punctuation is correct. Write *NC* if the end punctuation is not correct.

1. Seaman was an amazing dog? _____

2. Pull the boats along the shore. _____

3. Load the equipment in the first boat! _____

4. Only three beaver pelts for this fine dog! _____

5. Cross the river upstream! _____

Directions Write a word or phrase that will make these sentences the kind named in ( ).

6. _____ is the largest dog I've ever seen! (exclamatory)

7. _____ about the adventures of Lewis and Clark. (imperative)

8. _____ tip the boat! (exclamatory)

9. _____ stay on deck. (imperative)

10. _____ the rope tightly. (imperative)

Home Activity Your child learned about imperative and exclamatory sentences. With your child, listen to a favorite television show and have your child identify examples of imperative and exclamatory sentences. Have your child write two declarative and two interrogative sentences about something he or she did today.

© Pearson Education, Inc., 4

Long *a* and *i*

Spelling Words				
sigh	right	weigh	eight	detail
height	spray	braid	bait	grain
slight	thigh	tight	raisin	trait
highway	frighten	dismay	freight	sleigh

Rhyme Time Complete the rhymes with a list word from the box.

Soccer Score

The chances of scoring seemed **(1)**_____.

Young Pee Wee lacked weight, strength, and **(2)**____.

He fell down with a **(3)**____.

The ball bounced off his **(4)**____,

And it soared through the goal on the **(5)**____.

Fishing Trip

The fisherman left home at **(6)**____

And patiently set out with his **(7)**____.

But the fish just weren't bitin'.

Did the fisherman **(8)**____

Those fish that refused to be **(9)**____?

Winter Drive

As we drove down the icy **(10)**____

With our windshield covered with **(11)**____,

We started to **(12)**____

The idea of a **(13)**____.

It was slow going, to our **(14)**____.

1. _____
2. _____
3. _____
4. _____
5. _____

6. _____
7. _____

8. _____
9. _____

10. _____
11. _____
12. _____
13. _____
14. _____

Word Groups Write the missing list word that belongs in each group.

15. ponytail, pigtails,

_____

16. wheat, rice,

_____

17. feature, characteristic,

_____

18. fig, date,

_____

19. aspect, fact,

_____

20. taut, close fitting,

_____

School + Home

Home Activity Your child spelled words with *ai*, *eigh*, *ay*, and *igh*. Say a list word and ask your child to write it.

© Pearson Education, Inc., 4

Main Idea

Main Idea

Supporting Details

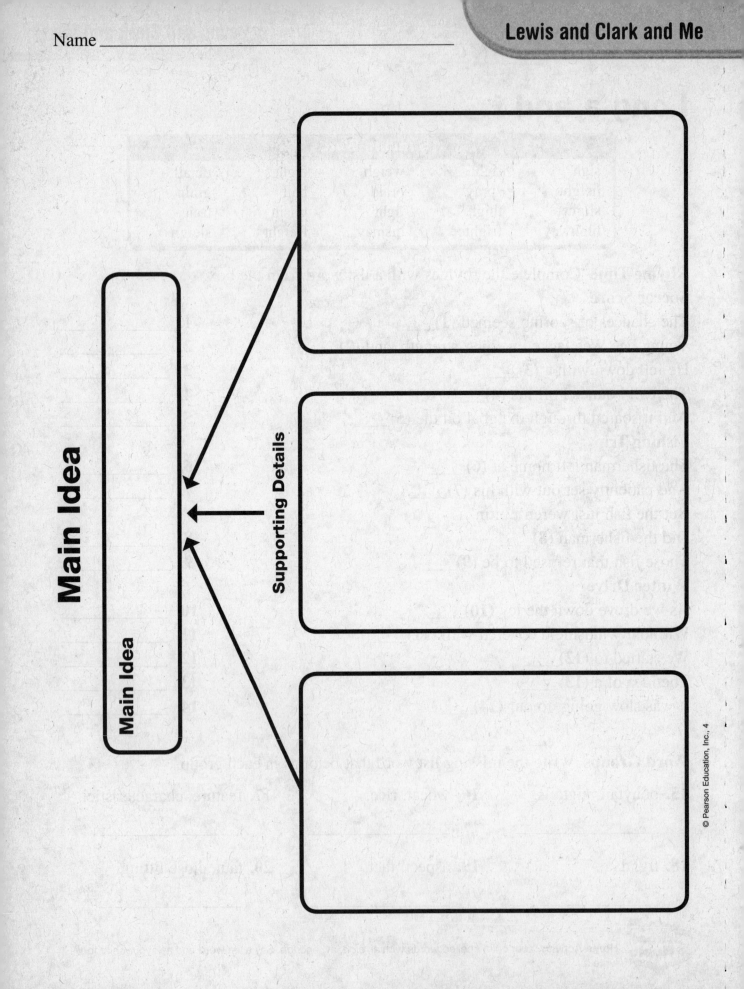

© Pearson Education, Inc., 4

Vocabulary • Word Endings

- An **ending** is a letter or letters added to the end of a base word. Recognizing an ending will help you figure out the word's meaning.
- The ending *-ed* is added to a verb to make it past tense. The ending *-ing* is added to a verb to make it tell about present or ongoing actions.

Directions Read the following passage about a journey. Look for words ending in *-ed* and *-ing.* Then answer the questions below.

Enrique yearned for the unsettled land of the West. He was tired of living in such a busy town. So one day he packed up his things and headed for the docks. He started his journey migrating by boat. He planned to meet his uncle downriver. His uncle was also moving west and had offered him a ride on his wagon. When he arrived at the wharf, Enrique hopped off the boat and headed into town. The scent of freshly baked bread was in the air, which made him hungry. Enrique stopped to scan the row of shops for the bakery. Just then, Enrique heard his name being called from across the street. It was his uncle. "Are you ready for the journey of a lifetime?" asked his uncle. Enrique shouted, "More than you know!"

1. What does *yearned* mean? How does the ending change the base word?

_____

2. What does *migrating* mean? What is the base word?

_____

3. Rewrite the ninth sentence in the passage so that it uses the word *scanning.*

_____

4. If you added *-ed* to the noun *scent,* what kind of word does *scent* become?

_____

5. Write a sentence using an *-ed* and an *-ing* word.

_____

_____

 Home Activity Your child identified and used word endings to understand words in a passage. Have your child make a list of common verbs. Ask your child to change the meaning of the word by adding *-ed* and *-ing* to each word.

© Pearson Education, Inc., 4

Skim and Scan

To **scan** is to move one's eyes quickly down the page, seeking specific words and phrases. Scanning is used to find out if a resource will answer a reader's questions. Once a reader has scanned a document, he or she might go back and skim it.

To **skim** a document is to read the first and last paragraphs as well as using headings and other organizers as you move down the page. Skimming is used to quickly identify the main idea. You might also read the first sentence of each paragraph.

Directions Scan the passage to answer the questions below.

School's largest yard sale. Northside School will hold its largest yard sale ever on Saturday, March 16. It will be located on the soccer field from 9 a.m. until 4 p.m. **Raising money for a class field trip.** The school is holding the sale to collect money for a class field trip to study the route taken by Lewis and Clarke. This is a cross-country trip, and the students need money for transportation, food, and lodging.

Toys, clothing, and furniture for sale. Students' families will set up booths on the field. We've heard reports that many of the items for sale will be toys, games, clothes, furniture, and antiques. **Come early for the best selection.** It is best to arrive at the sale early to have the best pick of items. But, if you are not an early bird, you might find some half-price bargains at the end of the day.

1. When you scan this passage, what helps you find specific information?

_____

2. In which paragraph would you find out if antiques will be for sale?

_____

3. In which paragraph would you find out why the yard sale is being held?

_____

4. In which paragraph would you find out the best time to go to the sale?

_____

5. Can you find out about the prices of items by scanning this passage?

_____

© Pearson Education, Inc., 4

Name _____

Directions Skim this letter to answer the questions below.

Dear Mr. Lewis and Mr. Clark,

I am a student at Gardner School in Portland, Oregon. My class is getting ready for a field trip that will cover part of the route you took to the Pacific Ocean.

I can hardly imagine a two-year journey across half of the country without a car, train, or airplane. I think I would have gotten tired and lonely. I would have missed my home and family.

But it must have been an amazing trip. Were you excited to see new landscapes? Were the people who you met along the way different from what you expected?

Did you learn a lot from them? I think I would have liked traveling on horseback and in canoes.

I wonder, were you ever scared? Did you worry about getting lost or getting sick? Were the wild animals frightening? You didn't have a map, although you had about 40 people traveling with you.

I can't wait to see the route you took with my own eyes!

Sincerely,

Justin

6. What is a good way to skim this letter?

_____

7. What is the topic of this letter?

_____

8. Is the letter about the modern-day city of Portland? How can you tell?

_____

_____

9. Does the letter indicate if Justin is impressed by Lewis and Clark's journey? How can you tell?

_____

_____

10. Is Justin excited about the trip? What in the letter gave you that impression?

_____

Home Activity Your child learned about scanning and skimming to help find a main idea or information. Look at a newspaper or magazine with your child and have him or her skim it to find the main idea. Then ask your child to scan it for a particular piece of information.

© Pearson Education, Inc., 4

Long *a* and *i*

Proofread Directions Read the following directions for making a wood puppet. Circle five misspelled words and write them correctly on the lines. Change the sentence fragments to a complete sentence and write the sentence.

Spelling Words	
sigh	slight
right	thigh
weigh	tight
eight	raisin
detail	trait
height	highway
spray	frighten
braid	dismay
bait	freight
grain	sleigh

Make sure you all ways work carefully with tools.
Measure wood for the hight you want.
Sand the wood in the direction of the grain.
Cut ate pieces for jointed arms and legs.
Spray on paint.
Braid some wool for hair.
Glue the hair on tite.
Add detale.
Make sure the puppet. Works
with right and left hands.

Frequently Misspelled Words
vacation
always
might

1. _____ 2. _____
3. _____ 4. _____
5. _____ 6. _____
_____

Finish the Sentences Circle the underlined list word that is spelled correctly. Write the word.

7. The <u>freight</u> <u>frate</u> train has over 150 cars.   7. _____
8. This kind of <u>raysin</u> <u>raisin</u> has no seeds.   8. _____
9. The horses pulled the <u>sleigh</u> <u>slay</u>.   9. _____
10. The <u>thy</u> <u>thigh</u> bone is the strongest bone in the body.   10. _____
11. Your answer is <u>rite</u> <u>right</u>.   11. _____
12. Generosity is a good <u>treight</u> <u>trait</u> to have.   12. _____
13. "I forgot my homework," he said with <u>dismay</u> <u>dismeigh</u>.   13. _____
14. "Bring it in tomorrow," his teacher said with a <u>sy</u> <u>sigh</u>.   14. _____

© Pearson Education, Inc., 4

Home Activity Your child identified misspelled words with *ai*, *eigh*, *ay*, and *igh*. Take turns quizzing each other on the spelling words.

Imperative and Exclamatory Sentences

Directions Read the passage. Then read each question. Circle the letter of the correct answer.

The Camp

(1) This is a great place to camp for the night? (2) Where is that dog? (3) Bosco, come here now. (4) Fetch a squirrel for us. (5) Watch out for that big old bear. (6) i will unpack the cooking equipment. (7) We have beans and cold water for supper too.

1 What change, if any, should be made in sentence 1?

A Change *This* to **That.**

B Change *camp* to **sleep.**

C Change the question mark to an exclamation.

D Make no change.

2 What change, if any, should be made in sentence 3?

A Change *now* to **at once.**

B Change *Bosco* to **Dog.**

C Change the period to a question mark.

D Make no change.

3 What change, if any, should be made in sentence 4?

A Change *Fetch* to **fetch.**

B Change *a squirrel* to **our supper.**

C Change *a squirrel for us* to **us a squirrel.**

D Make no change.

4 What change, if any, should be made in sentence 5?

A Change *Watch out for* to **Look for.**

B Change *Watch out* to **Watch out!**

C Change the period to an exclamation.

D Make no change.

5 What change, if any, should be made in sentence 6?

A Change *cooking equipment* to **pots.**

B Change *will* to **won't.**

C Change *i* to **I.**

D Make no change.

© Pearson Education, Inc., 4

Home Activity Your child prepared for taking tests on imperative and exclamatory sentences. Ask your child to write an example of each kind of sentence and to explain what makes it imperative or exclamatory.

Literary Elements: Character, Setting, and Plot

- **Characters** are the people in the story.
- The **setting** is where and when the story takes place.
- The **plot** is the sequence of events.

Directions Read the following passage. Then fill in the chart and answer the questions below.

In the 1870s the Dunton family, the first settlers, came to build our town. At the time, it looked very different from the busy place it is today. Wild horses and buffalo roamed the plains. When the settlers came, they plowed the fields and built homesteads. In town they built schools and churches.

Later on, the railroad came to town. People from China, such as the Lees, came to help construct the railroad tracks. Instead of moving on after the work was done, the Chinese families stayed in the town to raise their families. That is how our town grew up with a mix of many peoples.

Characters	Setting	Plot
1.	2.	3.

4. Is the narrator of the story first person or third person? How do you know?

_____

5. How do you think many towns started up? What points in the story help you know this?

_____

_____

Home Activity Your child identified the characters, setting, and plot in a passage. Tell a story about how your own town developed.

© Pearson Education, Inc., 4

Writing • Parody

Key Features of Parody

- imitates another work, usually with humor or exaggeration
- follows the style and voice of the original work
- makes a clear connection with the characters, setting or subject of the original work

Lewis and Clark and NOT ME

"Look alive! Here's buyers."

Our owner pointed at the men walking toward us on the dock. Seaman, the Newfoundland dog next to me, wagged his tail. I could tell he liked these people. Leon, the parrot on my other side, squawked loudly. But I just closed my eyes and waited for them to move on. The last thing I wanted was to be bought by these strangers.

"What's this one's name," the tallest man said and pointed at me.

"Sir, that's Tuffy. And she's a charmer," my owner said.

Charmer! Who's he kidding, I thought to myself.

The man tried to pet me and asked, "How would you like to come with me on an adventure? You'd be the first cat to explore the Missouri River."

EOOWWW! River! That's water! I don't get near water. How could I tell this man that my idea of adventure is to chase a mouse, then curl up on a sofa and sleep.

I budged Seaman with my head. Do something, you silly dog! Make him notice you.

Seaman took the clue and barked happily.

"Well, who do we have here?" the man asked and smiled at the dog.

Thank goodness, I thought to myself. I closed my eyes and went back to sleep.

1. Reread the selection. Select one example that shows this parody is a humorous imitation of *Lewis and Clark and Me*.

_____

_____

_____

2. Underline aspects of the characters and setting that are like the original story.

© Pearson Education, Inc., 4

Name _____

Vocabulary

Directions Choose the word from the box that best
completes each sentence. Write the word on the line.

**Check the Words
You Know**

___badger
___bank
___bristled
___jointed
___patched
___ruffled
___rushes

1. The furry _____ waddled down
   the forest path.

2. The little animal's coat _____,
   or stood up stiffly, when it picked up the scent of
   the dogs.

3. At the river's _____, it stopped
   for a drink of water.

4. We could hardly see it through the tall grasses and _____.

5. A woodpecker sat in the _____ place of a tree where two
   branches formed a kind of crook.

6. A deer sniffed at the flowers with _____ silky petals that grew
   along the river.

Directions Circle the word that has the same or nearly the same meaning as the word
or words in each group.

8. bank   edge   cliff   path

9. rushes   seaweed   sod   marsh grasses

10. patched   painted   mended   chopped

Write an E-mail Message

Pretend you have just moved to a new part of the country. On a separate sheet of paper,
write an e-mail message to a friend back home explaining how you have adapted to life
in this new place. Use as many vocabulary words as you can.

Home Activity Your child identified and used vocabulary words from *On the Banks of Plum Creek*. With
your child, look at a book about plant and animal life. Use some of the vocabulary words to describe what
you see.

© Pearson Education, Inc., 4

Complete Subjects and Predicates

Every sentence has a **subject** and a **predicate**. The **subject** is the part of the sentence that tells whom or what the sentence is about. All the words in the subject are called the **complete subject.** The **simple subject** is the most important word in the complete subject. A simple subject can be more than one word, as in *Plum Creek*.

Complete Subject	<u>The mud from the river</u> squished beneath her feet.
Simple Subject	The <u>mud</u> from the river squished beneath her feet.

The **predicate** is the part of the sentence that tells what the subject is or does. All the words in the predicate are called the **complete predicate**. The **simple predicate**, or **verb**, is the most important word in the complete predicate. A simple predicate can be more than one word, as in *was going*.

Complete Predicate	The mud from the river <u>squished beneath her feet.</u>
Simple Predicate	The mud from the river <u>squished</u> beneath her feet.

A **compound subject** is made up of two or more simple subjects. A **compound predicate** is made up of two or more simple predicates.

Compound Subject	<u>Mary</u> and <u>Laura</u> swept the floor.
Compound Predicate	The bees <u>buzzed</u> and <u>bumbled</u> in the wind.

Directions Look at the letters after each sentence. Circle the complete subject when you see *CS,* the simple subject when you see *SS,* and the compound subject when you see *SSS.* Circle the complete predicate when you see *CP,* the simple predicate when you see *SP,* and the compound predicate when you see *PPP.*

1. Huge water bugs skated on top of the water. SS

2. She pulled the rushes apart. SP

3. They went down a bank toward the willows. CP

4. Tall willows stood on one side of the pool. CS

5. Ma and Mary cooked dinner. SSS

Home Activity Your child learned about subjects and predicates. Ask your child to find sentences in a newspaper or magazine. Have him or her identify the simple subject and simple predicate in each sentence.

© Pearson Education, Inc., 4

Long e and o

Spelling Words				
sweet	each	three	least	freedom
below	throat	float	foam	flown
greet	season	croak	shallow	eagle
indeed	rainbow	grown	seaweed	hollow

Opposites Write the list words that have the opposite or almost opposite meaning to the words below.

1. sour
2. most
3. sink
4. dismiss
5. newborn
6. solid
7. above
8. all
9. deep
10. limits

1. _____
2. _____
3. _____
4. _____
5. _____
6. _____
7. _____
8. _____
9. _____
10. _____

Words in Context Write a list word from the box to complete each sentence.

11. The ocean waves were white with ____.
12. Twins describe two people, and triplets describe ____ people.
13. Spring is my favorite ____.
14. When I was sick, I had a sore ____.
15. Some ocean plants are called ____.
16. When I lost my voice, I could only ____ like a frog.
17. The bald ____ is the national bird of the United States.
18. Spelling is serious business, ____.
19. I saw a ____ after the thunderstorm.
20. By the time I got the camera, the bird had ____ away.

11. _____
12. _____
13. _____
14. _____
15. _____
16. _____
17. _____
18. _____
19. _____
20. _____

School + Home

Home Activity Your child wrote words with long e spelled ee or ea and long o spelled oa and ow. Say a word from the list and have your child write the word.

© Pearson Education, Inc., 4

T-Chart

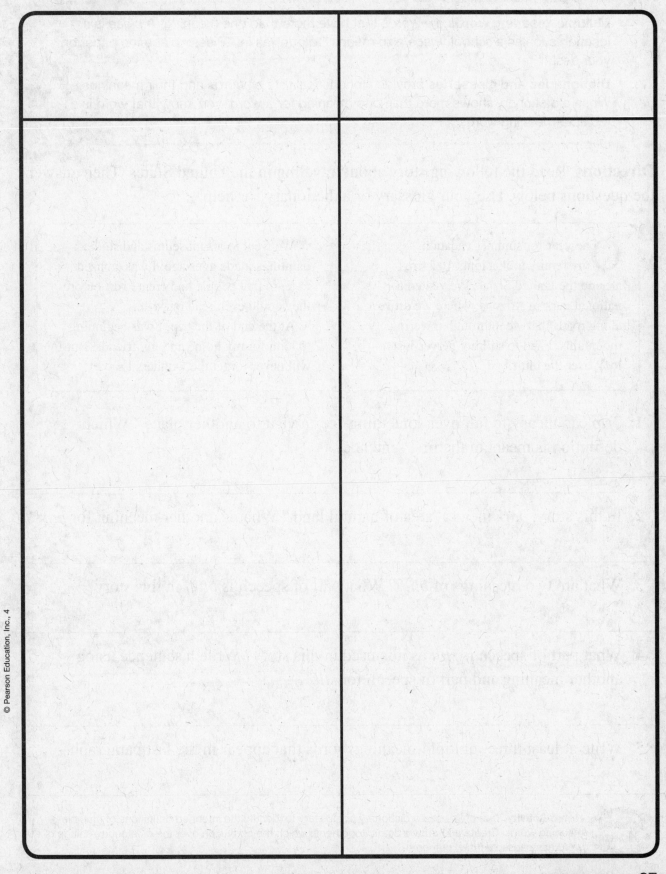

© Pearson Education, Inc., 4

Vocabulary • Multiple-Meaning Words

- **Multiple-meaning words** are words that have more than one meaning. A *place* is a location such as a school. *Place* also means "to put," as in, "Please place the paper on your desk."

- **Dictionaries and glossaries** provide alphabetical lists of words and their meanings. When a dictionary shows more than one meaning for a word, you know that word is a multiple-meaning word.

Directions Read the following story about traveling in the United States. Then answer the questions below. Use your glossary or a dictionary for help.

> One year for summer vacation, my family took a long road trip around the United States. We visited a national park in Arizona, where we drove along roads that went through towering mountains. I had to still my nerves just to look over the bluff.
>
> We went to art museums and studied paintings made ages ago. I was amazed to learn that people had created art before they could even read or write.
>
> At the end of the trip, I was beginning to long for my home and my friends. But I will never forget the wonders I saw.

1. *Trip* can mean "to fall over something" or "a visit to another place." Which definition is meant in the first sentence?

_____

2. In this story, *park* means "area of natural land." What is another meaning for *park*?

_____

3. What are two meanings of *bluff*? What part of speech is *bluff* in this story?

_____

4. What part of speech is *still* as it is used in this story? Write a sentence using another meaning and part of speech for *still*.

_____

_____

5. Write at least three multiple-meaning words that appear in the last paragraph.

_____

 School + Home **Home Activity** Your child used a dictionary or glossary to identify the intended definitions of multiple-meaning words. Create and draw a comic together in which the confusion over the different meanings of a word has caused a funny outcome.

© Pearson Education, Inc., 4

Name _____

Electronic Media

- There are two types of electronic media—computer and non-computer. Computer sources include computer software, CD-ROMs, DVDs, and the Internet. Non-computer sources include audiotapes, videotapes, films, filmstrips, television, and radio.

- To find information on the Internet, use a search engine and type in your keywords. Be specific. It's a good idea to use two or more keywords.

Directions Use the list of electronic media below to answer the questions about the research topic, "Animals of the Prairies." Take notes from the information you find to make a brochure or poster on your topic.

> **Electronic Media Source List**
> - The U.S. Fish & Wildlife Service (Web site)
> - National Public Radio "Environment" podcasts at NPR.org
> - DVD episode "The Great Plains" in the *Planet Earth* DVDs
> - Your state or local university's links to wildlife Web sites such as the Minnesota Cooperative Fish and Wildlife Research Unit

1. Which sources would you look at first to find out about badgers?

_____

_____

2. Why would the *Planet Earth* episode "The Great Plains" help you find out about many animals?

_____

3. Which keywords might you use to search online for prairie animals?

_____

4. At which Web site might you learn about the prairie animals of Laura Ingalls's time?

_____

_____

5. Where might you go to download podcasts?

_____

© Pearson Education, Inc., 4

Directions Use the Internet search results found on a search engine to answer the questions below.

WEB SEARCH

Results 1-4 of about 25,000

Search Results

Other Animals & Plants

Information on shorebirds of the Great Plains

Planet Earth

"Great Plains" video by David Attenborough

Great Plains

Before any people arrived in the Great Plains, there were the animals.

Great Plains Toad: Nature Snapshots from Minnesota

About the same size but more sharply marked than the widespread American toad, the Great Plains toad can be found along Minnesota's western border.

---

6. Where could you find a quote by the biologist David Attenborough?

_____

7. At which Web site might you find out about ancient animals of the Great Plains?

_____

8. Which keywords might you use to search online for toads in Minnesota?

_____

9. At which Web site might you learn about shorebirds of the Great Plains?

_____

10. Which keywords might you use to find a list of episodes of the video series *Planet Earth*?

_____

 Home Activity Your child learned about electronic media. With your child, review the rules of safe Internet searching and how to find helpful articles on the Internet.

© Pearson Education, Inc., 4

Name _____

Long e and o

Proofread a Menu The restaurant owner is frantic! The new menus have errors that must be fixed before dinner tonight. Circle five misspelled words and write them correctly. Rewrite the sentence that has a capitalization error.

Spelling Words	
sweet	greet
each	season
three	croak
least	shallow
freedom	eagle
below	indeed
throat	rainbow
float	grown
foam	seaweed
flown	hollow

Seewead salad with vinegar and sesame seeds

Thre delight dish: shrimp, beef, and chicken

Hole crispy fried rainbow trout with lemon
butter sauce

White hollo mushroom caps stuffed with
crabmeat

Fresh vegetables in seeson

Chocolate cake with sweet whipped cream

Rootbeer float (vanilla or chocolate ice cream)

Coffee with hot milk foam

our Food is Organically grown.

Frequently Misspelled Words

whole
know

1. _____   2. _____

3. _____   4. _____

5. _____   6. _____

Proofread Words Circle the correctly spelled word. Write the word

7.	leest	least	lest	7. _____
8.	egle	eagle	eegle	8. _____
9.	shallow	shalloe	shallo	9. _____
10.	greet	grete	graet	10. _____
11.	throte	throwt	throat	11. _____
12.	floan	flown	flone	12. _____
13.	beloa	below	belo	13. _____
14.	freedowm	fredom	freedom	14. _____
15.	indeed	indead	indede	15. _____

Home Activity Your child identified misspelled words with *ee*, *ea*, *oa*, and *ow*. Ask your child to use each list word in a sentence.

© Pearson Education, Inc., 4

Complete Subjects and Predicates

Directions Read the passage. Then read each question. Circle the letter of the correct answer.

At Plum Creek

(1) Mary's sister, Laura, went to the creek too. (2) The yellow butterflies flew onto the girls' hands. (3) The girls played. (4) Water rushed and bubbled over the rocks. (5) The big yellow daisies bloomed in the grass. (6) Laura and Mary waded in the pool.

1 What change, if any, could be made in sentence 1 to change a complete subject into a simple subject?

  A Change *creek* to **creek and field.**

  B Change *Mary's sister, Laura,* to **Mary and Laura.**

  C Change *Mary's sister, Laura,* to **Laura.**

  D Make no change.

2 What change, if any, could be made in sentence 2 to change a complete predicate to a simple predicate?

  A Change *flew onto the girls' hands* to **flew away.**

  B Change *flew onto the girls' hands* to **flew.**

  C Change *flew onto the girls' hands* to **sat on the girls' hands.**

  D Make no change.

3 What change, if any, could be made in sentence 3 to change a simple predicate into a complete predicate?

  A Change *played* to **played in the water.**

  B Change *played* to **played and swam.**

  C Change *The girls* to **Laura and Mary.**

  D Make no change.

4 What change, if any, could be made in sentence 5 to change a complete subject to a simple subject?

  A Change *The big yellow daisies* to **The daisies and blue flags.**

  B Change *The big yellow daisies* to **The big yellow flowers.**

  C Change *The big yellow daisies* to **The daisies.**

  D Make no change.

5 What change, if any, could be made in sentence 6 to change a simple predicate to a complete predicate?

  A Change *waded in the pool* to **waded.**

  B Change *waded in the pool* to **swam in the pool.**

  C Change *waded* to **swam.**

  D Make no change.

© Pearson Education, Inc., 4

 Home Activity Your child prepared for taking tests on subjects and predicates. Ask your child a question (*What did you eat for lunch? When did you get home?*). Have him or her write the answer in a complete sentence and identify the subject and predicate.

Author's Purpose

- The **author's purpose** is the reason or reasons for writing. An author may write to persuade, to inform, to entertain, or to express ideas and feelings.
- The kinds of ideas in the text, and the way the author organizes and states these ideas, can help you determine the purpose.

Directions Read the following passage. Then complete the diagram below.

When I smelled chili cooking in the kitchen, I knew I was in trouble. This wasn't just ordinary chili. This was "fibber's chili," which was invented by my great-aunt. She fed this chili to anyone she thought had told a fib or a lie. "One bite," she used to say, "and they can't help but tell you the whole truth."

I knew my mom was making it for me now. Why? Yesterday I kicked a soccer ball into a window, and it broke. Of course, then I told my mother that the window smashed when a bird flew into it. I suppose now I could tell her that I'm too sick to eat. But then she'd serve me fibber's chili a second time! I've got to get up my courage and tell the truth.

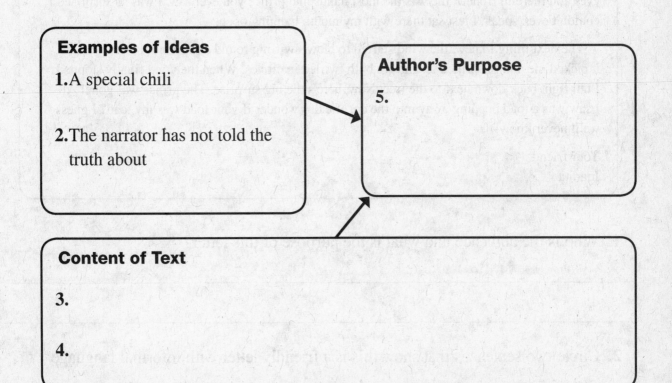

Examples of Ideas

1. A special chili

2. The narrator has not told the truth about

Author's Purpose

5.

Content of Text

3.

4.

School + Home **Home Activity** Your child identified the author's purpose in a text. Have your child choose something to write in a letter to a friend or relative. What would your child's purpose be, given the subject matter, and how could information be presented to serve that purpose? Then have your child write the letter.

© Pearson Education, Inc., 4

Writing • Friendly Letter

Key Features of a Friendly Letter

- usually includes five parts: heading, salutation, body, closing, and signature
- heading may include only the date
- written in a friendly voice, often to someone you know well

---

August 23, 20___

Dear Reba Jo,

    Wait till I tell you what happened to me last week. There I was out in the field picking corn. I had been picking corn for what seemed to me to be hours. It was really only about 30 minutes, but the sun was hot that day. Well, I decided to take a little nap. I walked over to a big shade tree at the end of the cornfield. I leaned up against the tree and I started to drift off.

    Suddenly I heard this voice — deep, but kind of croaky.

    "Well, young lady. It looks like you're sleeping on the job," the voice said. I snapped open my eyes and there in front of me was the most handsome prince you ever saw. I was so surprised I couldn't even speak. I just sat there with my mouth hanging open.

    The next thing I knew, the wind started to blow, swirling round and round. It blew so hard it picked me and the prince up and we both twirled in circles. When the wind finally stopped, I fell right back down next to the tree. Now, here's the big surprise. The prince was gone! All I saw was a toad hopping away into the cornfield. I wonder if your toad was my toad? I guess we'll never know!

Your friend,
Juanita

---

1. Who is the audience and what is the purpose of this letter?

_____

_____

2. Circle two sentences that show this is a friendly letter with informal language.

© Pearson Education, Inc., 4

Name _____

Vocabulary

Directions Draw a line to connect each word on the left with its definition on the right.

1. riverbed   a large area of level or rolling land with grass but few or no trees

2. favor   a channel in which a river flows or used to flow

3. prairie   an agreement to trade; deal

4. lassoed   act of kindness

5. bargain   roped; caught with a lasso

Directions In each statement below, the first pair of words has a certain relationship (such as the same meaning). To complete the statement, add a word that gives the second pair of words the same relationship as the first pair. For example, *neat* is to *messy* (opposite meanings) as *happy* is to *sad* (opposite meanings). Choose the word from the box and write it on the line to the left.

_____   6. *Laughed* is to *cried* as *whispered* is to _____.

_____   7. *Remembered* is to *recalled* as *angered* is to _____.

_____   8. *Tree* is to *forest* as *grass* is to _____.

_____   9. *Train* is to *track* as *river* is to _____.

_____   10. *Disagreement* is to *fight* as *deal* is to _____.

Check the Words You Know

___bargain
___favor
___lassoed
___offended
___prairie
___riverbed
___shrieked

Write a Fairy Tale

On a separate sheet of paper, write your own fairy tale about making a bargain. Use as many vocabulary words as you can.

Home Activity Your child identified and used vocabulary words from *The Horned Toad Prince*. Together, create additional analogies, as shown in the second activity, to use with the vocabulary words.

© Pearson Education, Inc., 4

Name _____

Compound Sentences

A **compound sentence** is made up of two simple sentences joined by a comma
and a connecting word such as *and, but,* or *or.*

Simple Sentences	Fairy tales are very old.
	Children still enjoy them.
Compound Sentence	Fairy tales are very old, *but* children still enjoy them.

The two sentences in a compound sentence must have ideas that make sense together.

Directions Write *S* after each simple sentence and *C* after each compound sentence.
Do not confuse a compound subject or predicate with a compound sentence.

1. Fairy tales and other old stories are sometimes very scary. _____

2. Witches, giants, or trolls can give little children nightmares. _____

3. Fairy tale heroes are often in danger, but they usually win in the end. _____

4. Often a poor girl marries a prince, or a poor boy marries a princess. _____

5. The dragon is killed, and everybody lives happily ever after. _____

Directions Join each pair of simple sentences to make a compound sentence. Use the
word *and, but,* or *or.* Do not forget to add a comma.

6. The hero was small and young. He was very brave.

_____

7. She fell in love with the prince. He fell in love with her.

_____

8. You can fight the dragon. You can run away.

_____

9. He saw the woman in the tower. He wanted to save her.

_____

10. The wolf knocked on the pigs' door. They wouldn't let him in.

_____

 Home Activity Your child learned about compound sentences. Encourage him or her to show you how the
words *and, but,* and *or* can link simple sentences to form compound sentences.

© Pearson Education, Inc., 4

Long e

Spelling Words				
prairie	calorie	honey	valley	money
finally	movie	country	empty	city
rookie	hockey	collie	breezy	jury
balcony	steady	alley	trolley	misty

Rhymes Write the list word that rhymes with the underlined word.

1. Are you <u>ready</u>? Take it slow and ____.
2. Go to Main and First Streets, <u>Molly</u>. That's where you can catch the ____.
3. He paid a lot of <u>money</u> for the big jar of ____.
4. Let's make a <u>tally</u> of the number of cars in the ____.
5. Buffaloes are big and <u>hairy</u>. They used to roam across the ____.
6. "He's guilty!" the lawyer said with <u>fury</u> to the ____.
7. It was a <u>pity</u> he couldn't take a trip to the ____.
8. Sailing boats is <u>easy</u> when the wind is strong and ____.
9. "You're one smart <u>cookie</u>," said the coach to the ____.

1. _____
2. _____
3. _____
4. _____
5. _____
6. _____
7. _____
8. _____
9. _____

Synonyms Write the list word that means the same thing as the word or phrase.

10. raised porch
11. unit of energy
12. film
13. sheep dog
14. ice game
15. cash
16. vale
17. at last
18. nation
19. hazy
20. unfilled

10. _____
11. _____
12. _____
13. _____
14. _____
15. _____
16. _____
17. _____
18. _____
19. _____
20. _____

© Pearson Education, Inc., 4

Home Activity Your child wrote words that end with the long e sound spelled *ie, ey,* or *y.* Ask your child to say sentences using list words.

Name ______________________________

Outline Form A

Title ______________________________

A. ______________________________

1. ______________________________
2. ______________________________
3. ______________________________

B. ______________________________

1. ______________________________
2. ______________________________
3. ______________________________

C. ______________________________

1. ______________________________
2. ______________________________
3. ______________________________

© Pearson Education, Inc., 4

Vocabulary • Synonyms and Antonyms

- Sometimes when you are reading, you see a word you don't know. To help you, the author may give you a **synonym** or an **antonym** as a context clue for the word.
- Synonyms are words with the same or similar meanings, such as *large* and *big.* A synonym is often set off by commas and preceded by the word *or* or *like.*
- Antonyms are words with opposite meanings, such as *happy* and *sad.* An antonym is often preceded by the words *instead of* or *rather than.*

Directions Read the following passage. Then answer the questions below.

Once upon a time, there lived an old man. One day, the man took a walk and came upon two boys fighting, a big boy and a little boy. The little boy shrieked, or screeched, that the big boy had not carried off his half of a bargain.

"The deal," he screamed, "was that we would both dig for the treasure—not just me!" The little boy was obviously offended, or insulted, to be doing all the work. "I'm not asking for favors. I just want you to do your share of the digging," he said.

The boys stopped fighting when they saw the old man standing before them. The old man reached in his pocket and took out the largest ruby the boys had ever seen.

"You should be friends instead of enemies," said the man. "If you agree never to fight again, I will show you a treasure that is a million times greater than the one you are digging for."

1. What synonym for *shrieked* does the author use? How do you know?

_____

2. Where in the passage is the antonym for *friends?* How do you know?

_____

3. In the passage, what is the synonym for *offended?*

_____

4. Which two antonyms describe the boys?

_____

© Pearson Education, Inc., 4

Home Activity Your child identified synonyms (words that mean the same thing) and antonyms (words that are opposite in meaning) that appear within the context of a passage. Play a naming game with your child by taking turns saying words that have the same or the opposite meaning of the given word.

Illustration/Caption/Label

- **Illustrations** and pictures can help readers understand information about characters and events in a story or a subject in a nonfiction article.

- A **caption** is the text that explains or gives more information about an illustration or picture. Captions usually appear below or to the side of the image.

- **Labels** also use text to provide information about illustrations and pictures. They can appear inside the image or above or below it.

Directions Study the illustrations and captions below.

prickly pear cactus

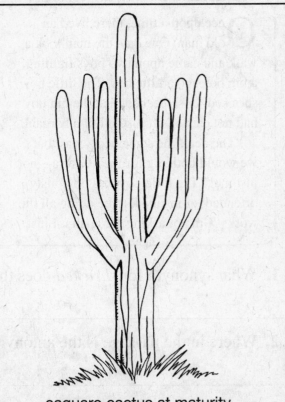

saguaro cactus at maturity

The prickly pear cactus, which grows in the American Southwest, has flat stems called pads. These stems are good at holding in water. For this reason, desert animals try to eat them. However, the prickly pear cactus protects itself with sharp, pointy spines that keep animals away.

The very large saguaro cactus grows from a very small seed. It takes many years for the saguaro to grow to its full size. These plants sometimes live 150 years. At that age, a saguaro may measure up to fifty feet high.

© Pearson Education, Inc., 4

Directions Use the illustrations and captions to answer the questions.

1. What is shown in these illustrations?

_____

2. What do the illustrations themselves show about the differences between the prickly pear cactus and the saguaro cactus?

_____

3. How large can a saguaro cactus grow?

_____

4. How does the prickly pear cactus protect itself? How do you know?

_____

5. Why does the caption for the saguaro cactus include a detail about its seed, even though the illustration does not show this detail?

_____

_____

6. If the illustration of the prickly pear showed the kinds of animals that try to eat the plant's pads, what new information might the caption include?

_____

7. What label might be added to the first illustration? Where would you place it?

_____

8. What label might be added to the second illustration? Where would you place it?

_____

9. What kind of article might include these illustrations?

_____

10. Write a new caption that could be used for both images at once.

_____

© Pearson Education, Inc., 4

Home Activity Your child learned how to analyze illustrations and captions. Read a nonfiction article that contains no illustrations. Together, discuss what illustration you could add to help the reader understand the information in the article.

Long e

Proofread an Ad Jan wrote this ad to sell her dog. Circle five misspelled words. Write the words correctly. Then write the sentence that has a capitalization mistake correctly.

Dog for Sale

This colly is a honey of a dog! Very nice and steadey. Likes to play ball and hockie too. We're not asking a lot of monie for this fine Dog. He needs a good home because we are probablie moving to the city.

Call: 555-888-1234

Spelling Words

prairie	rookie
calorie	hockey
honey	collie
valley	breezy
money	jury
finally	balcony
movie	steady
country	alley
empty	trolley
city	misty

Frequently Misspelled Words

finally
probably

1. _____   2. _____
3. _____   4. _____
5. _____
6. _____
_____

Correct the Sentences Cross out the misspelled list word in each sentence. Write the word correctly.

7. Please put the trash cans in the ally.
8. It took the pioneers a long time to cross the prairy.
9. Every spring, we put our potted plants on the balconie.
10. The mistie fog made it hard to see the road.
11. The long trip is finallee over.
12. The mailbox was emptie.
13. The rokie had a successful season.
14. I like huney on my toast.
15. The moovy was funny.
16. I take the troley to the shops.

7. _____
8. _____
9. _____
10. _____
11. _____
12. _____
13. _____
14. _____
15. _____
16. _____

© Pearson Education, Inc., 4

Home Activity Your child identified misspelled words that end with the long e sound spelled *ie*, *ey*, and *y*. Say a list word and spell it, stopping before the letter or letters that spell the long e sound at the end of the word. Have your child complete the word.

Compound Sentences

Directions Read the passage. Then read each question. Circle the letter of the correct answer.

The Hat in the Well

(1) Reba Jo lives on the prairie, and she loved roping. (2) Once her hat blew off and falls into a well. (3) Reba Jo was scared, but she wants her hat. (4) The toad made an offer that Reba Jo accepted. (5) The toad got her hat, and she had to kiss him.

1 What change, if any, should be made in sentence 1?

  A Change the comma to a period.

  B Change *lives on the prairie* to **loves the prairie and roping.**

  C Change *lives* to **lived.**

  D Make no change.

2 What change, if any, should be made in sentence 2?

  A Change *blew* to **is blown.**

  B Change *falls* to **fell.**

  C Change *falls into a well* to **blew into a well.**

  D Make no change.

3 What change, if any, should be made in sentence 3?

  A Change *wants* to **wanted.**

  B Change *wants* to **wanting.**

  C Change *but* to **and.**

  D Make no change.

4 What change, if any, should be made in sentence 4?

  A Change *made* to **gave.**

  B Change *that* to **and.**

  C Change the period to a question mark.

  D Make no change.

5 What change, if any, should be made in sentence 5?

  A Change *and* to **but.**

  B Change *got her hat* to **gets her hat.**

  C Change *got her hat* to **got her hat and kissed her.**

  D Make no change.

© Pearson Education, Inc., 4

Home Activity Your child prepared for taking tests on compound sentences. Say *but, and,* or *or* and have your child say a compound sentence using each word as a link.

Main Idea and Details

- The **main idea** is the most important idea from a paragraph, passage, or article.
- **Details** are small pieces of information that tell more about the main idea.

Directions Read the following passage. Then complete the diagram below.

Several people helped make Yellowstone National Park a protected place. In the 1600s and 1700s, fur trappers came through the area. They noticed its amazing features, such as geysers that shoot hot water high into the air. When they returned to towns and camps, they told stories about what they had seen.

Soon expeditions were organized to explore Yellowstone. The expedition led by Ferdinand Hayden in 1871 included a photographer and an artist who captured the beauty of Yellowstone in their pictures. They showed their pictures to Congress. In 1872, President Grant signed a law that made sure Yellowstone would be protected forever by making it the first national park.

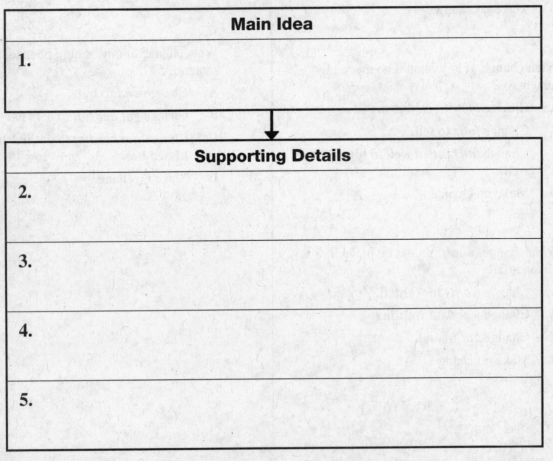

Main Idea

1.

Supporting Details

2.

3.

4.

5.

Home Activity Your child read a short passage and identified the main idea and supporting details. Work with your child to create a graphic organizer that identifies the main idea and supporting details of an article about a natural area.

© Pearson Education, Inc., 4

Writing • Personal Narrative

Key Features of Personal Narrative

- tells about a personal experience
- written in the first person
- usually organized in the order in which events occurred

How I Learned To Ride a Bike

I remember the day I learned to ride a bike. At first it started out like any other Saturday. I woke up around 10:00. Next I had breakfast. Then I got dressed and called my best friend, Roger, to see if he wanted to go to the park. He did.

So then I went to the park. Roger and I always meet by the swings. Roger can walk to the park, but this time he took his bike. He knew I didn't like it when he took his bike because I didn't know how to ride.

"Sorry about the bike," he said, "but I have to go to buy some milk after we play. I didn't want to walk all of the way there and back."

"No, problem," I said. Then Roger and I went off to play.

First we went on the swings. They were right there. Next we ran over to the climbing bars. Then we went to shoot some baskets on the basketball court. Finally it was time to go home.

"You want to come with me to the store?" asked Roger. "I'll let you try riding my bike if you want."

"Very funny," I said. "You know I can't ride a bike."

"I bet you can if you really try," said Roger. "My bike is small for you. You can just put your feet down on the ground when you start to lose your balance."

I didn't think it sounded like a bad idea, so I tried. First, I got on the bike. I could stand easily. Next I started to pedal very slowly. Roger ran next to me. If started to lose my balance, I just put my foot on the ground to keep from falling. I did this over and over all the way to the store. By the time we got there I was actually riding. Finally, I knew how to ride a bike!

1. Describe three events in the narrative using time-order words:

First, I _____

Next, I _____

Finally, I _____

2. What is the main topic of this narrative?

_____

© Pearson Education, Inc., 4

Vocabulary

Directions Choose the word from the box that best matches each definition. Write the word on the line to the left.

Check the Words You Know

____glacier
____impressive
____naturalist
____preserve
____slopes
____species
____wilderness

_____ 1. a mass of ice moving very slowly down a mountain or along a valley

_____ 2. a wild place with few or no people living in it

_____ 3. to keep from harm or change

_____ 4. a person who studies living things

_____ 5. a set of related living things with similar characteristics

Directions Choose the word from the box that best matches the meaning of each underlined word. Write the word on the line to the left.

_____ 6. We went skiing down the snow-covered <u>mountains</u>.

_____ 7. The scenery in the national park was <u>magnificent</u>.

_____ 8. The park rangers want to <u>keep changes from happening in</u> the park.

_____ 9. Long ago a <u>large sheet of ice</u> covered this whole area.

_____ 10. We camped out in a <u>wild, isolated</u> area.

Write a Poem

On a separate sheet of paper, write a poem about your favorite natural place. Use as many vocabulary words as you can.

Home Activity Your child identified and used vocabulary words from *Letters Home from Yosemite.* Read a nonfiction article about a natural place with your child. Have your child create sentences in response to the article using the vocabulary words.

© Pearson Education, Inc., 4

Clauses and Complex Sentences

A **clause** is a group of words with a subject and a verb. A **dependent clause** begins with a word such as *because* or *when*. It cannot stand alone as a sentence. An **independent clause** can stand alone.

Dependent Clause	when I was eight
Independent Clause	My family visited Yosemite.

A sentence made up of a dependent clause and an independent clause is a **complex sentence**.

Complex Sentences	When I was eight, my family visited Yosemite.
	My family visited Yosemite when I was eight.

Other words that often introduce a dependent clause are *since, although, if, until, unless, as, after,* and *before*. When a dependent clause comes first in a complex sentence, it is followed by a comma.

Directions Write *I* if the underlined group of words is an independent clause. Write *D* if it is a dependent clause.

1. People visit Yosemite <u>because it is so beautiful</u>. _____

2. <u>When you see El Capitan</u>, you'll be amazed. _____

3. If you go there, <u>visit Yosemite Falls</u>. _____

4. <u>You will probably see a bear</u> before you leave. _____

5. <u>After I returned</u>, I read a book about the park. _____

Directions Combine each pair of simple sentences. Use the word in ( ). Write the complex sentence.

6. I'll visit all the national parks. I'm grown up. (when)

_____

7. I'm only ten years old. I have to travel with my family. (since)

_____

Home Activity Your child learned about clauses and complex sentences. Encourage him or her to show you how words such as *because, when, although,* and *if* can link simple sentences to form complex sentences.

© Pearson Education, Inc., 4

Long *u*

Spelling Words				
usual	huge	flute	mood	smooth
threw	afternoon	scooter	juice	cruise
truth	bruise	cruel	excuse	pupil
groove	confuse	humor	duty	curfew

Antonyms Write the list word that has the opposite or nearly
the opposite meaning as the word.

1. kind   1. _____
2. evening   2. _____
3. rough   3. _____
4. dishonesty 4. _____
5. caught   5. _____

Synonyms Write the list word that has the same or nearly
the same meaning as the word.

6. atmosphere 6. _____
7. instrument 7. _____
8. ridge   8. _____
9. sail   9. _____
10. forgive   10. _____

Definitions Write the list word that fits the definition.

11. _____ the time when children must be indoors
12. _____ a student
13. _____ discolored skin caused by an injury
14. _____ a riding toy with a platform, wheels, and a handlebar
15. _____ funny or amusing quality
16. _____ liquid taken from fruit or vegetables
17. _____ enormous
18. _____ a task a person is required to do
19. _____ ordinary
20. _____ perplex, mix up

Home Activity Your child wrote words with long *u* sounds spelled *u-consonant-e, ew, oo, ui,* and *u.*
Say a list word and have your child write it.

© Pearson Education, Inc., 4

Scoring Rubric: Personal Narrative

	4	3	2	1
Focus/Ideas	Clear, focused narrative with engaging topic and descriptive details	Focused narrative with good topic and some details	Narrative has some unclear or off-topic details	Narrative lacking clarity or development
Organization	Well-organized paragraphs that tell events in chronological order.	Good paragraphs with events largely in chronological order.	Some events out of chronological order	No paragraphs, no chronological order
Voice	Lively, engaging voice that speaks to readers	Lively and engaging most of the time	Tries to be lively and engaging.	Neither lively nor engaging
Word Choice	Exact, descriptive, and time-order transition words to convey vivd impressions	Clear language; conveys strong impressions and generally suggests time-order	Some vague or repetitive words	Incorrect or limited word choice
Sentences	Varied sentences, including complex sentences	Smooth sentences, some complex	Too many short, choppy sentences	Many fragments and run-ons
Conventions	Excellent control and accuracy; independent and dependent clauses used correctly	Good control, few errors; independent and dependent clauses mostly used correctly	Weak control; independent and dependent clauses used somewhat, though not totally, correctly	Serious errors that obscure meaning; independent and dependent clauses not used correctly

© Pearson Education, Inc., 4

Name _____

Vocabulary • Suffixes

- A **suffix** is a word part added to the end of a **base word** to change its meaning. You can use a suffix to figure out the meaning of an unfamiliar word.
- The suffix *-ist* can make a word mean "one who is an expert in." The suffix *-ive* means "tending or inclined to _____."

Directions Read the following passage. Then answer the questions below.

On our sunrise hike through the extensive wilderness, the naturalist told us that the park was filled with many species of animals. It was impressive to think that so many different animals could live in the same place. She also told us that to preserve the park, we needed to leave it as if we had never been there. We couldn't take any flowers or plants with us, and we shouldn't leave our garbage there either. Unfortunately, visitors in the past had not been so careful. Restoring the park to its natural state is a creative job.

1. What is the suffix in the word *extensive?* What does it tell you about the meaning of the word?

_____

2. What does *naturalist* mean? How do you know?

_____

_____

3. What does *impressive* mean? How do you know?

_____

4. What does the word *creative* mean?

_____

5. Write two other words that end in either *-ist* or *-ive.*

_____

 Home Activity Your child read a short passage and identified suffixes to understand words in a passage. Read an article with your child. Help your child to identify and circle the suffixes added to words in the article.

© Pearson Education, Inc., 4

Print Sources

- Libraries contain many sources of information for students to use. You can use a library database or a card catalog to identify and locate these materials. In both cases, you can search for materials by author, title, or subject.
- **Print sources** include encyclopedias, newspapers, magazines, dictionaries, and other reference books.

Directions Study this school's list of available print resources.

Newspapers	**Encyclopedias**
Hillside School News (school newspaper)	*Encyclopedia of History Makers,* vol. I
Hillside Streets (community paper)	*Encyclopedia of the Nation,* vol. I–X
Daily Globe (metropolitan city paper)	*Encyclopedia of Nature,* vol. I–II
	Encyclopedia of Science, vol. I–IV
	Encyclopedia of Women, vol. I–II
Magazines	
History for Young People	**Dictionaries**
Mathematics Today	*Kenner's Dictionary of Common Words and Phrases*
The Natural World	*The Student's Dictionary*
Go Go Go Travel Monthly	*Theisen's Dictionary of Medicine*
Sports U.S.A.	

© Pearson Education, Inc., 4

Directions Imagine that you are writing a report on Yosemite National Park. Use the list of print sources to answer the questions below.

1. What print source would you use first for your report on Yosemite? Explain.

_____

2. Why might a newspaper not be the first place you look for information?

_____

_____

3. What magazine(s) might have information you could use for your report?

_____

4. Which source(s) might have interesting photographs for your report?

_____

5. How might you use a dictionary while writing your report?

_____

6. Suggest a topic you might check in a library's card catalog for information.

_____

7. Name three listed sources unlikely to have much information on Yosemite.

_____

8. Which encyclopedia might help you find information on animals in Yosemite?

_____

9. How might you use an author's name to find information for this report?

_____

_____

10. What print sources would have up-to-date information on a fire at Yosemite?

_____

_____

Home Activity Your child learned about print sources. Take a trip together to your local library. Find and browse through the sections of print sources.

© Pearson Education, Inc., 4

Long *u*

Proofread a Script Read the script that a DJ will read on the radio. Circle six spelling errors and write the words correctly. Add quotation marks where they are needed.

> **DJ:** Good afternune, listeners. Today, we're taking a crewse down memory lane. I'm going to play some smoothe sounds from the past. But first, here's a word from our sponsor.
>
> **Commercial Spot:** Is it breakfast as usual? How about a huge energy boost? Drink some OranGee orange juce today. Don't confuse it with other breakfast drinks!
>
> **DJ:** Now, it's time for the news! A high schewl pupil suffered a huge bruze when he fell off his scooter. I have no clue what happened, said the student.

1. _____	2. _____	
3. _____	4. _____	
5. _____	6. _____	

Proofread Words Circle the word that is spelled correctly. Write the word.

7. Abby likes to read stories that have some **humor hewmor**.   7. _____
8. The captain **thrue threw** a life jacket to each passenger.   8. _____
9. "There is no **excus excuse** for this mess," said Mom.   9. _____
10. It's always a good idea to tell the **truth trueth**.   10. _____
11. "Don't stay out past **curfoo curfew**," Dad warned.   11. _____
12. The **huge hug** truck rattled the windows as it passed our house.   12. _____

Spelling Words

usual
huge
flute
mood
smooth
threw
afternoon
scooter
juice
cruise

truth
bruise
cruel
excuse
pupil
groove
confuse
humor
duty
curfew

Frequently Misspelled Words

school
too

Home Activity Your child identified misspelled words with *u-consonant-e*, *ew*, *oo*, *ui*, and *u*. Ask your child to use list words to make up a radio announcement or commercial.

© Pearson Education, Inc., 4

Clauses and Complex Sentences

Directions Read the passage. Then read each question. Circle the letter of the correct answer.

Camping in Yosemite

(1) When the tourists arrive. (2) There are many cars. (3) Don't tease the animals, and they should not bother you. (4) Before going to sleep, pitch your tent. (5) We went too near the falls, we got soaking wet. (6) If there are bobcats and bears, we don't see any. (7) When I am hiking, I saw a large brown animal.

1 What change, if any, should be made in sentences 1 and 2?

  A Change the period in sentence 1 to a comma and change *There* to **there.**

  B Change *tourists arrive* to **tourist arrives.**

  C Change *There are many cars* to **many cars arrive.**

  D Make no change.

2 What change, if any, should be made in sentence 3?

  A Change the comma to a period.

  B Change *and* to **but.**

  C Change the period to a question mark.

  D Make no change.

3 What change, if any, should be made in sentence 5?

  A Change *we got soaking wet* to **We got soaking wet.**

  B Change the comma to a comma plus the word **so.**

  C Change the period to an exclamation.

  D Make no change.

4 What change, if any, should be made in sentence 6?

  A Change *If there are bobcats and bears* to **There are bobcats and bears.**

  B Change *don't* to **didn't.**

  C Change the comma to a period.

  D Make no change.

5 What change, if any, should be made in sentence 7?

  A Change *am* to **go.**

  B Change *am* to **was.**

  C Change the comma to a period.

  D Make no change.

Home Activity Your child prepared for taking tests on clauses and complex sentences. Say *clause* and then *sentence* and have your child say a clause and then a sentence using it.

© Pearson Education, Inc., 4

Short Vowels VCCV

Spelling Words				
admire	magnet	contest	method	custom
rally	soccer	engine	sudden	finger
accident	mitten	intend	fabric	flatten
rascal	gutter	mammal	happen	cannon

Synonyms Write the list word that is a synonym for each word.

1. quick _____

2. occur _____

3. scoundrel _____

4. squash _____

5. cloth _____

6. respect _____

7. habit _____

8. competition _____

9. plan _____

10. technique _____

Definitions Write the list word beside its definition.

11. object that attracts iron _____

12. unlucky event that harms _____

13. a large gun on a fixed base _____

14. a sport played by kicking a round ball _____

15. animal that produces milk for its young _____

16. to come together _____

17. a roadside channel _____

18. a part of the hand _____

19. a machine that uses energy _____

20. a kind of glove _____

© Pearson Education, Inc., 4

Home Activity Your child spelled words with the short vowel pattern VCCV. Have your child point out list words with short vowel *a* in the first syllable. Repeat for each vowel.

Declarative and Interrogative Sentences

Directions Write *D* if the sentence is declarative. Write *I* if the sentence is interrogative.

1. Have you read this book? _____

2. I'll leave my dog outside. _____

3. Would you like to visit the library? _____

4. There were wild animals in old Florida. _____

5. Can you write a story like this? _____

Directions Read each sentence and add the correct end punctuation. Then write whether each sentence is declarative or interrogative.

6. The librarian was old and frail

_____

7. Can you guess what happened

_____

8. She told the story over and over

_____

9. I threw the book at the bear

_____

10. Do you believe the bear took the book

_____

Directions Change each sentence to the kind named in ( ). Write the new sentence.

11. When is the storyteller at the library? (declarative)

_____

12. Most students like hearing stories. (interrogative)

_____

© Pearson Education, Inc., 4

Long *a* and *i*

Spelling Words				
sigh	right	weigh	eight	detail
height	spray	braid	bait	grain
slight	thigh	tight	raisin	trait
highway	frighten	dismay	freight	sleigh

Classifying Write the list word that fits each group.

1. arm, neck, hand, _____
2. laugh, cry, yawn, _____
3. pole, line, hook, _____
4. one, five, twelve, _____
5. avenue, street, lane, _____
6. length, width, depth, _____
7. prune, apricot, cherry, _____
8. scare, startle, spook, _____
9. wash, dry, comb, _____
10. skis, snow fort, sled, _____

1. _____
2. _____
3. _____
4. _____
5. _____
6. _____
7. _____
8. _____
9. _____
10. _____

Alphabetize Read the words. Write the list word from the box that comes between them in a dictionary.

11. freezer	_____	French	
12. go	_____	group	
13. slam	_____	sloop	
14. tomb	_____	trip	
15. dish	_____	displace	
16. tiara	_____	time	
17. week	_____	window	
18. sport	_____	spring	
19. depot	_____	develop	
20. reserve	_____	ring	

right
detail
grain
slight
dismay
spray
freight
tight
weigh
trait

© Pearson Education, Inc., 4

Home Activity Your child spelled words with long *a* and *i* spelled *ai*, *eigh*, *ay*, and *igh*. Ask your child to name all the ways he or she can spell long *a* and long *i* and write an example word for each spelling.

Imperative and Exclamatory Sentences

Directions Write *E* if the sentence is exclamatory. Write *I* if the sentence is imperative.

1. Check the maps and supplies.　　　　　　　_____

2. This dog can save a drowning man!　　　_____

3. Pay for the supplies.　　　　　　　　　　_____

4. I've never seen animals like these!　　　　_____

5. Keep a log of where we stop.　　　　　　　_____

Directions Read each sentence. Write *C* if the end punctuation is correct. Write *NC* if the end punctuation is not correct.

6. Say farewell to your families.　　　　　　_____

7. This is the journey of a lifetime!　　　　　_____

8. There will be breathtaking sights.　　　　_____

9. You must be able to swim.　　　　　　　　_____

10. I was so excited to be there.　　　　　　_____

Directions Write the correct end punctuation for each sentence. Then write *E* if it is an exclamatory sentence and *I* if it is an imperative sentence.

11. The trip may take years　　　　　　　　_____

12. The Missouri River has many dangerous rapids _____

13. Let the dog stay on deck　　　　　　　　_____

14. Pull toward the bank　　　　　　　　　　_____

15. Sit, Bosco　　　　　　　　　　　　　　_____

© Pearson Education, Inc., 4

Long e and o

Spelling Words				
sweet	each	three	least	freedom
below	throat	float	foam	flown
greet	season	croak	shallow	eagle
indeed	rainbow	grown	seaweed	hollow

Word Patterns Fill in the missing letters to write a list word.

1. S H __ L __ O __
2. __ A __ N B O __
3. __ __ E E __ __ M
4. __ E A S __ __
5. S __ __ W __ D
6. __ __ R O __ __
7. __ O L __ __ W
8. __ N __ E E __
9. __ __ C H
10. __ L __ __ T
11. G __ O W __

Crossword Puzzle Use the clues below to solve the puzzle.

Across
  2. welcome
  4. many white bubbles
  5. opposite of *above*
  7. opposite of *sour*

Down
  1. frog sound
  3. large, powerful bird
  4. fly, flew, _____
  6. opposite of *most*

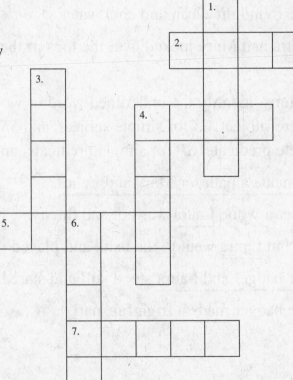

© Pearson Education, Inc., 4

Home Activity Your child spelled words with long *e* and *o* spelled *ee*, *ea*, *oa*, and *ow*. Read each list word. Have your child tell the spelling of the long vowel sound in the word.

Complete Subjects and Predicates

Directions Circle the simple subject and the simple predicate of each sentence.

1. Laura thought she would not go into the deep water.

2. Slowly Laura grasped a willow stick.

3. The fierce white teeth snapped at her nose.

4. She thought the day would never end.

5. Mary was learning how to read.

Directions Read each sentence. Underline the complete subject of each sentence. Underline the complete predicate twice. Write *SSS* if the subject is a compound subject. Write *PPP* if the predicate is a compound predicate. Write *N* if there is neither a compound subject nor a compound predicate.

6. The steep and grassy bank was muddy. _____

7. The animal stood still and stared at her. _____

8. She slid out of bed and walked across the floor. _____

9. She found the clean and cool water. _____

10. Laura and Mary looked over the tops of the grasses. _____

Directions Identify the underlined word or words in each sentence. Write *CS* for complete subject, *SS* for simple subject, and *SSS* for compound subject. Write *CP* for complete predicate, *SP* for simple predicate, and *PPP* for compound predicate.

11. Pa made a path for Mary and Laura. _____

12. After a while Laura was hot and thirsty. _____

13. Pa and Laura went to the bank and played with Mary. _____

14. The badger and Laura stood still and stared at each other. _____

15. The badger made a frightful snarl. _____

© Pearson Education, Inc., 4

Long e

Spelling Words				
prairie	calorie	honey	valley	money
finally	movie	country	empty	city
rookie	hockey	collie	breezy	jury
balcony	steady	alley	trolley	misty

Finish the Sentences Circle the underlined list word that is spelled correctly. Write the word.

1. My favorite dog is the border <u>colley</u>   <u>collie</u>.

1. _____

2. Sam and I went to a <u>hockey</u>   <u>hockie</u> game.

2. _____

3. The kitten ran into the <u>ally</u>   <u>alley</u>.

3. _____

4. The <u>jurie</u>   <u>jury</u> listened carefully to the lawyer.

4. _____

5. Crops in the <u>vally</u>   <u>valley</u> were green and healthy.

5. _____

6. That <u>movie</u>   <u>movey</u> about sailors was exciting.

6. _____

7. Some <u>praire</u>   <u>prairie</u> grasses grow ten feet tall.

7. _____

8. Tea with <u>honie</u>   <u>honey</u> is delicious.

8. _____

9. <u>Finaley</u>   <u>Finally</u> it was time to go.

9. _____

10. Let's sit on the <u>balcony</u>   <u>balconey</u> tonight.

10. _____

Word Clues Write the list word that matches the clue.

11. The glass is half full or half ____.

11. _____

12. Fresh air and wide open spaces

12. _____

13. It's often like this after a rain.

13. _____

14. Sailors hope for this condition.

14. _____

15. It can be burned and counted.

15. _____

16. Metal or paper, it spends either way.

16. _____

17. Bright lights, crowded streets

17. _____

18. He's the new guy on the team.

18. _____

19. If you stick to one speed, you're this.

19. _____

20. It can get you where you want to go.

20. _____

© Pearson Education, Inc., 4

School + Home

Home Activity Your child used words with the long e sound spelled *ie*, *ey*, and *y*. Say each list word and spell it incorrectly. Have your child tell you the correct spelling.

Compound Sentences

Directions Write *S* if the sentence is a simple sentence. Write *C* if the sentence is a compound sentence. Do not confuse a compound subject or predicate with a compound sentence.

1. *The Horned Toad Prince* is based on an old fairy tale.   _____

2. It is about a frog and a princess.   _____

3. A princess was by a spring, and she lost her golden ball.   _____

4. Just then a frog wandered by.   _____

5. The frog offered help to the princess.   _____

6. The princess must be kind, or she would not get the ball.   _____

7. The frog found the ball, but the princess ran away with it.   _____

8. The frog hopped after her and found her in her palace.   _____

9. The princess slammed the door, but the king let the frog in.   _____

10. The princess had given her word, and she must keep it.   _____

Directions Write the word you would use (*and, but,* or *or*) to join each pair of simple sentences into a compound sentence.

11. The frog had to sleep in the palace. He would never become a prince.

    _____

12. The princess did not like the frog. She let him sleep on her pillow.

    _____

13. On the third morning she awoke. She was amazed.

    _____

14. She looked for an ugly frog. She saw a handsome prince.

    _____

15. The prince and princess went off together. They lived happily ever after.

    _____

© Pearson Education, Inc., 4

Long *u*

Spelling Words				
usual	huge	flute	mood	smooth
threw	afternoon	scooter	juice	cruise
truth	bruise	cruel	excuse	pupil
groove	confuse	humor	duty	curfew

Words in Context Write a list word from the box to complete each sentence.

1. When I fell, I got a _____ on my knee.

2. Hap moved quickly through traffic on his ____.

3. The pitcher _____ the ball 95 miles per hour.

4. Julie played a solo on her _____.

5. Salsa music puts me in a good _____.

6. Most people like _____ with their breakfast.

7. A comic needs a good sense of _____.

8. Bad directions might _____ you.

9. I usually get sleepy in the middle of the _____.

10. A horse is large, but an elephant is _____.

1. _____

2. _____

3. _____

4. _____

5. _____

6. _____

7. _____

8. _____

9. _____

10. _____

Word Scramble Unscramble the list words and write the letters on the lines.

11. suula _____

12. frecuw _____

13. clure _____

14. sceuxe _____

15. goover _____

16. scrieu _____

17. uhttr _____

18. tudy _____

19. lippu _____

20. mthoso _____

Home Activity Your child used words with long *u* spelled *u*-consonant-*e*, *ew*, *oo*, *ui*, and *u*. Say each list word and have your child spell it. Then have him or her use it in a sentence.

© Pearson Education, Inc., 4

Clauses and Complex Sentences

Directions Write *I* if the underlined group of words is an independent clause. Write *D* if it is a dependent clause.

1. When miners first arrived, <u>Native Americans were living in Yosemite.</u> _____

2. Later, tourists flocked to the valley <u>because it was so beautiful.</u> _____

3. <u>As more people visited,</u> the area suffered. _____

4. <u>People arrived in Yosemite by horse</u> before there was a railroad. _____

5. The land was unprotected <u>until the federal government gave it to California.</u> _____

Directions Write the clause in the sentence that is named in ( ).

6. Since cars were not allowed at first, most early visitors came by train. (dependent)

_____

7. After cars were permitted, the park became even more crowded. (independent)

_____

8. The area was covered with dust because the roads were unpaved. (independent)

_____

9. Some roads became one way when traffic got too bad. (dependent)

_____

10. Visitors walked more after cars were banned from some areas. (independent)

_____

Directions Combine each pair of simple sentences. Use the word in ( ) to begin each sentence. Write the complex sentence. Remember to add a comma after a dependent clause when it comes first.

11. Yosemite has many visitors. You can get away from the crowds. (although)

_____

_____

12. You want a great experience. Go to Yosemite. (if)

_____

© Pearson Education, Inc., 4

Notes for a Personal Narrative

Directions Fill in the graphic organizer with information about the event or experience that you plan to write about.

Summary

What happened? _____

When? _____

Where? _____

Who was there? _____

Details

Beginning

Middle

End

© Pearson Education, Inc., 4

Name _____

Words That Tell About *You*

Directions Your feelings probably changed during the course of the experience described in your personal narrative. Choose two or three words from the word bank to describe how you felt at different times. For each word, explain why you felt that way. Then use vivid details that *show* how you felt.

angry	excited	proud	sad
disappointed	embarrassed	satisfied	curious
nervous	anxious	delighted	upset

I felt _____

Reason: _____

And here's how I looked and acted: _____

_____

I felt _____

Reason: _____

And here's how I looked and acted: _____

_____

I felt _____

Reason: _____

And here's how I looked and acted: _____

_____

© Pearson Education, Inc., 4

Combining Sentences

When you write, you can combine short simple sentences to make compound or complex sentences. A compound sentence has two independent clauses—groups of words that can stand alone as sentences—joined by a word such as *and, but, or, nor, yet,* and *so.* A complex sentence has one independent clause and one dependent clause—a group of words that cannot stand alone as a sentence—joined by a word such as *if, when, because, although, since,* or *as.* Remember, the two sentences you combine must make sense together.

Directions Use the word in ( ) to combine the two sentences. Remember to use a comma when necessary.

1. I want to be an actor. I think I could be a good one. (and)

_____

_____

2. Acting is fun. You can pretend to be someone else. (because)

_____

_____

3. I applied to an acting workshop. I haven't heard back yet. (but)

_____

_____

4. I'm only eleven. I have a long way to go. (so)

_____

_____

5. I graduate. I may move to Hollywood. (after)

_____

_____

© Pearson Education, Inc., 4

Peer and Teacher Conferencing
Personal Narrative

Directions After exchanging drafts, read your partner's narrative. Refer to the Revising Checklist as you make notes about your partner's narrative. Write your comments or questions on the lines. Offer compliments as well as suggestions for revisions. Take turns talking about each other's draft using your notes. Give your partner your notes.

Revising Checklist

Focus/Ideas
☐ Is the personal narrative focused on one important experience?
☐ Are there enough details about the experience?

Organization
☐ Do time-order words and paragraphs help organize the sequence of events?

Voice
☐ Is the narrative interesting and lively?

Word Choice
☐ Does vivid language help show rather than tell about the writer's feelings?

Sentences
☐ Are there both simple and compound sentences? Have short, choppy sentences been combined to make compound or complex sentences?

Things I Thought Were Good

_____

_____

Things I Thought Could Be Improved

_____

_____

Teacher's Comments

_____

© Pearson Education, Inc., 4

Cause and Effect

- A **cause** is why something happens.
- An **effect** is what happens.

Directions Read the following passage. Then complete the diagram.

Today's soccer game was full of action! Tina kicked the ball to Michael, but she kicked it too hard. Michael's kick made the ball go out of bounds. Jackie, on the other team, had the chance to throw it in. She threw the ball so hard, it almost went into Tina and Michael's goal. Andre, the goalie, jumped to the side and blocked it. He kicked it back into the field. Michael tripped while running and couldn't get to the ball. This left the ball right in front of Jackie. Jackie gave it one swift kick, sending the ball soaring past Andre and into the goal.

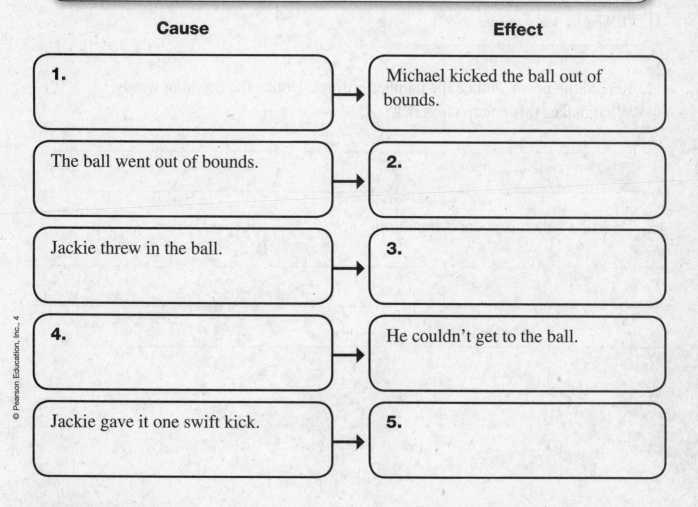

Cause

Effect

1.

→ Michael kicked the ball out of bounds.

The ball went out of bounds.

→ 2.

Jackie threw in the ball.

→ 3.

4.

→ He couldn't get to the ball.

Jackie gave it one swift kick.

→ 5.

© Pearson Education, Inc., 4

School + Home

Home Activity Your child identified causes and effects in a short passage. Read an article about a sporting event with your child. Ask your child to identify causes and effects in the article you read.

Writing • Limerick

Key Features of Limerick

• has 5 lines

• first line introduces a person and a place

• lines 1, 2, and 5 rhyme; lines 3 and 4 rhyme

• is usually humorous

Alien Race

There once was an alien from space
Who knew he was going to race
The kids in the school
Whom he thought very cool.
He won, but left not a trace.

1. Reread the poem. Notice the number of lines. Notice the rhyming words. What makes this poem a limerick?

_____

_____

2. Describe why this poem is humorous.

_____

_____

© Pearson Education, Inc., 4

Vocabulary

Directions Choose the word from the box that best matches each definition. Write the word on the line to the left.

_____ 1. not able to speak

_____ 2. hit sharply away

_____ 3. was filled with wonder

_____ 4. a ring or round band

_____ 5. incredible

Check the Words You Know

___fouled
___hoop
___jersey
___marveled
___rim
___speechless
___swatted
___unbelievable

Directions Choose the word from the box that best matches each clue. Write the word on the line to the left.

_____ 6. You might wear this while playing a sport.

_____ 7. This is part of a basketball hoop.

_____ 8. This is when someone made an unfair play in a sport.

_____ 9. This is what you are when you don't have anything to say.

_____ 10. This is something you thought was not possible.

Write a News Report

On a separate sheet of paper, write a news report about a sporting event. Use as many vocabulary words as you can.

Home Activity Your child identified and used vocabulary words from *What Jo Did*. Work with your child to make a crossword puzzle with the words and to write original clues for it.

© Pearson Education, Inc., 4

Common and Proper Nouns

- A **noun** is a word that names a person, place, or thing.
- A **common noun** names any person, place, or thing.
- A **proper noun** names a particular person, place, or thing. Proper nouns begin with capital letters.

  Common Nouns   That <u>girl</u> plays <u>basketball</u> at our <u>school</u>.
  Proper Nouns   <u>Sandy</u> will play for <u>Centerville</u> on <u>Friday</u>.

Some proper nouns have more than one word, such as *Boston Celtics*. Some include titles that tell what a person is or does, such as *Aunt Rosa* or *Captain Edwards*.

Directions   One of the underlined words in each sentence is a noun. Circle the noun. Write *C* if it is a common noun and *P* if it is a proper noun.

1. Dr. James Naismith <u>invented</u> the game of <u>basketball</u>.   _____
2. He <u>worked</u> at the <u>YMCA Training School</u> in Springfield, Massachusetts. _____
3. Naismith, a <u>teacher</u>, wanted to find a game <u>to</u> play inside in winter.   _____

Directions   Underline the three nouns in each sentence. Then write each noun under the correct heading in the chart.

4. The first game of basketball was played in Massachusetts.
5. Soon people all over the world were playing the sport.
6. In 1936, basketball was played at the Olympic Games in Berlin.
7. Today, many cities compete every winter in the National Basketball Association.
8. I watch our team at the stadium every weekend.

Common Nouns	Proper Nouns

© Pearson Education, Inc., 4

Home Activity Your child learned about common and proper nouns. Have your child name people, places, or things around the house and say whether th names are common or proper nouns.

Name _____

Adding -s and -es

Spelling Words				
monkeys	friends	plays	supplies	taxes
holidays	months	companies	costumes	sandwiches
hobbies	daisies	delays	scratches	counties
teammates	memories	bunches	batteries	donkeys

Multiple Meanings Some words can be either a noun (name of a person, place, or thing) or a verb (word that shows action). Write the list word that begins with the given letter and can be used to complete both sentences.

1. The traffic **d**____ made everyone late.
   When the bus breaks down, it **d**____ our arrival.

1. _____

2. The cat **s**____ the rug to sharpen its claws.
   I got these **s**____ when I fell off my bike.

2. _____

3. The government adds **t**____ to most things we buy.
   Running marathons **t**____ my energy.

3. _____

4. The army **s**____ troops with food, clothing, and shelter.
   Have you bought everything on your list of school **s**____?

4. _____

5. *Romeo and Juliet* and *Hamlet* are **p**___ by Shakespeare.
   The harpist **p**____ soft music at weddings.

5. _____

6. It gets crowded when everyone **b**____ up by the door.
   Ten **b**____ of grapes were passed out to the team.

6. _____

Adding -s or -es Add -s or -es to make each word plural. Write the word.

7. monkey _____
8. holiday _____
9. costume _____
10. battery _____
11. sandwich _____
12. company _____
13. county _____
14. daisy _____
15. donkey _____
16. friend _____
17. hobby _____
18. memory _____
19. teammate _____
20. month _____

Home Activity Your child spelled words that end with -s or -es. Say the singular form of the list word and have your child say and spell its plural form.

© Pearson Education, Inc., 4

Writing • Shape Poem

Key Features of Shape Poem

• takes the shape of the subject of the poem

• uses words and spaces to create the shape

• creates a mental picture of the topic that the shape represents

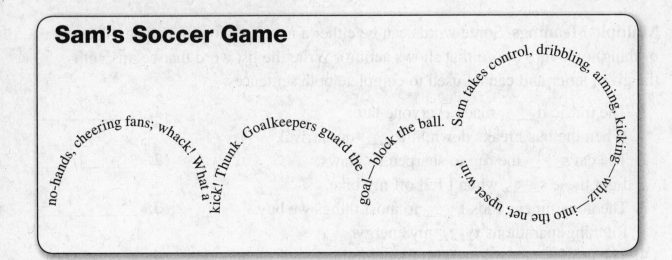

Sam's Soccer Game

no-hands, cheering fans; whack! What a kick! Thunk. Goalkeepers guard the goal—block the ball. Sam takes control, dribbling, aiming, kicking—whiz—into the net; upset win!

1. Reread the poem. What makes this poem a shape poem?

_____

_____

2. Think about the words and phrases in the poem and create a mental picture of the poem. What other descriptive words and soccer phrases might you add to this poem?

_____

_____

© Pearson Education, Inc., 4

Vocabulary • Prefixes and Suffixes

- **Prefixes** and **suffixes** have their own meanings and are added to base words. They change the meanings of base words.

- The prefix *un-* means "the opposite of _____" or "not _____." The suffix *-able* means "able to be _____ed." The suffix *-less* means "without _____."

Directions Read the following passage about a basketball game. Look for the prefix *un-* and the suffixes *-able* and *-less* as you read. Then answer the questions below.

> It was the most unforgettable basketball game I ever saw. When the referee said a foul had been made against our star player, I was speechless. The fans for our team were unable to stop yelling. It was useless to try to quiet them. They couldn't believe we were so lucky. We had played an unbelievable game and we were tied with a few seconds to go. It was up to our guard at the free-throw line. As I uncovered my eyes, I saw the effortless shot soar through the hoop like a bird. We won!

1. What does *unbelievable* mean? What are its prefix and suffix?

_____

2. What does *useless* mean? Does it have a prefix or suffix?

_____

3. How are *speechless* and *effortless* alike? What does each word mean?

_____

_____

4. What does *unforgettable* mean? What are its prefix and suffix?

_____

5. Write a sentence using two words that have a prefix or a suffix. Tell the meaning of those words.

_____

_____

Home Activity Your child identified and used prefixes and suffixes to understand words in a passage. With your child, make a list of words associated with a favorite sport or activity. Ask your child how the meanings change when you add a prefix, a suffix, or both.

© Pearson Education, Inc., 4

Chart/Table

- **Charts** show data or information visually. Most charts have titles and use a combination of words and numbers. A chart often takes the form of a list, diagram, or table.

- A **table** is a special kind of chart that shows information in rows and columns. A single box in a table is often called a **cell**.

- Charts and tables can be created easily using word-processor software.

Directions Examine the images below from the ZipWriter word processor program. Then answer the questions.

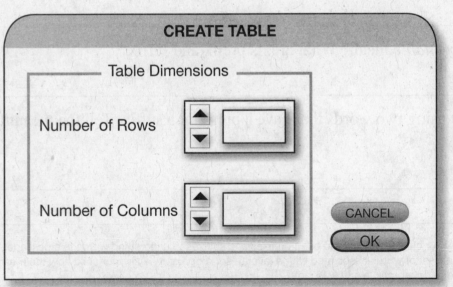

| ZipWriter | EDIT | **TABLE** | FORMAT |

Create Table . . . ⇧ ⌘ T

Insert Row ▶

Delete Row ▶

Insert Column ▶

Delete Column ▶

Join Cells ▶

Divide Cells ▶

Borders and Backgrounds ▶

This is the Table menu in ZipWriter.

CREATE TABLE

Table Dimensions

Number of Rows ▲ ▼

Number of Columns ▲ ▼

CANCEL

OK

This is the Create Table window. It appears when you select the Create Table command from the Table menu.

© Pearson Education, Inc., 4

1. You want to create a table showing 31 students' high scores at a certain video game. How many columns would you ask for in the Create Table window?

_____

2. What command in the Table menu would you use to erase an extra row?

_____

3. Now you want to add another column to the table to show each student's high score at a different game. What command from the Table menu would you use?

_____

4. How would you make a cell that stretched all the way across the top of the table?

_____

5. When you finish your table, you decide you want to put a heavy line between each column. Where on the Table menu do you think you would find the tools to do this?

_____

6. Imagine you want to show the score for each of four rounds of a certain video game, plus the total after four rounds for each person who plays it. How many columns would you need? Why?

_____

_____

7. Two new students join the class. What should you do to update your table?

_____

8. One student leaves the class. How would you remove his or her data?

_____

9. How would you dismiss the Create Table window if you did not want it?

_____

10. For what purpose might a person create a table like this?

_____

© Pearson Education, Inc., 4

 Home Activity Your child read a table and answered questions about it. Together, draw a table (either by hand or using a computer) to show your family's activities each day during the course of a week. Before drawing the table, have your child decide how many columns and rows you will need.

Adding -s and -es

Proofread a Dialogue Read the dialogue and circle five spelling mistakes. Then write the words correctly. Cross out the punctuation error and write the sentence correctly.

> **Rick:** Which plays are you trying out for.
>
> **Hal:** I want to be in the one about six silly monkeyes.
>
> **Kim:** I'm sure the costumees are itchy.
>
> **Hal:** You're right! All that furry stuff probably scratches alot.
>
> **Kim:** Ami, one of my friends, wants to try out, too. Acting is one of her hobbys.
>
> **Rick:** Well, I hope we all have good memores.

1. _____   2. _____

3. _____   4. _____

5. _____

6. _____

Proofread Words Circle the correctly spelled word. Write the word.

7. taxs	taxse	taxes	7. _____
8. countys	counties	counteys	8. _____
9. months	monthes	monthies	9. _____
10. batterys	batteryes	batteries	10. _____
11. teamates	teammates	teammats	11. _____
12. supplies	supplys	supplyes	12. _____
13. frinds	frends	friends	13. _____
14. scratches	skratches	scrathes	14. _____
15. daysies	daisies	dasies	15. _____

Spelling Words

monkeys
friends
plays
supplies
taxes
holidays
months
companies
costumes
sandwiches

hobbies
daisies
delays
scratches
counties
teammates
memories
bunches
batteries
donkeys

Frequently Misspelled Words

a lot
because

© Pearson Education, Inc., 4

Home Activity Your child identified misspelled words with *-s* and *-es* endings. Ask your child to use the words in Exercises 7–15 in sentences.

Common and Proper Nouns

Directions Read the passage. Then read each question. Circle the letter of the correct answer.

Basketball

(1) The inventor of Basketball was born in Canada. (2) While living in Massachusetts, dr. Naismith wrote thirteen rules for basketball. (3) One rule is that a player must not run with the ball. (4) Basketball became very popular. (5) Boston and Chicago have great teams. (6) Not all basketball players are american. (7) Basketball a popular sport in Asia.

1 What change, if any, should be made in sentence 1?

  A   Change *Basketball* to **basketball.**

  B   Change *Canada* to **canada.**

  C   Change *The inventor of Basketball* to **basketball's inventor.**

  D   Make no change.

2 What change, if any, should be made in sentence 2?

  A   Change *Massachusetts* to **massachusetts.**

  B   Change *dr.* to **Dr.**

  C   Change *thirteen rules for basketball* to **Thirteen Rules for Basketball.**

  D   Make no change.

3 What change, if any, should be made in sentence 5?

  A   Change *Boston and Chicago* to **boston and chicago.**

  B   Change *Boston and Chicago* to **boston, chicago.**

  C   Change *Boston and Chicago* to **Boston, Chicago.**

  D   Make no change.

4 What change, if any, should be made in sentence 6?

  A   Change *american* to **American.**

  B   Change *players* to **Players.**

  C   Change the period to a question mark.

  D   Make no change.

5 What change, if any, should be made in sentence 7?

  A   Change *Basketball a popular sport* to **basketball, a popular sport.**

  B   Change *popular sport* to **Popular Sport.**

  C   Change *Basketball a popular sport* to **Basketball is a popular sport.**

  D   Make no change.

© Pearson Education, Inc., 4

Home Activity Your child prepared for taking tests on common and proper nouns. Say *common noun* or *proper noun* and have your child say a noun of the correct kind.

Name _____

Draw Conclusions

- **Drawing a conclusion** is forming an opinion based on what you already know or on the facts and details in a text.

- Check an author's conclusions or your own conclusions by asking: Is this the only logical choice? Are the facts accurate?

Directions Read the following passage. Then complete the diagram below by finding facts and details to support a conclusion.

A cowboy's job changed with the seasons. In the fall, the cowboys brought cattle roaming on the open land to the ranch. They branded the cattle, so they could keep track of them. Then during the winter months, the cowboys fed the cattle and raised them.

When spring arrived, the ranchers chose the cattle they wished to sell. Next, the cowboys would take the cattle on a long journey to a busy town so that others could buy the cattle. After the cowboys sold the cattle, they rested a little while before they started the process all over again.

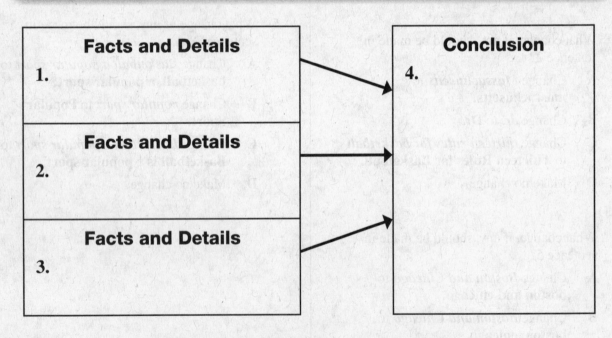

Facts and Details
1.

Facts and Details
2.

Facts and Details
3.

Conclusion
4.

5. How would you decide if the facts and details are accurate?

_____

Home Activity Your child read a short passage and drew a conclusion using facts or details. Tell your child about a job you once had. Have your child draw a conclusion about this job based on the facts and details you provide.

© Pearson Education, Inc., 4

Writing • News Article

Key Features of a News Article

- reports real current events
- begins with a headline and a byline
- gives the most important information in the lead
- includes supporting sentences with facts, details, and explanations
- often includes text features, such as photos and captions

Glenview School Elects Student Council

By Dan Clark

Last week the 540 students at Glenview School went to the polls to vote. They cast ballots for their Student Council officers. They also elected their grade level representatives. They knew they were electing officers who would represent them on the Student Council for the rest of the school year.

All grades participated in the election. The candidates for President and Vice President visited every classroom to give a campaign speech. They explained to fellow students why they should be elected. Fourth grader Anthony Taylor said he cast his votes for the candidates he thought were the smartest students. "If a kid is a top student, they know how to listen to others, and come up with smart solutions to our problems," he said. "That is what we need at Glenview School."

We interviewed Roberta Ruiz, the new President, to find out what she thinks the issues facing the Student Council will be. She listed better food in the cafeteria, more clubs and after-school activities, and environmental issues as her top concerns, and the things she promised to work on if elected.

The President, the three Vice-Presidents, and the grade-level representatives will be busy if they tackle all of the problems that Roberta listed. The new Student Council agreed that they were elected to make life at Glenview School better for everyone. "Yes, we can," they echoed each other. "We learned that from the President of the United States."

© Pearson Education, Inc., 4

1. Reread the news article. Name two features that make it a news article.

_____

_____

2. What is the main point or focus of the article?

_____

_____

Vocabulary

Directions Choose the word from the box that best matches each definition. Write the word on the line to the left.

_____ 1. people who were raised in the city but vacation on a ranch

_____ 2. metal points worn on a horse rider's boot heel

_____ 3. small, wolf-like animal

_____ 4. the act of driving or bringing cattle together from long distances

_____ 5. shouting or crying out in a noisy way

Check the Words You Know

___bawling
___coyote
___dudes
___roundup
___spurs

Directions Choose the word from the box that best completes each sentence. Write the word on the line to the left.

_____ 6. Juan heard a calf ____ in the middle of the night.

_____ 7. He got dressed, put on his ____, and ran to his horse.

_____ 8. A hungry-looking ____ had frightened the herd.

_____ 9. Juan had to quickly do a ____ to get the cattle to safety.

_____ 10. There was so much noise, the ____ visiting the ranch came outside to see what was going on.

Write a Pep Talk

On a separate sheet of paper, write a pep talk a cowboy would give other cowboys before going on a long journey to do a cattle roundup. Use as many vocabulary words as you can.

© Pearson Education, Inc., 4

Home Activity Your child identified and used vocabulary words from *Coyote School News*. With your child, create a word search using the words from this selection.

Regular Plural Nouns

- **Singular nouns** name one person, place, or thing. **Plural nouns** name more than one person, place, or thing.
- Add *-s* to form the plural of most nouns.
  bird/birds   snake/snakes   monkey/monkeys
- Add *-es* to form the plural of nouns that end in *ch, sh, s, ss,* or *x*.
  finch/finches   dish/dishes   gas/gases   dress/dresses   box/boxes
- To form the plural of nouns that end in a consonant followed by a *y*, change the *y* to *i* and add *-es*.
  butterfly/butterflies   puppy/puppies

Directions Underline the plural noun in each sentence.

1. Texas has many cattle ranches.

2. A cowboy rides after cows.

3. A cowboy can throw a rope within inches of his target.

4. Wild ponies also live in the Southwest.

5. Many movies have been made about the Old West.

Directions Write the singular form of each noun.

6. outlaws _____

7. stories _____

8. patches _____

9. foxes _____

10. saddles _____

11. coyotes _____

12. losses _____

© Pearson Education, Inc., 4

 School + Home **Home Activity** Your child learned about regular plural nouns. Point to objects around the house. Ask your child to say the nouns and their plural forms. Then have them explain how the plurals were formed.

Irregular Plurals

Spelling Words				
videos	feet	potatoes	themselves	lives
leaves	cliffs	men	halves	moose
radios	sheep	cuffs	beliefs	patios
children	tornadoes	tomatoes	hoofs	loaves

Words in Context Write a list word to complete the sentence.

1. When the siren sounded, people turned on their ____.   1. _____
2. The weather report warned that ____ were on the way.   2. _____
3. Then the ____ on the trees began to sway.   3. _____
4. The wind could lift a person off his or her ____.   4. _____
5. Even grown ____ and women feared the powerful storm.   5. _____
6. After the storm, people walked out onto their ____.   6. _____
7. They wanted to see the damage for ____.   7. _____
8. The tornado had divided the town into two ____.   8. _____
9. In one half, the houses were stacked up like ____ of bread. 9. _____
10. In the other half, even ____ on their vines had not been   10. _____
    disturbed.
11. The neighbors pushed up their ____ and went to work.   11. _____
12. Everyone was grateful that no ____ had been lost.   12. _____

Definitions Write the list word that matches the definition.

13. values and ideals   13. _____
14. young people   14. _____
15. steep rocks   15. _____
16. pictures on monitors   16. _____
17. large members of the deer family 17. _____
18. starchy foods with dark skins   18. _____
19. horses' feet   19. _____
20. wooly animals   20. _____

Home Activity Your child wrote irregular plural words. Say the singular form of each spelling word. Ask your child to say and spell the plural form.

© Pearson Education, Inc., 4

Story Predictions Chart

When?	Where?	Who?	What?

© Pearson Education, Inc., 4

Vocabulary • Unknown Words

- **Dictionaries** and **glossaries** provide alphabetical lists of words and their meanings.
- Sometimes looking at the words around an unknown word can't help you figure out the word's meaning. If this happens, use a dictionary or glossary to find the meaning.

Directions Read the following passage. Then answer the questions below.

> At the crack of dawn, my uncle went around to the tents to wake up the dudes at the ranch. Today they were going on a roundup and needed to get everything ready before they left. The dudes sat down for breakfast and then got dressed for the trip. Some of them had never ridden a horse before, so putting on their chaps and spurs took a lot of time. They heard some cattle bawling far in the distance. Before long, the group headed out into the open plains.

1. How would you define *dudes* by looking at the words that are around it?

_____

2. Look up *dudes* in a glossary or dictionary. How is the meaning that you looked up different from the meaning you thought it had by looking at the words around it?

_____

_____

3. How would you define *bawling* by looking at the words that are around it?

_____

4. Look up *bawling* in a glossary or dictionary. How is the meaning that you looked up different from the meaning you thought it had by looking at the words around it?

_____

_____

5. Look up *roundup* in a glossary or dictionary. What part of speech is it?

_____

© Pearson Education, Inc., 4

Home Activity Your child read a short passage and used a dictionary or glossary to understand unknown words. Have a conversation about your day with your child. When your child hears an unknown word, help your child to find the word's meaning in a dictionary.

Newspaper/Newsletter

Newspapers are daily or weekly publications printed on large sheets of paper folded together. They include such sections as current news, advertisements, feature stories, and editorials. **Newsletters** are short publications for groups and include news that interests the groups' members.

Directions Use this index from a school newspaper to answer the questions below.

1. In what section would you find information about the mayor's upcoming visit to the school?

   _____

   _____

2. On what page would you find the score of the last basketball game?

   _____

3. On what page would you find comments from students about last week's newspaper?

   _____

4. In what section would you find comics or cartoons?

   _____

5. Would the school newspaper be a good place to find out information about world events? Why or why not?

   _____

   _____

© Pearson Education, Inc., 4

Name _____

Directions Use the school newspaper article to answer the questions below.

Gallup Ranch School to Have New Bus

Most of the students who attend Gallup Ranch School have to take the bus in the morning. The surrounding ranches are too far away for students to be able to walk or ride a bicycle to school. Since the bus has to start out early to make all of its stops, many students have to wake up very early in the morning to catch the bus. Teachers are aware of the problem, and that is why they have asked for funding from the county government. Just yesterday, the principal of the school announced that the county will buy us a second bus. Now there will be two bus routes instead of one, and students won't have to be on the bus so long.

6. What does the headline of this article tell you about the article?

_____

_____

7. Why do you think a school newspaper would include an article like this?

_____

_____

8. Where would you expect to find an article like this in a school newspaper?

_____

_____

9. Name the *who, what,* and *when* in this article.

_____

_____

_____

10. What kind of group might include this story in their newsletter? Explain.

_____

_____

© Pearson Education, Inc., 4

Home Activity Your child learned about using newspapers/newsletters as resources. Work with your child to create a family newspaper. Challenge your child to think of the sections to include in the newspaper and the topics to write about in the articles.

Name _____

Irregular Plurals

Proofread an E-mail The computer's spelling and grammar check isn't working. Circle five misspelled words. Add the missing period.

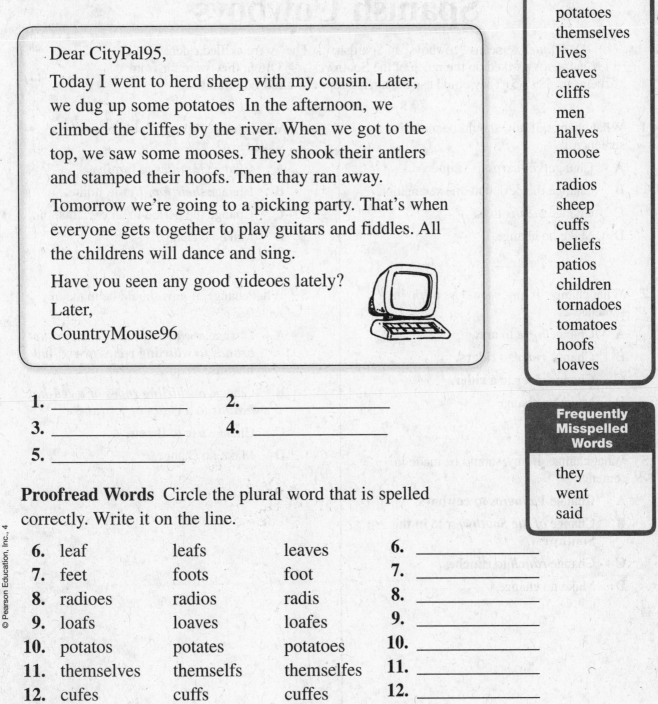

Dear CityPal95,

Today I went to herd sheep with my cousin. Later, we dug up some potatoes In the afternoon, we climbed the cliffes by the river. When we got to the top, we saw some mooses. They shook their antlers and stamped their hoofs. Then thay ran away.

Tomorrow we're going to a picking party. That's when everyone gets together to play guitars and fiddles. All the childrens will dance and sing.

Have you seen any good videoes lately?

Later,
CountryMouse96

Spelling Words

videos
feet
potatoes
themselves
lives
leaves
cliffs
men
halves
moose

radios
sheep
cuffs
beliefs
patios
children
tornadoes
tomatoes
hoofs
loaves

1. _____   2. _____
3. _____   4. _____
5. _____

Proofread Words Circle the plural word that is spelled correctly. Write it on the line.

Frequently Misspelled Words

they
went
said

6. leaf	leafs	leaves	6. _____
7. feet	foots	foot	7. _____
8. radioes	radios	radis	8. _____
9. loafs	loaves	loafes	9. _____
10. potatos	potates	potatoes	10. _____
11. themselves	themselfs	themselfes	11. _____
12. cufes	cuffs	cuffes	12. _____

Home Activity Your child identified misspelled irregular plural words. Say each spelling word. Ask your child to explain how the plural was formed.

© Pearson Education, Inc., 4

Regular Plural Nouns

Directions Read the passage. Then read each question. Circle the letter of the correct answer.

Spanish Cowboys

(1) *Vaqueros* means "cowboys" in Spanish. (2) They were skilled rider. (3) Vaqueros worked on the ranch of the Southwest. (4) Often, they were far from their families. (5) They could use a whirling ropes or a red-hot brands.

1 What change, if any, should be made in sentence 1?

    A   Change *Vaqueros* to **vaqueros.**

    B   Change the period to an exclamation.

    C   Change *means* to **is.**

    D   Make no change.

2 What change, if any, should be made in sentence 2?

    A   Change *were* to **are.**

    B   Change *rider* to **riders.**

    C   Change *rider* to **a rider.**

    D   Make no change.

3 What change, if any, should be made in sentence 3?

    A   Change *Vaqueros* to **cowboys.**

    B   Change *of the Southwest* to **in the Southwest.**

    C   Change *ranch* to **ranches.**

    D   Make no change.

4 What change, if any, should be made in sentence 4?

    A   Change *families* to **family.**

    B   Change *their families* to **home.**

    C   Change the period to an exclamation.

    D   Make no change.

5 What change, if any, should be made in sentence 5?

    A   Change *a whirling ropes or a red-hot brands* to **whirling ropes or red-hot brands.**

    B   Change *a whirling ropes or a red-hot brands* to **a ropes or a brands.**

    C   Change *use* to **throw.**

    D   Make no change.

© Pearson Education, Inc., 4

Home Activity Your child prepared for taking tests on regular plural nouns. Read a brief passage to your child from a book. Ask him or her to identify any plural nouns in the passage and say how they were formed.

Name _____

Draw Conclusions

- **Drawing a conclusion** is forming an opinion based on what you already know or on the facts and details in a text. Facts and details are the small pieces of information in an article or story.
- Facts and details "add up" to a conclusion. Conclusions formed by the author or the reader must make sense.

Directions Read the following passage. Then complete the diagram and answer the question.

Big projects are almost never done by just one person. This is true both in school and in work. Different people have different skills that help a project be successful. Some people are great at organizing, while other people are excellent speakers. When you put them together, they form a team.

The right people should do the right jobs, of course. That way, all team members can do quality work quickly. A good team can be effective. Sharing the work in this way is one of the best types of cooperation. Effective teams have built skyscrapers, put people in space, and filmed blockbuster movies.

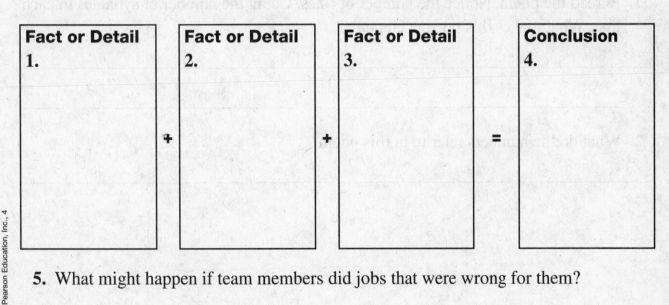

Fact or Detail 1.		Fact or Detail 2.		Fact or Detail 3.		Conclusion 4.
	+		+		=	

5. What might happen if team members did jobs that were wrong for them?

_____

School + Home **Home Activity** Your child drew a conclusion using facts or details in a passage. Talk to your child about ways your family works together to get things done. Ask your child to draw a conclusion about the role of teamwork in your home.

© Pearson Education, Inc., 4

Writing • Cinquains

Key Features of Cinquains

- five-line poems that do not rhyme
- the first and fifth line contain two syllables
- the second line contains four syllables
- the third line contains six syllables
- the fourth line contains eight syllables

The Talent Show

Six sing,
two dance, four play
musical instruments.
Three tap their feet and beat a drum.
Great show!

1. Reread the poem. Notice the number of lines. Count the number of syllables in each line. What makes this poem a cinquain?

_____

_____

2. What do the numbers refer to in this poem?

_____

© Pearson Education, Inc., 4

Vocabulary

Directions Choose the word from the box that best completes each sentence. Write the word on the line to the left.

_____ 1. Anabelle hoped she could learn all her lines in the ____ by December.

_____ 2. I shop for clothes with my friend Josh, who gives great fashion ____.

_____ 3. Their flight cancelled, the family had to make other ____ to get home.

_____ 4. Her plans to rule the world hit a ____ when the superheroes burst into her hideout.

_____ 5. Ellen and her brother Holden were excited to learn that they were ____ of Blackbeard.

Check the Words You Know

___advice
___argument
___arrangements
___descendants
___dishonest
___script
___snag

Directions Choose the word from the box that best matches each clue. Write the word in the puzzle.

Across

6. later generations of family
7. plans and schedules
8. emotional disagreement

Down

9. obstacle, problem area
10. not truthful

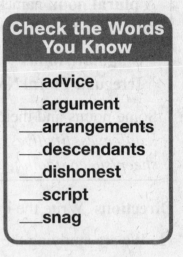

Write an E-mail Message

On a separate sheet of paper, write an e-mail message to a friend about what you discovered when you found a secret room in the building of the local historical society. Use as many vocabulary words as you can.

© Pearson Education, Inc., 4

Home Activity Your child identified and used vocabulary from *Scene Two*. With your child, talk about your family's history. Use as many of the vocabulary words as you can.

Irregular Plural Nouns

A **plural noun** names more than one person, place, or thing. Most nouns add -*s* to form the plural. An **irregular plural noun** has a special form for the plural.

Singular Nouns   The <u>man</u> saw a <u>wolf</u> and a <u>moose</u> on the prairie.
Irregular Plural Nouns The <u>men</u> saw some <u>wolves</u> and some <u>moose</u> on the prairie.

Some nouns and their irregular plural forms are *child/children, deer/deer, foot/feet, leaf/leaves, life/lives, loaf/loaves, man/men, moose/moose, mouse/mice, sheep/sheep, tooth/teeth, wolf/wolves,* and *wife/wives*.

Directions Write the irregular plural noun in each sentence.

1. We are studying the men who first settled in our area.   _____

2. They found wolves and other wild animals.   _____

3. Don't you admire the women who first went west?   _____

4. Their lives were not easy.   _____

5. Even children had to work hard.   _____

Directions If the noun is plural, write *P*. If it is singular, write its plural form. If the noun could be either singular or plural, write *S/P*.

6. loaves   _____

7. sheep   _____

8. moose   _____

9. leaves   _____

10. deer   _____

11. tooth   _____

12. mouse   _____

© Pearson Education, Inc., 4

Home Activity Your child learned about irregular plural nouns. Say the words *tooth, wife,* and *sheep,* and have your child say and spell the plural form of each word.

Words with *ar, or*

Spelling Words				
morning	forest	garbage	form	alarm
corner	story	argue	backyard	start
partner	storm	Florida	apartment	sport
force	forward	sharp	garden	Arkansas

Missing Words Write a list word to finish each chapter title. Use capital letters.

Household Ecology

Chapter 1: Make Nature Your **(1)**____

Chapter 2: Grow a Healthy **(2)**____

Chapter 3: Birds as **(3)**____ Visitors

Chapter 4: Turn Kitchen **(4)**____ into Gold

Chapter 5: Your Own Woody **(5)**____

Stories from the South

Chapter 1: "The **(6)**____ Traveler"

Chapter 2: "**(7)**____ Swamps"

Chapter 3: "Early **(8)**____ Fishing in the Carolinas"

Your New Apartment

Chapter 1: House or **(9)**____?

Chapter 2: How NOT to **(10)**____ with Your Landlord

1. _____
2. _____
3. _____
4. _____
5. _____
6. _____
7. _____
8. _____
9. _____
10. _____

Multiple Meanings Read the definitions. Write the list word that fits both meanings.

11. _____ a shape or to make

12. _____ sudden fear or a warning device

13. _____ the place where two walls come together or to trap

14. _____ to begin or to jump in surprise or fright

15. _____ one floor of a building or a tale

16. _____ strong wind with heavy rain or snow or to show anger

17. _____ a game or contest or to wear

18. _____ ahead or bold

19. _____ having a thin, cutting edge or smart

20. _____ active power or to make someone act against his or her will

Home Activity Your child wrote words with *ar* and *or*. Spell a list word. Ask your child to say the word and then use it in a sentence.

© Pearson Education, Inc., 4

Writing • Free Verse

Key Features of Free Verse
- has no set number of lines or rhythmic patterns
- does not usually rhyme
- line length varies

The Geese

Geese call in the clean autumn air.
They fly like an arrow
that's soaring south.
They flee the freezing days to come.
We envy their flight as we make our journey to school.
Then comes one goose, a straggler, calling "Wait for me!"
Just like my little brother.

1. Reread the poem. What makes this poem free verse?

_____

_____

2. What words are examples of assonance in this poem?

_____

© Pearson Education, Inc., 4

Vocabulary • Prefixes

- A **prefix** is a word part added at the beginning of a base word to change its meaning.
- The prefix *re-* means "to do over" or "again."

Directions Read the following passage. Then answer the questions below.

My youth group hiked the Appalachian Trail last summer. The exercise and views were great, but what impressed me was our teamwork. After a week, we were able to rebuild our campsite every night in half an hour. And that's pretty fast for a bunch of kids who had been hiking all day! When we arrived at official camp areas, we pitched tents and prepared meals.

After dinner we passed around our digital camera to review pictures we had taken of the scenery that day. In good weather, we slept in sleeping bags under netting to enjoy the refreshing air. For some reason, rearranging all our equipment took an hour in the morning. When we left the campsite, we took all our trash with us and left no signs of our presence.

1. What is the prefix in the word *rebuild*? What does the word mean?

_____

2. What does the word *review* mean?

_____

3. Why does the author describe the night air as refreshing?

_____

_____

4. If you *rearrange* your bedroom, what do you do?

_____

5. Write a sentence using a word with the prefix *re-*.

_____

© Pearson Education, Inc., 4

Home Activity Your child identified the prefix *re-* to understand the meanings of new words. Have a conversation with your child and try to use as many words that begin with *re-* as you can. Count how many you can use in one sentence.

Advertisement

- All **advertisements** sell a product or service. Advertisers want their product or service to appear at its best or most appealing.

- There are four parts to an advertisement: a photo or other picture of what is being sold, a headline in large type that "yells" about the product, information about the product, and who makes the product or offers the service.

Directions Use this advertisement to answer the questions below.

Usher House Mystery Weekend Get-Away! A driving rain batters against the windows. A fire roars in the fireplace in the mansion's library, but it can't quite take the chill out of the air. Suddenly, as lightning flashes for an instant, the power goes out! Your fellow guests in the mansion shuffle about nervously in the dark. Just before the lights return, you hear a scream! Racing into the front hall, you see a woman standing by a broken window with her hand to her neck. Her diamond necklace is gone!

And so begins your Mystery Weekend Get-Away at the historic Usher House! Look for clues scattered around the mansion. Find secret passages. Work as a team with the other guests to solve the mystery. But remember—one of them committed the crime, and YOU have to figure out "whodunit!" Treat yourself to a weekend of mystery and suspense. Contact Usher Resorts, Inc., for more details or to book your weekend now!

1. What is this advertisement trying to sell?

_____

2. What is the headline of this advertisement?

_____

3. Who wants you to book the Weekend Get-Away?

_____

4. To whom might this ad appeal?

Home Activity Your child analyzed an advertisement for ways ads appeal to readers. Look through magazines with your child and talk about the kinds of appeals the ads use to get people to buy things.

© Pearson Education, Inc., 4

Directions Use the advertisement below to answer the questions.

Get your team some help...superhuman help!

Gone are the days of class projects suffering because your team has too much work to do! Now, using the Extreme TeamBot, class project cyborg, you and your teammates have an artificial life form to help you organize the project schedule, carry piles of heavy books back from the library, and make copies of hand-outs for the class. Extreme TeamBot never sleeps.

YOU command your cyborg by playing a computer game that controls its every move. When your parents ask you if you're playing a game or doing your homework, you can answer, "Both!" But wait, there's more! Extreme TeamBot is also an MP3 player and digital video projector! Order Extreme TeamBot today! Extreme ChoreBot is also available.

1. How does the headline grab your attention?

_____

_____

2. Why does the ad include a picture of the Extreme TeamBot?

_____

_____

_____

3. How is the Extreme TeamBot controlled?

_____

_____

4. What is the ad's purpose for saying "But wait, there's more!"?

_____

_____

_____

5. How would your teachers feel about students using the Extreme TeamBot?

_____

_____

_____

Home Activity Your child learned to identify the parts of an advertisement. Look through a newspaper or magazine with your child. Ask your child to indicate the different parts of the advertisements that appear in the periodical.

© Pearson Education, Inc., 4

Words with *ar, or*

Proofread a Travel Brochure Check the brochure before it goes to the printer. Circle six misspelled words. Write the words correctly. Then correct the sentence fragment.

All aboard! Daily sightseeing trains leave Tallahassee at six o'clock in the morening. Start your day right. With some delicious Flarida orange juice. Enjoy the view from the top storry of our observation car. Have lunch in everyone's favarit tearoom in Theodore, Alabama, and tour the graden. There's just time to hike in the forest around the Buffalo River before our last stop at Little Rock, Arkansaw.

1. _____   2. _____
3. _____   4. _____
5. _____   6. _____
7. _____

_____

Missing Letters Chose *ar* or *or* to complete each word. Then write the word.

8. _ _ gue   8. _____
9. ap _ _ tment   9. _____
10. sh _ _ p   10. _____
11. p _ _ tner   11. _____
12. g _ _ bage   12. _____
13. f _ _ ward   13. _____
14. sp _ _ t   14. _____
15. st _ _ m   15. _____
16. f _ _ ce   16. _____
17. g _ _ den   17. _____
18. al _ _ m   18. _____

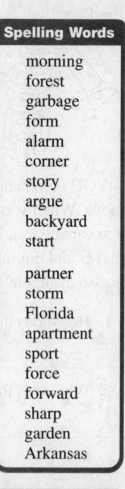

Spelling Words

morning
forest
garbage
form
alarm
corner
story
argue
backyard
start

partner
storm
Florida
apartment
sport
force
forward
sharp
garden
Arkansas

Frequently Misspelled Words

favorite
morning

Home Activity Your child identified misspelled words with *ar* or *or*. Say list words and spell them incorrectly. Have your child correct your mistakes.

© Pearson Education, Inc., 4

Irregular Plural Nouns

Directions Read the passage. Then read each question. Circle the letter of the correct answer.

Long Ago

(1) Lives was different in the old days. (2) The man went out and worked, but the women worked at home. (3) Their wife did the housework. (4) Not all child went to school. (5) Sometimes they saw mooses in the forest.

1 What change, if any, should be made in sentence 1?

  A Change *was* to **are.**

  B Change *Lives* to **life.**

  C Change *Lives* to **Life.**

  D Make no change.

2 What change, if any, should be made in sentence 2?

  A Change *went* to **goes.**

  B Change *man* to **men.**

  C Change *women* to **womans.**

  D Make no change.

3 What change, if any, should be made in sentence 3?

  A Change *wife* to **wifes.**

  B Change *did the housework* to **kept house.**

  C Change *wife* to **wives.**

  D Make no change.

4 What change, if any, should be made in sentence 4?

  A Change *child* to **child's.**

  B Change *child* to **children.**

  C Change *child* to **a child.**

  D Make no change.

5 What change, if any, should be made in sentence 5?

  A Change *mooses* to **moose.**

  B Change *mooses* to **moose's.**

  C Change *mooses* to **mooses'.**

  D Make no change.

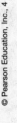© Pearson Education, Inc., 4

Home Activity Your child prepared for taking tests on irregular plural nouns. Have a discussion with your child about animals. Ask him or her to use the singular and plural forms of *goose, calf, wolf,* and *sheep.*

Fact and Opinion

- A **statement of fact** can be proved true or false. You can look in a reference book, ask an expert, or use your own knowledge and experience.

- A **statement of opinion** cannot be proved true or false. It is a belief or a judgment. It often contains a word of judgment, such as *best, should,* or *beautiful.* It may begin with the words *in my opinion* or *I believe.*

Directions Read the following passage. Then complete the table. Read each statement and answer the questions at the top of each column.

My family is going to visit an animal rescue shelter this weekend. Rescue shelters take in animals that have been abandoned or mistreated by people. My parents say my sister and I can choose a pet from the shelter, but we can't agree on what type of pet to get. Cats make the best pets because you can teach a cat to use a litter box. Dogs have to be walked three or four times a day, and that's too much trouble.

Of course, my sister wants a dog—a big one. Raising a puppy requires time to train them. My sister promises that she will take care of a dog every day, but I think she is too irresponsible. Besides, kittens are cuter than puppies. When we go the shelter to look at all the animals, I believe she'll change her mind.

Statement	Does it state a fact or an opinion?	If an opinion, what are the clue words? If a fact, how could you prove it?
Rescue shelters take in animals that have been abandoned or mistreated by people.	Fact	Contact animal shelters to find out where their animals come from.
A puppy requires time to train.	1.	2.
Kittens are cuter than puppies.	3.	4.

5. Find one sentence that contains both a statement of fact and a statement of opinion.

_____

Home Activity Your child identified statements of fact and statements of opinion in a short paragraph. Listen to or watch a news program with your child. Ask your child to tell you when he or she hears the news announcer expressing an opinion. Ask your child to explain why it is an opinion rather than a fact.

© Pearson Education, Inc., 4

Writing • Expository Composition

Key Features of Expository Composition

- gives information about real people, things, or events
- has an introduction that focuses the reader on the central idea
- has paragraphs with topic sentences and supporting details
- often includes text features

A Different Kind of Blood Donor

When you think of a blood donor, do you think of a big yellow cat with a hole in its ear drum, a tilted head, and balance problems? Probably not! But Nemo the cat spent a year of his life as a blood donor. He gave 22 packets of blood to help save cats all over the country.

Animal Blood Banks

When an animal is sick, or injured in a fight or accident, it may need to be given blood to survive. The blood supplies come from animal blood banks. These blood banks are ready to send blood quickly to help animals in need.

Who Are the Donors?

Most animal blood donors come from the Humane Society. The blood bank gives their potential donors a long physical exam and blood screening. If the animal is healthy and has a blood type that is needed, it becomes part of the blood bank community. The animals, like Nemo, are well fed and taken care of at the blood bank. Every few weeks a worker carefully takes their blood. The blood becomes part of the blood bank's supply.

A Remarkable Life

After a year, the animal donors at the blood bank are given up for adoption. Nemo was adopted into a happy home. He may not understand that he helped many other cats that were sick or injured. He may not understand that he is a remarkable cat. But those around him know how remarkable and special he and the other donor animals like him really are.

1. Reread the selection. What is the central idea of the selection?

_____

_____

2. Circle the facts and details that support the central idea.

© Pearson Education, Inc., 4

Vocabulary

Directions Choose the word from the box that best matches each definition. Write the word on the line to the left.

_____ 1. area of deep, water-filled sand or dirt that cannot support weight, so objects sink into it

_____ 2. unstable, about to fall apart

_____ 3. strength or determination against opposing force or conditions

_____ 4. feeling or trait causing a person to pursue a goal

_____ 5. filled with so much or many as to be unhealthy, dangerous, or irritating

Check the Words You Know
___ambition
___infested
___landslide
___quicksand
___resistance
___rickety
___roamed
___vast

Directions Choose the word from the box that best completes each sentence. Write the word on the line to the left.

_____ 6. The insect repellant allowed us some _____ against all the mosquitoes on our hike.

_____ 7. His mansion destroyed in the _____, the millionaire vowed to rebuild on the same hill because he likes the view.

_____ 8. Huge wind farms now cover_____ areas of desert that were once believed to be useless.

_____ 9. Her _____ to be the first female president was finally within reach after years of hard work.

_____ 10. The lost sheep _____ around the countryside for days.

Write a Journal Entry

On a separate sheet of paper, write a journal entry about an adventure you took with an animal on which you depended for help. Use as many vocabulary words as you can.

Home Activity Your child identified and used vocabulary words from *Horse Heroes*. Read a selection with your child. List any unfamiliar words and try to figure out the meaning of each word by using other words that appear around it. Use a dictionary when necessary.

© Pearson Education, Inc., 4

Singular Possessive Nouns

> A **possessive noun** shows ownership. A **singular possessive noun** shows that one person, place, or thing has or owns something. Add an apostrophe (') and the letter *s* to a singular noun to make it possessive.
>
> **Singular Noun**   The <u>horse</u> had a mane that was thick and brown.
> **Singular Possessive Noun**   This <u>horse's</u> mane was thick and brown.

Directions Write the possessive form of each underlined noun.

1. In the 1800s, <u>America</u> transportation was limited.

_____

2. <u>California</u> people needed ways to communicate with the East.

_____

3. A Pony Express <u>team</u> job was to carry mail quickly.

_____

4. A <u>rider</u> day was difficult.

_____

5. The <u>job</u> dangers included long, tiring rides.

_____

6. A <u>pony</u> ride might be 40 miles or more.

_____

7. The telegraph took over the <u>Pony Express</u> job.

_____

8. Today, a mail <u>carrier</u> job is not quite so difficult.

_____

Home Activity Your child learned about singular possessive nouns. Ask your child to write the names of family members as possessive nouns and to use them in sentences.

© Pearson Education, Inc., 4

Consonant Pairs *ng, nk, ph, wh*

Spelling Words

Thanksgiving	among	think	blank	graph
young	wheel	nephew	belong	whiskers
whisper	elephant	white	shrink	wharf
trunk	strong	blink	chunk	skunk

Context Clues Write a list word to complete each saying.

1. The ____ never forgets.
2. The squeaky ____ gets the oil.
3. He vanished in the ____ of an eye.
4. Its fleece was ____ as snow.
5. The wet dog was as smelly as a ____.
6. I ____ therefore I am.
7. The weightlifter is as ____ as an ox.
8. I ate until I felt as stuffed as a ____ turkey.

1. _____
2. _____
3. _____
4. _____
5. _____
6. _____
7. _____
8. _____

Classifying Write the list word that fits into each group.

9. shout, talk, ____
10. between, in, ____
11. empty, unused, ____
12. childlike, immature, ____
13. chart, map, ____
14. reduce, decrease, ____
15. briefcase, suitcase, ____
16. piece, slab, ____
17. uncle, grandfather, ____
18. join, fit, ____
19. pier, dock, ____
20. beard, mustache, ____

9. _____
10. _____
11. _____
12. _____
13. _____
14. _____
15. _____
16. _____
17. _____
18. _____
19. _____
20. _____

© Pearson Education, Inc., 4

Home Activity Your child spelled words with *ng, nk, ph,* and *wh*. Say a list word and have your child spell the word and use it in a sentence.

Outline Form A

Title _____

A. _____

   1. _____

   2. _____

   3. _____

B. _____

   1. _____

   2. _____

   3. _____

C. _____

   1. _____

   2. _____

   3. _____

© Pearson Education, Inc., 4

Vocabulary • Unknown Words

- **Dictionaries** and **glossaries** provide alphabetical lists of words and their meanings.

- Sometimes looking at the words around an unknown word can't help you figure out the word's meaning. If this happens, use a dictionary or glossary to find the meaning.

Directions Read the following story. Then answer the questions below.

The buffalo lifted his massive, wooly head and looked toward the sunset. An old and mighty bull, he was leader of a herd that roamed the wide, vast plains that spread out between the mountains. He did not usually need to think much, but tonight he was deep in thought. Strange humans had come to his lands. Only a few arrived in rickety wagons at first. Now the plains were infested with them.

The buffaloes' tough hides gave them resistance against the teeth of wolves and sometimes against the arrows of the First People. But the newcomers shot at his herd with sticks of fire. The ambition of these people seemed to be to conquer all the land and every creature on it. He wondered sadly if he could find a safe place to take his herd. He had to try. In the morning they would head west toward the Big Water beyond the mountains.

1. Which words around the word *vast* can help you figure out its meaning?

_____

2. What is the meaning of the word *rickety*? How did you determine its meaning?

_____

3. What words around the word *resistance* help you figure out its meaning?

_____

4. What is the meaning of the word *ambition*? How did you determine its meaning?

_____

_____

5. Use a dictionary or glossary to find the definition for one of the words you couldn't define using the words around it. Write the definition.

© Pearson Education, Inc., 4

Home Activity Your child identified unknown words that could be defined using a dictionary or glossary. Work with your child to identify unknown words in a newspaper or magazine article. Ask your child if he or she needs to use a dictionary to find the meaning of the words. If so, ask your child to look up at least one definition in a dictionary or glossary.

Graphs

- **Graphs** show data in visual form. Graphs can quickly show how one piece of information compares to other pieces of information. There are several types of graphs.
- A **bar graph** uses vertical or horizontal bars to show different amounts of something.
- A **circle graph** has a pie shape. It shows how something can be divided into parts.
- A **line graph** contains lines that connect a series of points on a graph. Line graphs are good for showing changes that happen over time.
- A **picture graph** uses pictures to show amounts or numbers of things.

Directions Bart, the blacksmith, wants to know who his best customers are. The number of horseshoes his customers needed in the past may also tell him how much business he can expect in the future. Study the bar graph and the circle graph below. Then answer the questions on the next page.

Number of Horseshoes Sold in One Month

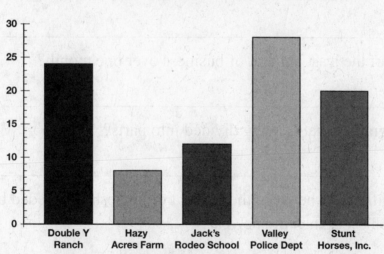

% of Total Horseshoes Needed in One Year

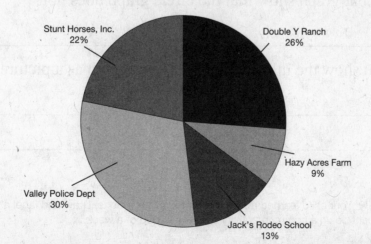

© Pearson Education, Inc., 4

Directions Use the graphs to answer the following questions.

1. How do you know what each graph shows?

_____

2. What unit is used in the bar graph to measure how much business Bart is doing?

_____

3. Whose names appear along the bottom of the bar graph?

_____

4. How is the information in each graph similar? How is it different?

_____

_____

5. Who needed the most horseshoes in one month?

_____

6. Who gave Bart the least amount of business over one month?

_____

7. In the circle graph, what is being divided into parts?

_____

8. What is the difference between the percent of horseshoes needed by Stunt Horses, Inc., and Double Y Ranch in one year?

_____

9. What does the bar graph show that the circle graph does not?

_____

10. How could you show the information in the bar graph as a picture graph?

_____

_____

Home Activity Your child learned about different kinds of graphs. Draw and label a line graph to show the hours you spent doing a common activity over the period of a week.

© Pearson Education, Inc., 4

Consonant Pairs *ng, nk, ph, wh*

Proofread a Poster Andy made a poster for the team fundraiser. Circle six words that are spelled incorrectly. Write the words correctly. Find the run-on sentence. Write it correctly.

Spelling Words

Thanksgiving
among
think
blank
graph
young
wheel
nephew
belong
whiskers

whisper
elephant
white
shrink
wharf
trunk
strong
blink
chunk
skunk

> Come to the white elefant sale!
>
> Wen: Friday after Thanksgivin
>
> Where: Kennedy School Gym
>
> Why: To buy sports equipment for youg boys' and girls' sports teams
>
> One person's junk is another person's treasure, so bring a chunk of change to spend. Your children, nieces, and nefews will benefit. Everyone is welcome!
>
> We need some stronge people to help with setup come early.

1. _____   2. _____

3. _____   4. _____

5. _____   6. _____

7. _____
   _____

Frequently Misspelled Words

where
when

Proofread Words Write the underlined words correctly. Then follow the directions. What you see may surprise you.

8. Draw a large red dot in the middle of a sheet of <u>graf</u> paper.   8. _____

9. Stare at the dot for 30 seconds. Don't <u>blin</u>!   9. _____

10. Then stare at a <u>blanc</u> wall for 15 seconds.   10. _____

11. A <u>wite</u> wall works best.   11. _____

12. What color dot do you <u>thik</u> you will see?   12. _____

School + Home **Home Activity** Your child identified misspelled words with *ng*, *nk*, *ph*, or *wh*. Ask your child to spell the words he or she did not write when answering the questions on this page.

© Pearson Education, Inc., 4

Singular Possessive Nouns

Directions Read the passage. Then read each question. Circle the letter of the correct answer.

Pony Express Riders

(1) The first Pony Express team heard the crowds cheers. (2) Brave riders were not scared of the jobs' risks. (3) The West weather made the trail dangerous. (4) The trail dangers were hidden. (5) A rider's adventure could last over two years.

1 What change, if any, should be made in sentence 1?

  A Change *crowds* to **crowds'**.

  B Change *crowds* to **crowd's**.

  C Change *cheers* to **cheer's**.

  D Make no change.

2 What change, if any, should be made in sentence 2?

  A Change *jobs'* to **jobs**.

  B Change *jobs'* to **job's**.

  C Change *risks* to **risky**.

  D Make no change.

3 What change, if any, should be made in sentence 3?

  A Change *West* to **west**.

  B Change *West* to **West's**.

  C Change *trail* to **trail's**.

  D Make no change.

4 What change, if any, should be made in sentence 4?

  A Change *were* to **are**.

  B Change *trail* to **trail'**.

  C Change *trail* to **trail's**.

  D Make no change.

5 What change, if any, should be made in sentence 5?

  A Change *rider's* to *riders'*.

  B Change *rider's* to **rider**.

  C Change *years* to **year**.

  D Make no change.

© Pearson Education, Inc., 4

Home Activity Your child prepared for taking tests on singular possessive nouns. Name two or three familiar objects in the house. Have your child write the possessive forms of these nouns and use them in sentences.

Main Idea and Details

- The **main idea** is the most important idea from a paragraph, passage, or article.
- **Details** are small pieces of information that tell more about the main idea.

Directions Read the following passage. Complete the diagram by stating the main idea and three supporting details. Then answer the question below the diagram.

> The President has a difficult job, but at least there are people to help the President along the way. These special people are called the Cabinet. The President gets to choose the members of the Cabinet, but the members of the United States Senate must approve them.
>
> Each member of the Cabinet represents a department of the government. Some examples of these departments are Education, Homeland Security, and Transportation. The Cabinet meets with the President to talk about issues that affect their departments. In these meetings, the President gets good advice on what decisions to make.

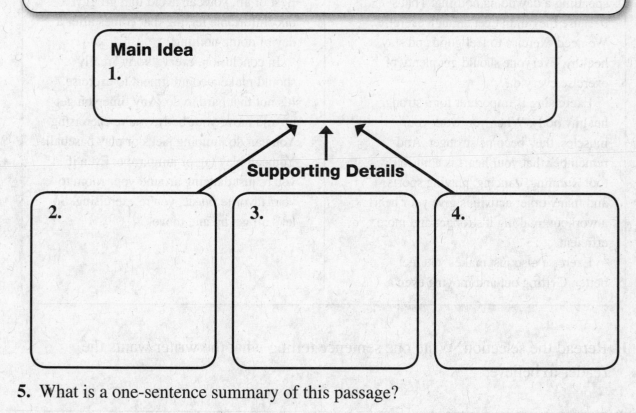

Main Idea

1.

Supporting Details

2.

3.

4.

5. What is a one-sentence summary of this passage?

_____

© Pearson Education, Inc., 4

Home Activity Your child used a graphic organizer to identify the main idea and supporting details of a passage. Work with your child to identify the main idea and supporting details for individual paragraphs in a magazine or newspaper article about government. Challenge him or her to summarize the entire article.

Writing • Argument/Persuasive Essay

Key Features of Argument/Persuasive Essay

- states the writer's opinion, or claim
- tries to influence the reader's opinion by developing an argument
- provides evidence that is supported by facts and examples
- provides a conclusion that is related to the opinion
- urges the reader to take action

Exercise: It's Good for You!

Have you ever had one of those days when you just sit around? How do you feel at the end of a day like that? Most people feel groggy and restless after spending a day doing nothing. That's because they didn't get enough exercise. We need exercise to feel good and stay healthy. Everyone should get plenty of exercise every day.

Exercising is important for a strong, healthy body. When you work your muscles, they become stronger. And remember that your heart is a muscle too! Running, dancing, playing sports, and many other activities give your heart a workout, making it stronger and more efficient.

Exercise also just makes you feel better. Getting out and moving even a little bit every day makes a person more alert. When you burn up some energy on the playground, it's easier to sit in the classroom and pay attention to the teacher. Best of all, you can avoid that groggy, uncomfortable feeling that comes after a day of doing nothing.

In conclusion, every "body" really should make a commitment to exercise. It's not that hard to do. Any time you get up and move your body, you're exercising. You can do jumping jacks or play baseball. You can play tag or jump rope. Even if you're just dancing around your room to your favorite music, you're exercising. So let's all get up and move!

1. Reread the selection. Write one sentence telling what the writer wants the reader to believe.

_____

_____

2. In paragraphs 2 and 3, underline the supporting facts.

© Pearson Education, Inc., 4

Vocabulary

Directions Choose a word from the box that best completes each sentence. Write the word on the line to the left.

_____ 1. A _____ person might look in a mirror all the time.

_____ 2. The President has much _____.

_____ 3. He behaved _____ as he took the oath.

_____ 4. The _____ is an important document.

_____ 5. Many people voted, so the election was a _____ success.

Check the Words You Know

___Constitution
___howling
___humble
___politics
___responsibility
___solemnly
___vain

Directions Choose the word from the box that best matches each numbered clue below. Write the letters of the word on the blanks. After you are finished, the boxed letters will spell a secret word.

6. seriously

7. government work

8. the act of taking care of someone

9. having too much pride

10. not proud

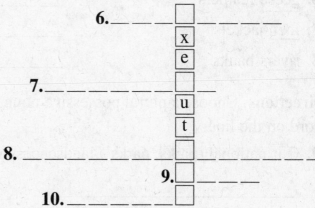

Write a Speech

Pretend you have just been elected President of the United States. On a separate sheet of paper, write a short speech you would give to the public. In the course of explaining how you will approach your new job, use as many vocabulary words as you can.

© Pearson Education, Inc., 4

Home Activity Your child identified and used vocabulary words from *So You Want to Be President?* Together, read an article about politics or government. Discuss the article, using as many vocabulary words from the selection as you can.

Name _____

Plural Possessive Nouns

A **plural possessive noun** shows that something is owned or shared by more than one person, place, or thing.

- Add an apostrophe (') to a plural noun that ends in *-s, -es,* or *-ies.*
  our <u>parks'</u> popularity   <u>animals'</u> rights
- Add an apostrophe (') and *-s* to a plural noun that does not end in *-s, -es,* or *-ies.*
  the <u>deer's</u> feeding ground   the <u>children's</u> vacation

Directions Write the possessive form of each underlined plural noun.

1. <u>highways</u> rest stops   _____

2. <u>teeth</u> cavities   _____

3. <u>states</u> laws   _____

4. <u>forests</u> trees   _____

5. <u>raccoons</u> paws   _____

6. <u>geese</u> feathers   _____

7. <u>men</u> jackets   _____

8. <u>rivers</u> banks   _____

Directions Choose a plural possessive noun to complete each sentence. Write the word on the line.

9. Our national (parks, parks') landscapes are known around the world.

_____

10. (Automobiles, Automobiles') exhausts can harm the wilderness.

_____

11. The (wolfs', wolves') fangs are very sharp.

_____

12. Park (rangers', ranger's) jobs are rewarding.

_____

© Pearson Education, Inc., 4

 Home Activity Your child learned about plural possessive nouns. Ask your child to explain the difference between singular and plural possessive nouns. Encourage your child to give examples using the words *boys, girls,* and *children.*

Words with *ear, ir, our, ur*

Spelling Words				
return	courage	surface	purpose	first
turkey	heard	early	turtle	birthday
journal	courtesy	nourish	purse	furniture
search	curtain	burrow	hamburger	survey

Missing Words Write two list words to complete each sentence correctly.

Baby Teddy is having his **(1)**____ **(2)**____ party today.

1. _____ 2. _____

We bought new **(3)**____ for my bedroom and a new **(4)**____ for the window.

3. _____ 4. _____

It takes **(5)**____ for a box **(6)**____ to cross a road.

5. _____ 6. _____

Mom had to **(7)**____ through her **(8)**____ to find a tissue.

7. _____ 8. _____

The **(9)**____ of **(10)**____ is to put others at ease.

9. _____ 10. _____

Like other birds, the **(11)**____ wakes **(12)**____.

11. _____ 12. _____

Analogies Write list words to complete each analogy.

13. *Bread* is to *sandwich* as *bun* is to ____.   13. _____
14. *Blanket* is to *warm* as *food* is to ____.   14. _____
15. *Eye* is to *saw* as *ear* is to ____.   15. _____
16. *Go* is to *come* as *leave* is to ____.   16. _____
17. *Read* is to *novel* as *write* is to ____.   17. _____
18. *Draw* is to *map* as *measure* is to ____.   18. _____
19. *Down* is to *dive* as *up* is to ____.   19. _____
20. *Bird* is to *nest* as *rabbit* is to ____.   20. _____

Home Activity Your child spelled words with *ear, ir, our,* and *ur.* Say a list word and have your child spell the word and use it in a sentence.

© Pearson Education, Inc., 4

Scoring Rubric: Argument/Persuasive Essay

Writing Traits	4	3	2	1
Focus/Ideas	Opinion, or claim, clearly stated; argument, facts, and details support the opinion	Opinion, or claim, is well stated; argument, facts, and details mostly support the opinion	Opinion, or claim, is not completely clear; argument not well developed and many facts and details do not support the opinion	No clear opinion, or claim; no argument and; few or no related facts and details
Organization	Ideas are in logical order, using transitions to link opinion and evidence	Ideas are in mostly logical order, using several transitions to link opinion and evidence	Order of ideas is unclear; transitions are weak or missing	No logical order or transitions to link opinion and evidence
Voice	Voice is lively and interesting	Voice is generally engaging	Voice is sometimes dull	Voice is flat and dull
Word Choice	Uses strong, descriptive words	Uses some strong, descriptive words	Few strong or descriptive words	Poor word choice
Sentences	No fragments, run-on sentences, or comma splices	One or two fragments, run-on sentences, or comma splices	Several fragments, run-on sentences, or comma splices	Many fragments, run-on sentences, or comma splices
Conventions	Few or no errors; correct use of plural possessive nouns	Few or no errors; correct use of plural possessive nouns	Many errors	Many serious errors

© Pearson Education, Inc., 4

Vocabulary • Unknown Words

- **Dictionaries** and **glossaries** provide alphabetical lists of words and their meanings.
- Sometimes looking at the words around an unknown word can't help you figure out the word's meaning. If this happens, use a dictionary or glossary to find the meaning.

Directions Read the following letter. Then answer the questions below. Use your glossary or a dictionary to help you with unknown words.

Dear Mr. President,
  I became interested in politics after studying the Constitution in school. I hope this doesn't sound vain, but I think I'm a pretty smart student, and I believe that my ideas are sound. I think that the government should take on the responsibility of making sure that every person in the country knows how

to read and write. Then everyone would be able to communicate better and solve problems easier. I solemnly believe this. Please look at the plan I've written on the following pages.

  Sincerely,
  Benita

1. Look up the word *Constitution* in your glossary. What part of speech is it?

_____

2. What is the meaning of the word *communicate?*

_____

3. Why does Benita want to avoid sounding *vain?*

_____

_____

4. The word *sound* can mean "vibrations that can be detected by hearing organs" or "sensible, reasonable." Which meaning is used in this letter? How do you know?

_____

_____

_____

Home Activity Your child used a glossary to identify the definitions of unknown words. Read a short story together. Create a glossary for the story by writing down all the unknown words and using the definitions from a dictionary.

© Pearson Education, Inc., 4

Time Line

A **time line** is a chart that shows a sequence of events. A time line uses a bar divided into periods of time to show the order of events.

Directions Study the time line below. Then answer the questions that follow.

Presidential Time Line

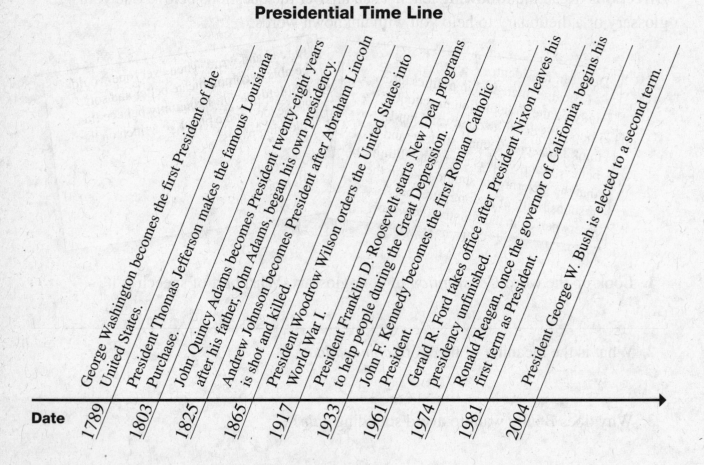

George Washington becomes the first President of the United States.

President Thomas Jefferson makes the famous Louisiana Purchase.

John Quincy Adams becomes President twenty-eight years after his father, John Adams, began his own presidency.

Andrew Johnson becomes President after Abraham Lincoln is shot and killed.

President Woodrow Wilson orders the United States into World War I.

President Franklin D. Roosevelt starts New Deal programs to help people during the Great Depression.

John F. Kennedy becomes the first Roman Catholic President.

Gerald R. Ford takes office after President Nixon leaves his presidency unfinished.

Ronald Reagan, once the governor of California, begins his first term as President.

President George W. Bush is elected to a second term.

Date 1789 1803 1825 1865 1917 1933 1961 1974 1981 2004

1. What information does this time line provide?

_____

_____

2. How are the dates organized on this time line?

_____

_____

3. According to the time line, what event happened most recently?

_____

© Pearson Education, Inc., 4

4. When did President Jefferson make the Louisiana Purchase?

_____

5. What happened in 1974 before Gerald R. Ford became President?

_____

6. What happened for the first time in 1961?

_____

7. How many years passed between the start of George Washington's presidency and President Wilson's decision to enter World War I?

_____

8. Why did Andrew Johnson become President?

_____

9. In what year did John Quincy Adams's father become President? How do you know?

_____

_____

10. How might you use this time line as you do research for a report on American Presidents?

_____

_____

_____

© Pearson Education, Inc., 4

Home Activity Your child learned about time lines and used a time line to answer questions. Together, read an encyclopedia entry about an American President. Write key facts about the President's life and career in a time line. Encourage your child to illustrate the time line with pictures, where appropriate.

Words with *ear, ir, our, ur*

Proofread a Journal Entry Samantha made mistakes as she wrote her journal entry. Circle six misspelled words and write them correctly. Insert quotation marks where they are needed.

> Today was my birthday! I was up very erly. Usually I run right down to breakfast, but today I was as slow as a tertle. As I walked into the kitchen, I herd my family yell, Surprise!
>
> My family gave me a new purse and this brand new jurnal! My friends took me out for a hambirger at lunch. For dinner, we had my favorite—turkey! The only present I have to retearn is a shirt that is too small.
>
> I'll write more tomorrow,
> Samantha

1. _____   2. _____
3. _____   4. _____
5. _____   6. _____

Spelling Words

return
courage
surface
purpose
first
turkey
heard
early
turtle
birthday

journal
courtesy
nourish
purse
furniture
search
curtain
burrow
hamburger
survey

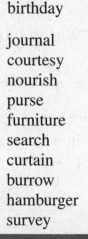

Proofread Words Circle the word that is spelled correctly. Write it on the line.

7. courage	corage	curage	7.	_____
8. searface	sirface	surface	8.	_____
9. curtesy	cirtesy	courtesy	9.	_____
10. survey	sourvey	sirvey	10.	_____
11. bourrow	birrow	burrow	11.	_____
12. curtain	courtain	curtin	12.	_____
13. perse	purse	pirse	13.	_____
14. pirpose	purpase	purpose	14.	_____

Frequently Misspelled Words

heard
our
are

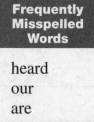

Home Activity Your child identified misspelled words with *ear, ir, our,* and *ur.* Ask your child to write *courtesy* and make up a journal entry about a time he or she was courteous.

© Pearson Education, Inc., 4

Plural Possessive Nouns

Directions Read the passage. Then read each question. Circle the letter of the correct answer.

The White House

(1) Presidents families live in the White House. (2) Their families lives are different from ours. (3) Servants take care of all the residents' needs. (4) Families bring their pets' to the White House. (5) The children pets have a great life.

1 What change, if any, should be made in sentence 1?

A   Change *Presidents* to **Presidents'**.

B   Change *Presidents* to **President's**.

C   Change *Presidents* to **President**.

D   Make no change.

2 What change, if any, should be made in sentence 2?

A   Change *families* to **family's**.

B   Change *families* to **family**.

C   Change *families* to **families'**.

D   Make no change.

3 What change, if any, should be made in sentence 3?

A   Change *residents'* to **resident's**.

B   Change *residents'* to **residents**.

C   Change *needs* to **need**.

D   Make no change.

4 What change, if any, should be made in sentence 4?

A   Change *pets'* to **pets**.

B   Change *pets'* to **pet**.

C   Change *pets'* to **pet's**.

D   Make no change.

5 What change, if any, should be made in sentence 5?

A   Change *children* to **child**.

B   Change *children* to **children's**.

C   Change *children* to **childrens**.

D   Make no change.

© Pearson Education, Inc., 4

Home Activity Your child prepared for taking tests on plural possessive nouns. Have your child prepare flash cards with a plural noun on one side and its possessive form on the other. Quiz him or her using the flash cards.

Adding -s and -es

Spelling Words				
monkeys	friends	plays	supplies	taxes
holidays	months	companies	costumes	sandwiches
hobbies	daisies	delays	scratches	counties
teammates	memories	bunches	batteries	donkeys

Naming Classes Write the list word that describes each group.

1. Fourth of July, Thanksgiving, Labor Day _____
2. hiking, collecting stamps, reading _____
3. flower shop, bank, grocery store _____
4. AA, AAA, D, 9-volt _____
5. July, February, October _____
6. ham and cheese, hamburger, peanut butter _____
7. pencils, paper, ruler, markers _____
8. howler, capuchin, marmoset _____
9. bananas, grapes, bouquets of flowers _____
10. pitcher, catcher, shortstop _____

Word Meanings Write the list word beside the phrase that means the same.

11. people who know and like you _____
12. dramas acted on the stage _____
13. money paid to a government _____
14. actors' clothing _____
15. long-eared relatives of the horse _____
16. things remembered _____
17. flowers with white or pink petals _____
18. areas into which a state is divided _____
19. marks or cuts made by sharp objects _____
20. makes late by slowing or stopping _____

© Pearson Education, Inc., 4

 School + Home **Home Activity** Your child learned to spell the plural forms of words by adding -s or -es. Write the singular form of each word and have your child tell if and how it changes to form the plural.

Common and Proper Nouns

Directions One of the underlined words in each sentence is a noun. Write the noun.

1. Women have <u>played</u> <u>basketball</u> for almost as long as men have.

_____

2. One of the <u>first</u> games was played at Smith College in <u>Massachusetts</u>.

_____

3. <u>At</u> first there were nine women on a <u>side</u>.

_____

4. The <u>court</u> was divided into <u>three</u> zones.

_____

5. Three <u>players</u> <u>would</u> play in each zone.

_____

Directions Two nouns are underlined in each sentence. Write the noun that is the kind named in ( ).

6. <u>Senda Berenson</u>, a physical education <u>teacher</u>, taught at Smith College. (common)

_____

7. The first college <u>game</u> was played at Smith College on <u>March</u> 21, 1893. (proper)

_____

8. The first intercollegiate game for <u>women</u> was played in <u>California</u>. (common)

_____

9. Stanford played <u>Berkeley</u> in the game then known as "basket <u>ball</u>." (proper)

_____

10. <u>Stanford</u> scored two <u>baskets</u> and won the game! (proper)

_____

© Pearson Education, Inc., 4

Irregular Plurals

Spelling Words				
videos	feet	potatoes	themselves	lives
leaves	cliffs	men	halves	moose
radios	sheep	cuffs	beliefs	patios
children	tornadoes	tomatoes	hoofs	loaves

Context Clues Choose a list word to complete each sentence. Write the word.

1. A strong wind blew the _____ off of trees. _____
2. The weather service sent out a warning for _____. _____
3. People sat in basements and listened to _____. _____
4. _____ and their parents waited patiently. _____
5. The furniture on _____ had to be put away. _____
6. Most people thought _____ lucky. _____
7. Going to the basement was a safety tip that saved many _____. _____
8. Over a meal of meat and _____, people smiled. _____
9. They rolled up the _____ of their sleeves and went to work. _____

Word Clues Write the list word that answers the clue.

10. Your socks are filled with these. _____
11. We get wool from them. _____
12. A baker makes these. _____
13. A tasty red food with *toes* in them. _____
14. You watch these after an event happens. _____

Watch the Ending Circle the correctly spelled list word.

15. patios   patioes
16. hoofs   hoofes
17. cliffs   clives
18. halfs   halves
19. loafs   loaves
20. beliefs   believs

Home Activity Your child learned irregular plural words. Have your child make flash cards with the singular form of each list word on one side and the plural form on the other. Use the cards to quiz each other.

© Pearson Education, Inc., 4

Regular Plural Nouns

Direction Write the two plural nouns in each sentence.

1. The cowboys of the Southwest were expert riders.

   _____

2. On horses or ponies, they were completely at home.

   _____

3. They worked on the big ranches, far from the cities.

   _____

4. Cowboys worked in many of the western and southwestern states.

   _____

5. They spent their days herding cows.

   _____

Directions Write each singular noun as a plural noun. Say the plural nouns.

6. trench _____

7. lady _____

8. road _____

9. dress _____

10. puppy _____

11. branch _____

12. family _____

13. brother _____

14. farm _____

15. box _____

© Pearson Education, Inc., 4

Words with *ar, or*

Spelling Words				
morning	forest	garbage	form	alarm
corner	story	argue	backyard	start
partner	storm	Florida	apartment	sport
force	forward	sharp	garden	Arkansas

Tried and True Sayings Write the list word that correctly completes each saying.

1. Happiness begins right in your own _____. _____

2. He is as _____ as a tack. _____

3. She can't see the _____ for the trees. _____

4. Sleep. Things will look better in the _____. _____

5. After a _____, a rainbow comes. _____

6. For every step _____, I take two steps back. _____

7. Let's begin again to make a fresh _____. _____

8. _____, the Natural State! _____

9. _____, it's the Sunshine State! _____

10. Thanks for being such a good _____. _____

Word Meanings Write the list word that fits each definition.

11. things thrown away _____

12. a home in a larger building _____

13. something's shape _____

14. angle where two walls meet _____

15. sudden feeling of fear _____

16. to disagree _____

17. power or strength _____

18. co-worker or associate _____

19. a tale of an event _____

20. a plot for growing vegetables _____

Home Activity Your child learned to distinguish words with *ar* and *or*. Have your child write list words and highlight *ar* and *or* in contrasting colors.

© Pearson Education, Inc., 4

Name _____

Irregular Plural Nouns

Directions Write the irregular plural noun in each sentence.

1. If we went back in time, our lives would be different. _____

2. Women would probably stay in their homes more. _____

3. Men might be out in the fields. _____

4. They would hitch their oxen to the wagons. _____

5. Their feet would be sore from heavy leather boots. _____

6. Guarding sheep and cows was an important job. _____

7. Wolves might grab a lamb for their suppers. _____

8. What would the children do? _____

9. They might look after the chickens and geese. _____

10. Maybe they would help the cats catch mice in the barns. _____

Directions If the noun is plural, write *P*. If it is singular, write its plural form. If the noun could be either singular or plural, write *S/P*. Say the plural forms.

11. moose _____

12. calf _____

13. teeth _____

14. shelf _____

15. wives _____

16. deer _____

17. ox _____

18. men _____

19. tooth _____

20. wife _____

© Pearson Education, Inc., 4

Consonant Pairs *ng, nk, ph, wh*

Spelling Words				
Thanksgiving	among	think	blank	graph
young	wheel	nephew	belong	whiskers
whisper	elephant	white	shrink	wharf
trunk	strong	blink	chunk	skunk

Antonyms Write the list word that has the opposite, or nearly the opposite, meaning as the word.

1. old _____
2. shout _____
3. weak _____
4. black _____
5. grow _____

Synonyms Write the list word that has the same, or nearly the same, meaning as the word.

6. beard _____
7. box _____
8. ponder _____
9. dock _____
10. with _____

Words in Context Write a list word from the box to complete each sentence.

11. Carl cut himself a large _____ of cheese. _____
12. The _____ uses a bad smell to keep predators away. _____
13. We eat a huge meal on _____ Day. _____
14. The wagon has a loose _____. _____
15. The zoo has monkeys and an _____. _____
16. Zach is my brother's son, or my _____. _____
17. The bright light made me _____ my eyes. _____
18. Write your answer on the _____ line. _____
19. Those marbles _____ to me; they are mine. _____
20. I made a _____ showing how I have grown. _____

© Pearson Education, Inc., 4

 Home Activity Your child learned words with consonant pairs *ng, nk, ph,* and *wh*. Have your child identify the consonant pair in each list word. Then help your child think of other words with these spellings.

Singular Possessive Nouns

Directions Write the possessive form of each underlined singular word.

1. <u>city</u> mail   _____

2. <u>mustang</u> rider   _____

3. <u>winter</u> storms   _____

4. <u>desert</u> trails   _____

5. <u>trip</u> dangers   _____

6. <u>Tschiffely</u> plan   _____

7. <u>Ecuador</u> forests   _____

8. <u>horse</u> back   _____

9. <u>Trigger</u> talents   _____

10. <u>movie</u> plot   _____

Directions Write the singular possessive noun in ( ) that completes each sentence.

11. It's fun to read about (history's, histories) horses.

    _____

12. (Californias, California's) mail was delivered by the Pony Express.

    _____

13. Both horse and rider were tired at (journeys, journey's) end.

    _____

14. Gato and Mancha were a Swiss (teachers, teacher's) horses.

    _____

15. That (cowboys, cowboy's) movies featured his horse, Trigger.

    _____

© Pearson Education, Inc., 4

Words with *ear, ir, our, ur*

Spelling Words				
return	courage	surface	purpose	first
turkey	heard	early	turtle	birthday
journal	courtesy	nourish	purse	furniture
search	curtain	burrow	hamburger	survey

Classifying Write the list word that fits each group.

1. chicken, pheasant, quail, _____ _____
2. desks, tables, beds, sofas, _____ _____
3. bedspread, screen, tablecloth, _____ _____
4. measure, examine, map out, _____ _____
5. lizard, snake, alligator, _____ _____
6. nest, cave, den, _____ _____
7. book, magazine, newspaper, _____ _____
8. hot dog, chicken salad, barbecue, _____ _____
9. bag, briefcase, pouch, _____ _____
10. fourth, third, second, _____ _____

Word Scramble Unscramble each list word and write it on the line.

11. thradiby _____
12. nuterr _____
13. sharce _____
14. greacuo _____
15. radeh _____
16. restucoy _____
17. furcesa _____
18. raley _____
19. hournis _____
20. ropesup _____

Home Activity Your child learned words spelled with *ear, ir, our,* and *ur*. Say each list word. Have your child explain the word's meaning and spell it aloud.

© Pearson Education, Inc., 4

Plural Possessive Nouns

Directions Write the possessive form of each underlined plural word.

1. <u>senators</u> duties   _____

2. <u>cities</u> monuments   _____

3. <u>states</u> rights   _____

4. <u>women</u> votes   _____

5. <u>parks</u> wildlife   _____

6. <u>wolves</u> howls   _____

7. <u>sheep</u> horns   _____

8. <u>families</u> vacations   _____

9. <u>feet</u> blisters   _____

10. <u>wives</u> conversations _____

Directions Write the plural possessive noun in ( ) that completes each sentence.

11. Three (President's, Presidents') pets once got together for a meeting.

_____

12. The (pets', pet's) idea was that they would run the country.

_____

13. The (dog's, dogs') job would be homeland security.

_____

14. The Roosevelt (children's, childrens') guinea pigs would run the hospitals.

_____

15. The white (mices', mice's) voices were so soft that no one heard them.

_____

© Pearson Education, Inc., 4

Main Ideas and Details Chart

Directions An expository composition has one or more main ideas. Each main idea is supported by one or more details. Fill in the chart with the main ideas and details for your expository composition.

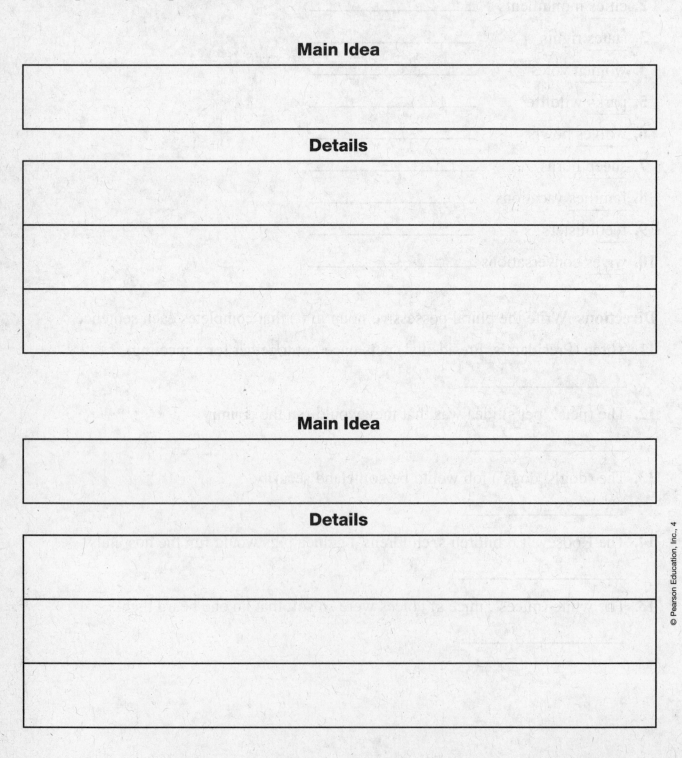

Main Idea

Details

Main Idea

Details

© Pearson Education, Inc., 4

Use Tables and Graphs

Directions Create a table to show several related facts from your expository composition. Use the table below or make another kind of chart if this table is not suitable for your facts.

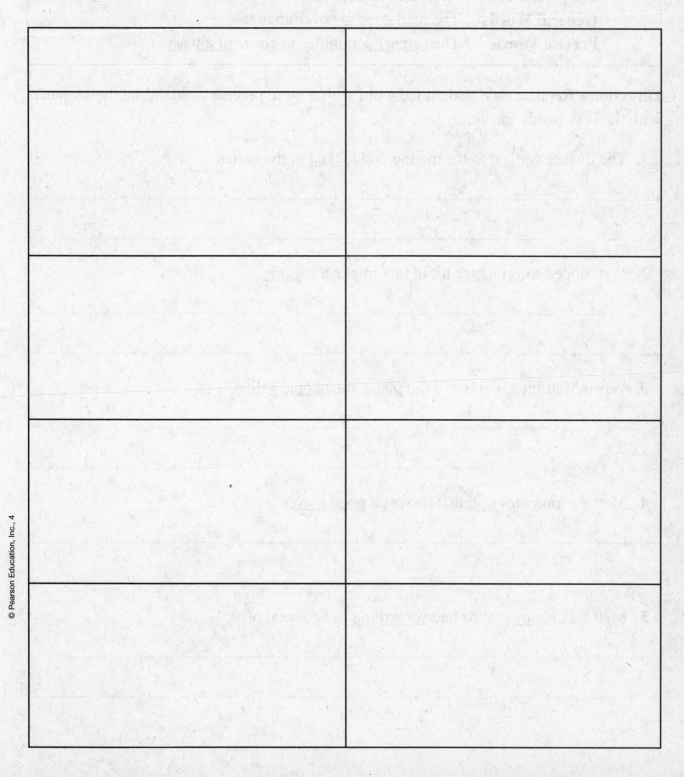

© Pearson Education, Inc., 4

Use Precise Words

Use precise words to help make your writing clearer, more coherent, and easier for your audience to read and understand. Replace vague nouns, verbs, and adjectives with more precise nouns, verbs, and adjectives.

| General Words | The <u>man</u> <u>goes</u> to cover an <u>area</u>. |
| **Precise Words** | The <u>catcher</u> <u>scrambles</u> to cover <u>first base</u>. |

Directions Replace each underlined word with a more precise word. Write the sentence with the new words shown.

1. The pitcher <u>walked</u> to the mound and <u>looked</u> at the batter.

_____

_____

2. Matt hoped to get a <u>nice</u> hit in this important <u>game</u>.

_____

_____

3. When Matt <u>hit</u> a ball out of the <u>place</u>, the <u>people</u> <u>yelled</u>.

_____

_____

4. Matt's teammates <u>said</u> that he was a <u>good</u> <u>player</u>.

_____

_____

5. Matt was <u>happy</u> that he had <u>something</u> to be proud of.

_____

_____

© Pearson Education, Inc., 4

Editing 1

Directions Edit these sentences. Look for errors in spelling, grammar, and mechanics. Use proofreading marks to show the corrections.

Proofreading Marks	
Delete (Take out)	⌐
Add	∧
Spelling	◯
Uppercase letter	≡
Lowercase letter	/

1. The school band needs money for a feild trip to chicago.

2. Band members plans to have car washes on sevral weekends.

3. Every band member will wash cars to help pay for their trip

4. David brings the buckits, detergent and scrub brushes.

5. Moniques' towels and sponges is just what they need.

6. Sumi makes beutiful signs, to post where customers can see it.

7. Principal sanchez lets the students use the school's three garden hose.

8. because so many came to help Monique had to run home and get more towels!

Now you'll edit the draft of your expository composition. Then you'll use your revised and edited draft to make a final copy of your composition. Finally, you'll share your written work with your audience.

© Pearson Education, Inc., 4

Graphic Sources

- A **graphic source** shows or explains information in the text. Pictures, maps, charts, time lines, and diagrams are all graphic sources.

Directions Study the following table. Then answer the questions below.

Chicago, IL Temperature and Precipitation Averages

Month	Temperature (High)	Precipitation (Inches)
January	22°	4.78"
March	45°	6.70"
May	68°	3.65"
July	84°	3.70"
September	73°	5.85"
November	47°	4.01"

1. What does this table show? _____

_____

2. In what month is it most likely to rain or snow? _____

_____

3. Based on the table, what do you think the weather is like in Chicago in December?

_____

_____

4. How could this table be of value in planning an outdoor event in Chicago?

_____

_____

5. What other graphic source could you use to show this information?

_____

_____

Home Activity Your child identified information from a graphic source. Work with him or her to identify other graphic sources in newspapers or magazines. Together, take information from a newspaper or magazine article and create a graph or table to show it.

© Pearson Education, Inc., 4

Writing • Narrative Poem

Key Features of Narrative Poems

• tells a story in sequence and includes main character(s)

• can include meter, rhymes, and refrains

• uses language playfully

Carl from Sweden

In Sweden in 1707,
Carl von Linné was born one day in May.
Known as Carolus Linnaeus,
His work would be famous one day.

He named our plants and animals,
He gave them Latin names.
So the man called Carl Von Linné,
Became known by his Latin name.

Carl's father had a garden, with
Plants and flowers, wild and tame.
As a little boy Carl loved them all.
He knew each one needed a name.

He named our plants and animals,
He gave them Latin names.
So the man called Carl Von Linné,
Became known by his Latin name.

1. Who is the main character and what story does this narrative poem tell?

_____

_____

2. What are the words that rhyme in the third stanza?

_____

© Pearson Education, Inc., 4

Vocabulary

Directions Choose the word from the box that best matches each clue.
Write the word on the line.

_____ **1.** making by hand or machine

_____ **2.** the continued action of a
weight or other force

_____ **3.** a person learning a trade or
an art from a skilled worker

_____ **4.** any substance used in or
produced by chemistry

_____ **5.** the air that surrounds the earth

Check the Words You Know
___apprentice
___atmosphere
___chemical
___club
___essay
___manufacturing
___pressure
___scales

Directions Choose the word from the box that best completes each sentence below.
Write the word on the line shown to the left.

_____ **6.** Maya and I joined the photography _____.

_____ **7.** Maya photographed the _____ of the fish.

_____ **8.** Avoid too much _____ on the camera's shutter button.

_____ **9.** Maya wrote a short _____ about her visit to the fish
market.

_____ **10.** I wrote about clouds in the _____.

Write a Poem

On a separate sheet of paper, write a poem about your favorite type of weather. Use as
many vocabulary words as you can.

Home Activity Your child identified and used words from the story *The Man Who Named the Clouds.*
Review the definitions with your child and talk about other meanings for each word. Work together to use
the words in sentences.

© Pearson Education, Inc., 4

Name _____

Action and Linking Verbs

The main word in the predicate of a sentence is a verb. Verbs that show actions are called **action verbs.** Most verbs show actions you can see. Some verbs, such as *think* and *wonder,* show actions you cannot see.

Action Verbs   Luke <u>finished</u> school at age fifteen.
Luke <u>thought</u> the clouds needed names.

Linking verbs do not show actions. They tell what the subject is or what the subject is like. Common linking verbs are forms of the verb *to be,* such as *am, is, are, was,* and *were.* Verbs such as *seem, appear, become,* and *feel* can also be linking verbs.

Linking Verbs   Luke's school <u>was</u> a religious boarding school.
He <u>felt</u> that there were seven types of clouds.

Directions Circle the verb in each sentence.

1. Wind usually moves from west to east.

2. Some clouds appear like animals in the sky.

3. Luke was unhappy at his first job.

4. His father loaned him money.

5. He filled the shelves with books.

6. Luke wondered about names for the clouds.

7. Some names were not exact enough.

8. At first, Luke described three main cloud shapes.

Directions Underline action verbs. Circle linking verbs.

9. Many people still wonder about the clouds.

10. Some weather reports describe the day's clouds.

11. Tall cumulonimbus clouds often bring thunderstorms.

12. Cirrus clouds are very thin.

Home Activity Your child learned about action and linking verbs. Ask your child to tell you something that happened today. Have your child identify action and linking verbs in his or her account.

© Pearson Education, Inc., 4

Adding *-ed* and *-ing*

Spelling Words				
watched	watching	danced	dancing	studied
studying	stopped	stopping	dried	drying
happened	happening	noticed	noticing	robbed
robbing	slipped	slipping	hurried	hurrying

Definitons Write a list word to fit each definition. If the verb in the definition ends with *-ed*, write an *-ed* word. If the verb ends with *-ing*, write an *-ing* word.

1. raced

_____

2. paying attention

_____

3. occurring

_____

4. reviewed for a test

_____

5. ended

_____

6. falling on ice

_____

7. moved to music

_____

8. observed

_____

9. stealing

_____

10. dehydrated

_____

Complete the Sentence Read the base word at the beginning of each sentence. Write the correct form of the base word to complete the sentence.

11. **hurry** Did you see anyone _____ by here lately?

12. **happen** No I didn't. What _____?

13. **stop** Well, I heard cars _____ quickly.

14. **dance** People seemed to be _____ around in front of the bank.

15. **rob** Then I realized they were shouting that the bank had been _____.

16. **notice** Soon I _____ the sound of sirens.

17. **study** I saw police _____ the crime scene.

18. **slip** The thief had _____ away.

19. **watch** Now the police are _____ the bank's videotape.

20. **dry** Soon the criminal will be _____ his tears in jail.

11. _____

12. _____

13. _____

14. _____

15. _____

16. _____

17. _____

18. _____

19. _____

20. _____

© Pearson Education, Inc., 4

Home Activity Your child wrote words with *-ed* and *-ing* endings. Say a list word and have your child spell the list word aloud.

Name _____

Story Sequence A

Title _____

Beginning

↓

Middle

↓

End

© Pearson Education, Inc., 4

Vocabulary: Context Clues

- You might read a word whose meaning you know, but the word doesn't make sense in the sentence. The word may have more than one meaning. You can use **context clues** to decide which meaning the author is using.

Directions Read the following passage about the Weather Club. Then answer the questions below. Look for context clues as you read.

Twice a month, Carlos and Tina meet with the Weather Club. Here, club members learn about patterns and changes in the weather. They learn how clouds are formed and what causes lightning. Members also use different scales, such as those on thermometers and barometers, to gather information about the atmosphere. A barometer measures air pressure. Carlos and Tina are learning how air pressure, or the force exerted by the atmosphere, affects weather. For example, low pressure, can signal an impending, or coming, storm. As apprentice meteorologists, they are becoming experts in the study of weather.

1. What does the word *club* mean in this passage? What clues helped you figure this out?

_____

2. What is another meaning of *club?*

_____

3. What does the word *pressure* mean in this passage? What clues helped you figure this out?

_____

4. What is another meaning for *pressure?*

_____

5. *Scale* can mean "a series of marks along a line used in measuring" or "one of the thin, hard plates found on some fish and reptiles." How is it used in the passage? How can you tell?

_____

Home Activity Your child learned to use context clues to choose the correct meaning of a multiple meaning word. With your child, take turns coming up with words that have more than one meaning. One says a word that the other uses in two sentences, each revealing one possible meaning of the word.

© Pearson Education, Inc., 4

Almanac

An **almanac** is a book that is published every year. It contains calendars, weather information, and dates of holidays. It also contains charts and tables of current information about subjects such as city population and recent prize winners in science, literature, or sports.

Directions Review this information from an almanac.

Fall Facts

- Fall usually lasts from September 22 (or 23) to December 21 (or 22).
- September 22 (or 23) has equal hours during the day and night.
- December 21 (or 22) is the shortest day of the year.
- Fall, also called autumn, is a time for harvesting crops.
- Fall is a popular time for festivals celebrating crops.

Fall Holidays

Holiday	Date	Common Image
Columbus Day	second Monday in October	ship
Halloween	October 31	pumpkin
Thanksgiving	fourth Thursday in November	turkey

Fall Leaves

- Some trees have leaves that turn yellow (instead of orange or red) each autumn. Examples include birch, tulip poplar, hickory, and redbud trees.
- During the fall in the United States, the most brilliant leaf colors appear in the New England states.

Peak Times to See Colorful Leaves

State	Time
Maryland	September and early October
North Carolina	mid-September to mid-October
New York	mid-September to early November
Maine	end of September to mid-October
West Virginia	early October to end of November
Georgia	late October
Kentucky	October and most of November

© Pearson Education, Inc., 4

Name _____

Directions Use the information from the almanac to answer the following questions.

1. Which section gives information about trees and leaf colors?

_____

2. What are the three holidays listed in this part of the almanac?

_____

3. What is the shortest day of the year?

_____

4. An image of a ship is often used to indicate which holiday?

_____

5. How is the table labeled "Peak Times to See Colorful Leaves" arranged?

_____

6. In which states can people best view leaves changing color on Thanksgiving?

_____

7. Give two examples of trees whose leaves change only to yellow.

_____

8. About how long is autumn, according to the information given in the almanac?

_____

9. Which is more likely to be useful when planning a vacation: an almanac or an encyclopedia?

_____

10. For what reasons might you choose an almanac over a dictionary to find information about autumn?

_____

_____

Home Activity Your child studied an almanac and answered questions about its use. With your child, look at the almanacs in a library's reference section. Choose a topic and find out what kinds of information on this topic can be found in an almanac.

© Pearson Education, Inc., 4

Name _____

Adding -ed and -ing

Proofread a Story Read the story. Circle six misspelled words and write them correctly. Rewrite the sentence that has a punctuation error.

Spelling Words

watched
watching
danced
dancing
studied
studying
stopped
stopping
dried
drying

happened
happening
noticed
noticing
robbed
robbing
slipped
slipping
hurried
hurrying

A Dancer Dreams

After Katrina put on her costume, she stoped to look into the mirror.

"Maybe tonight I'll be notised, she said softly.

Katrina had been studing dancing for most of her fourteen years. She wacht other dancers become famous. Katrina hoped that would happen to her soon.

She struck her most graceful pose in front of the mirror. Then she openned the door and hurryed out to the stage.

1. _____   2. _____

3. _____   4. _____

5. _____   6. _____

7. _____

Frequently Misspelled Words

swimming
stopped
happened
slipped
opened

Proofread Words Write the misspelled list word correctly.

8. driing _____   9. happing _____

10. sliped _____   11. danceed _____

12. robed _____   13. hurryng _____

14. noticeing _____   15. studyed _____

16. stoping _____   17. hapened _____

18. robing _____   19. dryed _____

Home Activity Your child identified misspelled words with -ed and -ing endings. Say a base word, and have your child add the endings and spell the list words.

© Pearson Education, Inc., 4

Action and Linking Verbs

Directions Read the passage. Then read each question. Circle the letter of the correct answer.

Cloud Watch

(1) Many people is interested in the clouds. (2) Clouds come in many different shapes. (3) Long ago, people keeps journals about weather and clouds. (4) Luke Howard studyd clouds, temperature, and rainfall. (5) He write an essay on the classification of clouds. (6) Luke named seven kinds of clouds.

1 What change, if any, should be made in sentence 1?

   A Change *is interested* to **are interested.**

   B Change *is interested* to **was interested.**

   C Change *is interested* to **is interesting.**

   D Make no change.

2 What change, if any, should be made in sentence 2?

   A Change *come* to **came.**

   B Change *come* to **comes.**

   C Change *shapes* to **shape.**

   D Make no change.

3 What change, if any, should be made in sentence 3?

   A Change *keeps* to **keeping.**

   B Change *keeps* to **kept.**

   C Change *keeps* to **keep.**

   D Make no change.

4 What change, if any, should be made in sentence 4?

   A Change *studyd* to **studied.**

   B Change *studyd* to **has studyd.**

   C Change *studyd* to **have studyd.**

   D Make no change.

5 What change, if any, should be made in sentence 5?

   A Change *write* to **had writed.**

   B Change *write* to **wrote.**

   C Change *write* to **writes.**

   D Make no change.

© Pearson Education, Inc., 4

Home Activity Your child prepared for taking tests on action and linking verbs. Have your child write action and linking verbs on index cards. Ask your child to use these verbs in sentences as you hold up the cards one at a time.

Fact and Opinion

- A **statement of fact** can be proved true or false by doing research.
- A **statement of opinion** cannot be proved true or false. It is a belief or a judgment. It often contains a word of judgment, such as *best, should,* or *beautiful.* It may begin with the words *In my opinion* or *I believe.*

Directions Read the following passage. Then complete the table. Read each statement and answer the questions at the top of each column.

People and their pets have special relationships. Many people believe that their pets are a part of their families. Some people dress their animals in colorful clothes and buy expensive food for them to eat.

Pets also help people in many ways. For instance, pets can cheer up people who are sick or living alone. Barking dogs protect people and their homes. In addition, Seeing Eye™ dogs guide their blind owners. These dogs are trained to stop walking if they sense a dangerous situation and to avoid low branches and other obstacles. Whether the animals are companions or trained partners, animal experts feel that it's important to treat them kindly.

Statement	Does it state a fact or an opinion?	If an opinion, what are the clue words? If a fact, how could you prove it?
Seeing Eye™ dogs guide their blind owners.	1.	2.
Many people believe that their pets are a part of their family.	3.	4.

5. Write a statement of fact from the passage. How could you prove it?

_____

_____

Home Activity Your child identified statements of fact and statements of opinion in a short passage. Read an article or story about nature with your child. Ask your child to identify the facts and opinions in the article or story.

© Pearson Education, Inc., 4

Writing • Invitation

Key Features of Invitations

- include who is hosting or what the event is for, the time, and place
- use a tone that matches the audience and purpose of the event
- include RSVP information, date, salutation, and closing
- include directions and possibly a map to the event

Pool Party Invitation

June 24, 20___

Dear Max and Sam,

School's out – time to celebrate and dive into summer fun! Come help us break in our brand-new pool and enjoy the "taste" of summer!

Date: July 1

Place: Eva Chang's Grandparent's Home
1451 Main Street, Austin, TX (see map below)

Time: 2:00-4:00 p.m.

Please call me by May 1 at (512) 555-5555 to let me know if you can come. If it rains, we'll try to do it the following week, July 8—same time, same place! Remember to bring a towel and sunscreen—we'll supply water, treats, and fun!

Directions: From school, go right on Green Street and go straight until you get to the stop sign, which is Main Street. Turn right and go to the third house on your left, number 1451.

Sincerely,
Annabelle

© Pearson Education, Inc., 4

1. Is the tone of this invitation formal or informal? Circle the words that help set the tone.

2. Underline words that give important facts the reader needs.

3. What else does writer use to convey an informal and fun tone?

Vocabulary

Directions Choose the word from the box that best completes each sentence. Write the word on the line.

Check the Words
You Know

___biologist
___bluff
___lagoon
___massive
___rumbling
___tropical

Joan Ferguson looked out over the blue **1.** _____. She viewed the whales shooting air out of their blowholes. As the mist covered the air above the water, a low **2.** _____ sound echoed across the valley. Joan felt small as she observed the **3.** _____ mammals. She was a **4.** _____, or a scientist who studied animals. Joan came to the same **5.** _____ location every year.

Directions Circle the word or words with the same or nearly the same meaning as the first word in the group.

6. **rumbling**	deep sound	squeaky sound	sharp sound	silent
7. **bluff**	lake	creek	cliff	island
8. **massive**	tiny	bulky	salty	long
9. **biologist**	nurse	doctor	teacher	scientist
10. **lagoon**	pond	bluff	island	ocean

Write a Newspaper Article

On a separate sheet of paper write a newspaper article about an animal that returns to the same place every year. Remember to include a title, and use as many vocabulary words as you can.

Home Activity Your child identified and used vocabulary words from *Adelina's Whales*. Read a story about animals with your child. Point out unfamiliar words in the story. Challenge your child to find the meanings by looking at the words around the unfamiliar words.

© Pearson Education, Inc., 4

Name _____

Main and Helping Verbs

A verb that has more than one word is called a **verb phrase.** A verb phrase is made up of a **main verb** and one or more **helping verbs.** The main verb shows action. The helping verb or verbs tell more about the action. Common helping verbs are *am, is, are, was, were, will, would, should, has, have, had, do, does, did, can,* and *could.* In the following sentences, the main verb is underlined once and the helping verb is underlined twice.

> Scientists <u>are</u> <u>studying</u> animal migration.
> They <u>have</u> <u>tracked</u> salmon's journeys.

The helping verbs *am, is,* and *are* show present time. *Was* and *were* show past time. *Will* shows future time. The helping verbs *has, have,* and *had* show that an action started in the past. In the following sentences, the helping verb *has* shows action that started in the past, and the helping verb *will* shows future time.

> One turtle has traveled 7,000 miles.
> Scientists will follow it by satellite.

Directions Circle the verb phrase in each sentence.

1. I am studying the migration of sharks.

2. My team has put tags on sharks' fins.

3. The tags are sending radio signals to satellites.

4. Our computers have received information from the satellites.

5. We are collecting important information.

Directions Write the verb named in ( ).

6. These salmon could deposit thousands of eggs. (helping)

_____

7. The flashlight fish are looking for food. (main) _____

8. The turtle has returned to its home. (helping) _____

© Pearson Education, Inc., 4

Home Activity Your child learned about main and helping verbs. Ask your child these questions: *What are you doing now? What will you do tomorrow?* Have your child answer the questions in complete sentences and identify the main and helping verbs.

Homophones

Spelling Words				
two	to	too	piece	peace
break	brake	there	their	they're
threw	through	by	bye	beat
beet	thrown	throne	aloud	allowed

Word Meanings Write the list word that has the same or almost the same meaning as each word or phrase.

1. part
2. stop
3. finished
4. so long
5. rhythm
6. king's chair
7. spoken
8. they are
9. also
10. belonging to them

1. _____
2. _____
3. _____
4. _____
5. _____
6. _____
7. _____
8. _____
9. _____
10. _____

Missing Words Write a list word to complete each sentence.

11. Three is one more than ____.
12. The pitcher ____ the ball to first base.
13. I was afraid I had ____ my homework in the wastebasket.
14. Mom asked for some ____ and quiet.
15. Jon's face turns as red as a ____ when he blushes.
16. We aren't ____ to stay out after dark.
17. This book was written ____ my favorite author.
18. My brother is over ____ beside the car.
19. Sarah read her poem ____ the class.
20. You can take a ____ after you finish your chores.

11. _____
12. _____
13. _____
14. _____
15. _____
16. _____
17. _____
18. _____
19. _____
20. _____

© Pearson Education, Inc., 4

School + Home

Home Activity Your child wrote homophones. Use a list word in a sentence and have your child write the word.

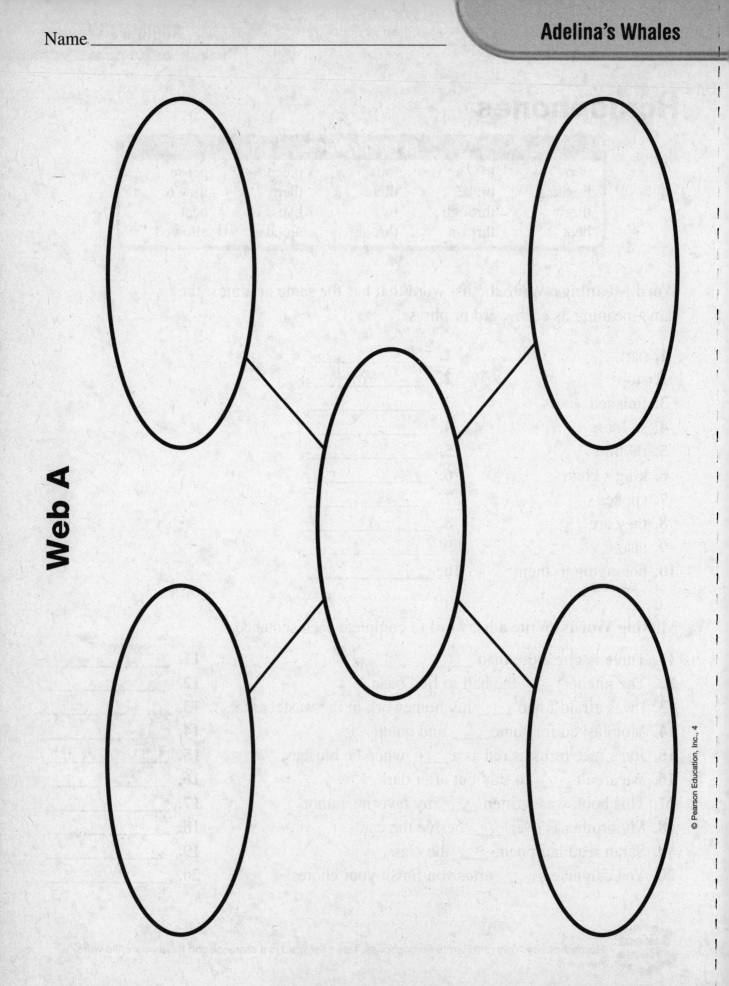

Web A

© Pearson Education, Inc., 4

Vocabulary • Multiple-Meaning Words

- **Multiple-meaning words** are words that are spelled the same but have different meanings, depending upon how they are used in a sentence.

- When you read, you may come to a word whose meaning you know, but that meaning does not make sense in the sentence. Use **context clues** to find the meaning.

Directions Read the following passage. Then answer the questions below.

The tropical island nation of Jamaica is wonderful to visit. Its weather is warm and sunny, although brief rain showers fall almost every day. The sound of thunder rumbling through the sky gives everyone time to take cover. Since it is sunny so much, it is a lovely place to go swimming.

There are many waterfalls and warm-water lagoons on the island. Some of the lagoons are hidden behind a bluff or a cluster of hills. At the beach, you might sit on the sand, read a book, and watch for the flukes of passing whales.

1. What does the word *bluff* mean in this passage? What clues can help you determine the correct definition?

_____

2. *Sand* can mean "tiny grains of stone and shell" or "what you do to make wood smooth." How is it used in the passage? How can you tell?

_____

3. *Beach* can mean "the sand at the ocean's edge" or "to wash up on shore." Which meaning does it have above? How do you know?

_____

4. *Flukes* can mean "parts of an animal" or "strokes of luck." How is it used in the passage? How can you tell?

_____

5. Why are context clues useful when you encounter multiple-meaning words?

_____

 Home Activity Your child identified and used context clues to understand multiple-meaning words used in a passage. Work with your child to identify other multiple-meaning words. Make a list of the words and take turns using them in sentences that employ the words' different meanings.

© Pearson Education, Inc., 4

The *Readers' Guide to Periodical Literature*

The ***Readers' Guide to Periodical Literature*** is a set of books that is an index of articles published in periodicals. Each volume lists articles published in a specific year. Within each volume, articles are listed alphabetically by author and subject. The introductory pages of each volume explain how to use the *Readers' Guide.*

Directions Look at the volumes of the *Readers' Guide to Periodical Literature* illustrated below. Then answer the questions that follow.

READERS' GUIDE TO PERIODICAL LITERATURE	READERS' GUIDE TO PERIODICAL LITERATURE	READERS' GUIDE TO PERIODICAL LITERATURE	READERS' GUIDE TO PERIODICAL LITERATURE	READERS' GUIDE TO PERIODICAL LITERATURE	READERS' GUIDE TO PERIODICAL LITERATURE	READERS' GUIDE TO PERIODICAL LITERATURE
1998	1999	2000	2001	2002	2003	2004
58	59	60	61	62	63	64

1. In what order are volumes organized? What volume will be published for 2005?

_____

2. If you were looking to read more about some whales that were saved in 2002, in which volume would you look?

_____

3. How would you use the *Readers' Guide* to find the most up-to-date information about whales?

_____

4. If you wanted to read articles about whales written by the biologist Dr. Joan Brady, why do you think you would check several volumes?

_____

5. How are the *Readers' Guides* important for research today?

_____

_____

© Pearson Education, Inc., 4

Name _____

Directions The entry below is similar to what you might see in the *Readers' Guide*.
Read it, then answer the questions that follow.

WHALES
   COMMUNICATION
      See also
     Animal behavior
     Marine animals
   Sharing information. K. Kleeman. il *Animal Quarterly* v.45 pp. 98–101 O '03
   Whales' habits. S. Romberg. il *The Animal Sanctuary* v.20 pp. 22–26 Mr '04
   ENDANGERED *See* Endangered species
   MIGRATION PATTERNS
      See also
     Animal migration
     Marine animals
   The dangerous journey for whales. K.T. Smith. *Nature Observers* v.150 pp. 210–222
    N '03
   Whales' yearly patterns. T.H. Finley. il *Whales and Their Ways* v.2 pp. 101–123 S '04

---

1. What main subject and subtopics are listed?

_____

_____

2. Name the magazine and article about how whales share information.

_____

_____

3. Where would you find more information about whale communication?

_____

_____

4. Which magazine has an article titled *Whales' Yearly Patterns*?

_____

5. Are there any listings about whales that are endangered? Where would you
   find them?

_____

_____

Home Activity Your child answered questions about the *Readers' Guide to Periodical Literature*. With your child, go to the library and look for articles about something that interests your child.

© Pearson Education, Inc., 4

Homophones

Proofread a Play Circle six spelling errors in the play. Write the words correctly on the lines. Find a sentence with a capitalization error and write it correctly.

Spelling Words

two
to
too
piece
peace
break
brake
there
their
they're

threw
through
by
bye
beat
beet
thrown
throne
aloud
allowed

Mr. Dario: A ball just went threw your window!

Mr. Chala: Did the window break?

Mr. Dario: Yes, I think a small peace cracked.

Mr. Chala: It's those neighbors playing they're game again!

Mr. Dario: I thought they weren't aloud to play by the house.

Mr. Chala: Soon Jim will be knocking on the door red as a beat.

Mr. Dario: well, children need to play too.

Mr. Chala: Yes, we were once children to.

1. _____ 2. _____
3. _____ 4. _____
5. _____ 6. _____
7. _____

Proofread Words Cross out the homophone that is spelled incorrectly. Write the correct homophone.

Frequently Misspelled Words

too   there
their   they're

8. Everyone cheered when the new queen sat on the thrown.   8. _____

9. Tony beet Alan in the big race.   9. _____

10. Always break at a stop sign.   10. _____

11. Shannon sat bye me at lunch.   11. _____

12. The football star volunteers to read allowed to preschoolers.   12. _____

© Pearson Education, Inc., 4

Home Activity Your child identified misspelled homophones. Ask your child to explain the meaning of several homophones.

Main and Helping Verbs

Directions Read the passage. Then read each question. Circle the letter of the correct answer.

Journey of the Whales

(1) The whales are swim north. (2) They have spend all winter in Baja. (3) A baby whale is following its mother. (4) The baby has growed fat on milk. (5) All the whales are moving slowly. (6) They will traveled many miles.

1 What change, if any, should be made in sentence 1?

   A   Change *swim* to **swimming.**

   B   Change *swim* to **swam.**

   C   Change *are* to **is.**

   D   Make no change.

2 What change, if any, should be made in sentence 2?

   A   Change *spend* to **spending.**

   B   Change *have* to **are.**

   C   Change *spend* to **spent.**

   D   Make no change.

3 What change, if any, should be made in sentence 3?

   A   Change *following* to **follows.**

   B   Change *is following* to **has following.**

   C   Change *following* to **followed.**

   D   Make no change.

4 What change, if any, should be made in sentence 4?

   A   Change *growed* to **grown.**

   B   Change *growed* to **groan.**

   C   Change *growed* to **growing.**

   D   Make no change.

5 What change, if any, should be made in sentence 6?

   A   Change *will traveled* to **will.**

   B   Change *will traveled* to **will travel.**

   C   Change *will traveled* to **will traveling.**

   D   Make no change.

© Pearson Education, Inc., 4

Home Activity Your child prepared for taking tests on main and helping verbs. Have your child write helping verbs on index cards. Hold up the cards one at a time and ask your child to use the helping verb with a main verb in a sentence.

Generalize

- A **generalization** is a broad statement or rule that applies to many examples.
- Clue words such as *all, most, always, usually,* or *generally* signal generalizations.
- You can test generalizations with knowledge you already have to see if they make sense.

Directions Read the following passage. Then complete the diagram by writing down generalizations and their clue words from the passage.

Tom and Jim always had fun when they went camping. They planned the fun things they would do on their trip for days. They liked to plan their camping trips for summer because the weather was usually good. Tom planned their daily hikes. He packed a light breakfast, some water, and a compass. Then he and Jim would usually hike an hour or two in the morning before the sun rose. They often found themselves on top of a hill where they could watch the sunrise and eat breakfast. Jim was responsible for building their campfires. He gathered sticks and wood and made sure that the fire pit was safe. Jim's campfires were built so well that they often burned late into the night. Usually they talked after dinner until the fire faded away. Tom and Jim's camping trips were always full of great memories.

Generalization	Clue Word?
Tom and Jim always had fun when they went camping.	always
1.	usually
2.	3.
4.	5.

School + Home **Home Activity** Your child identified generalizations and their clue words in a short passage. Have your child write a paragraph generalizing a topic. Challenge him or her to use the clue words from this passage in his or her paragraph.

200 **Comprehension**

© Pearson Education, Inc., 4

Writing • Myth

Key Features of Myth

- passed down by word of mouth and storytelling
- often explains why something in nature happens
- characters usually represent some part of nature

How Fin Made Day and Night

Long ago, there was a young giant named Fin who lived in the sky. When she was only two million years old, Fin was big enough to toss the sun through a hoop and throw the moon up and catch it. Once she tied a string around a planet and turned it into a yo-yo. Another time she batted a planet so far away that she never found it again.

Fin's favorite toy was Earth, which she loved to spin like a top. Sometimes she carried Earth in her pocket, where it was dark. Other times she left Earth too close to the sun and burnt the tops of its mountains.

The creatures on Earth never knew what to expect. However, as Fin grew older, she began to build clever structures with these heavenly bodies. She built herself a mobile for her room with the sun in the center, and with each planet on a track that circled it. She loved to watch the planets go round and round at different speeds.

As it happens, Earth did a full spin every 24 hours. As Earth traveled around the sun, the half that faced the sun was light, while the half faced that faced away from the sun was dark. Finally there was something the creatures of earth could depend on! They began to call the light time *Day* and the dark time *Night*. To this day, the mobile is one of Fin's favorite toys.

1. What does this myth explain about nature?

_____

_____

2. What important role does the giant Fin play in the myth?

_____

_____

_____

© Pearson Education, Inc., 4

Vocabulary

Directions Choose the word from the box that best matches each clue. Write the word on the line to the left.

_____ 1. flashed or beamed with light

_____ 2. shining brightly; sparkling

_____ 3. a person who lacks courage or is easily made afraid

_____ 4. gleaming faintly

_____ 5. anything spoken or sung all at the same time

> **Check the Words You Know**
>
> ___brilliant
> ___chorus
> ___coward
> ___gleamed
> ___shimmering

Directions Choose the word from the box that best completes each sentence below. Write the word on the line to the left.

_____ 6. The queen's necklace was set with _____ gems.

_____ 7. He looked into the well and saw the water _____ in the moonlight.

_____ 8. "I'm no _____," said Beatriz, as she climbed the ladder to the diving board.

_____ 9. The shiny guitar _____ in the store window.

_____ 10. Carolyn sat at the window and listened to the _____ of frogs greeting the sunset.

Write a Description

On a separate sheet of paper, write a description about the sky at night. Remember to include details about what you see. Use as many vocabulary words as you can.

Home Activity Your child identified and used vocabulary words from *How Night Came from the Sea: A Story from Brazil.* Read another story about day and night. Write poems with your child about the sky either during the day or at night.

© Pearson Education, Inc., 4

Subject-Verb Agreement

The **subject** and the **verb** in a sentence must work together, or **agree**.
To make most present tense verbs agree with singular nouns or *he, she,* or *it*, add
-s or *-es*. If the subject is a plural noun or *I, you, we,* or *they*, the present tense verb
does not end in *-s*.

Singular Subject   Ant tugs at his belt. He watches Bear.

Plural Subject   Animals talk in some stories. Ants and bears act like people.

Use *is* or *was* to agree with singular nouns. Use *are* or *were* to agree with plural
nouns.

Singular Subject   Bear is angry.

Plural Subject   Ants are small and stubborn.

Directions Write *Yes* if the subject and the verb in the sentence agree. Write *No* if the
subject and the verb do not agree.

1. Whone, the Changer, plant trees for forests. _____

2. He becomes tired of his work. _____

3. Bear's name is Chetwin. _____

4. Bears catches ants in rotten logs. _____

5. Some ants grows wings. _____

6. That anthill is very tall. _____

7. Thousands of ants lives there. _____

Directions Circle the verb in ( ) that correctly completes each sentence.

8. I (like, likes) the story about Ant's waist.

9. An insect (flys, flies) from its nest.

10. Bears (sleep, sleeps) through the cold winter months.

11. A good story (keep, keeps) us interested.

12. Ants and bears (are, is) very different creatures.

Home Activity Your child learned about subject-verb agreement. Ask your child questions with *does* and
do: What does a cow say? What do chickens say? Have your child show you how the verb in the answer
changes when the subject is singular and plural.

© Pearson Education, Inc., 4

Vowel Sound in *shout*

Spelling Words				
however	mountain	mound	scout	shout
couch	towel	ounce	coward	outdoors
flowerpot	scowl	browse	announce	hound
trout	drowsy	grouch	eyebrow	boundary

Rhymes Complete each sentence by writing two or more rhyming list words.

"If you (1)___, you'll scare the (2)___," said the (3)___.

1. _____ 2. _____ 3. _____

Now I can (4)____ that this tennis ball gives the most bounce per (5)____.

4. _____ 5. _____

The barking (6)____ jumped over the grassy (7)____.

6. _____ 7. _____

The neighborhood (8)____ had nothing nice to say about my comfortable new (9)____.

8. _____ 9. _____

"Oh, no. I forgot my beach (10)____," said Jackie with a (11)____.

10. _____ 11. _____

Classifying Write the list word that best completes each group.

12. seed, soil, ____   12. _____
13. scaredy-cat, chicken, ____   13. _____
14. eyelash, mustache, ____   14. _____
15. sleepy, tired, ____   15. _____
16. in the open, outside, ____   16. _____
17. but, although, ____   17. _____
18. peak, cliff, ____   18. _____
19. look around, glance, ____   19. _____
20. border, margin, ____   20. _____

Home Activity Your child wrote words with *ou* and *ow*. Challenge your child to spell the rhyming word groups from the Rhymes exercises on this page.

© Pearson Education, Inc., 4

Story Elements

Title _____

This story is about _____

_____
(name the characters)

This story takes place _____

_____
(where and when)

The action begins when _____

_____

_____

Then, _____

_____

_____

Next, _____

_____

_____

After that, _____

_____

_____

The story ends when _____

_____

_____

Theme: _____

_____

© Pearson Education, Inc., 4

Name_____

Vocabulary • Unfamiliar Words

- When you are reading and see an unfamiliar word, you can use **context clues,** or words around the unfamiliar word, to figure out its meaning.

Directions Read the following passage and look for context clues as you read. Then answer the questions below.

Wearing her mask and fins, Joy walked into the ocean. Joy had heard about the reef in the ocean, and she was excited to be visiting it. As she swam out to the reef, she could no longer hear the chorus of waves crashing on the beach. She looked under the water and saw different kinds of fish swimming around her. She was a bit afraid of the bigger fish, but Joy was not a coward! As she reached the edge of the reef, she saw something shimmering ahead. She swam closer to the coral and saw a fish shining with brilliant colors. Joy caught a quick movement to the side. A school of fish gleamed, their scales reflecting light like a million tiny mirrors. Joy knew she would never forget this day. She pulled out her camera and took a picture so she could share her journey with her friends.

1. Explain how you can use context clues to help determine the meaning of *chorus*.

_____

_____

2. What does *coward* mean? What clue helped you to determine the meaning?

_____

3. What does *shimmering* mean? What clues help you to determine the meaning?

_____

4. What does *gleamed* mean? What clues help you to determine the meaning?

_____

5. Write one word you did not know from the passage. What clues helped you to determine the meaning?

_____

_____

© Pearson Education, Inc., 4

Home Activity Your child identified and used context clues to understand new words in a passage. Read a story about the ocean or about taking a journey. Work with your child to identify unknown words in the story and the context clues to help understand those words.

Textbook and Trade Book

- A **textbook** teaches about a particular subject. These books are organized to help you find information quickly. Textbooks contain tables of contents, chapter titles, headings, subheadings, illustrations with captions, and vocabulary words.

- A **trade book** is any book that is not a textbook, periodical, or reference book. The skills you use for understanding trade books are a lot like those used for understanding textbooks.

Directions Use the following sample of a textbook to answer the questions below.

Earth Science   Unit 3
Chapter 4   The Sun
Lesson 2: Patterns of Day and Night
Vocabulary   rotates, terminator

The Terminator The Earth **rotates,** or turns, from day to night on a twenty-four hour basis. Night and day occur on a line called the **terminator.** The terminator is an imaginary vertical line that divides the Earth into night and day. The terminator's shape changes during the year as the length of days and nights changes.

    The sun can be seen rising on one part of the terminator and setting at another part. When the sun is rising, it is lit on the right side of the Earth; when it is setting, it is lit on the left side of the Earth. At times, the sun can been seen "skimming" the northern or southern hemisphere.

---

1. Why are the words *rotates* and *terminator* printed in **boldfaced type?**

_____

2. What type of textbook is this? What is the title of this chapter?

_____

3. Does the passage help you learn about day and night? Why or why not?

_____

_____

4. What is the subject of this section of the lesson? How can you tell?

_____

5. Why do textbooks divide information into units, chapters, lessons, and sections?

_____

© Pearson Education, Inc., 4

Name _____

Directions Use the following passage to answer the questions below.

Every night Karamo looked up and saw a twinkling light. It was in the same place in the sky every night, and Karamo wondered how it got there. Was it special? Why was it so bright? Karamo walked through the forest to his village. He found his grandfather sitting near the river's edge. He sat next to his grandfather and asked him about the star. Karamo's grandfather smiled and nodded his head. He knew which star Karamo was talking about. It was a special star. The story of how the star took its place in the sky is a famous story that many people know. Grandfather took a deep breath and began to tell the story of the star.

Long ago there was a boy called Moth, who lived in a village much like the one Karamo lived in. Moth was well known for his wisdom. As the boy grew older, the village's crops began to fail, and the boy went off to search for land with better soil. When he found a good site, he sent a huge white moth into the sky to flutter over his head. His friends and neighbors walked toward the moth until they reached the place Moth had found. That land became the village Karamo now lived in, and the moth turned into a twinkling star that still flutters over their heads today.

---

1. What is the subject of this story?

_____

_____

2. According to the grandfather, what do people believe about the twinkling star?

_____

_____

3. Do you think this passage comes from a trade book or a science textbook? Why?

_____

_____

_____

4. How would you describe the author's purpose?

_____

_____

_____

5. On a separate piece of paper, create your own legend about something in nature.

Home Activity Your child learned about textbooks and trade books and applied his or her knowledge to two sample passages. Together, browse through a textbook and discuss different parts of the book. Have your child identify titles and headings that show the book's organization. Invite him or her to explain the importance of different elements in a textbook.

© Pearson Education, Inc., 4

Vowel Sound in *shout*

Proofread a Dialogue Help Rita correct her dialogue. Circle six misspelled words and write them correctly. Add the missing punctuation mark.

Spelling Words

however
mountain
mound
scout
shout
couch
towel
ounce
coward
outdoors

flowerpot
scowl
browse
announce
hound
trout
drowsy
grouch
eyebrow
boundary

"You said this was a small mownd, but it's a mountain!" grumbled Rita.

"You're such a grouch!" said Andy.

"You don't have to announce it to everyone!" Rita replied.

"We have to do this to get our scowt badge," Chen reminded her.

"But I hate the owtdoors," Rita said with a scoul.

"I know! You'd rather be in your house on the couch," laughed Andy.

"All this walking is making me drousy, said Rita.

"Me, too," agreed Chen. "Let's walk threw the woods and go home."

---

1. _____   2. _____
3. _____   4. _____
5. _____   6. _____

Proofread Words Cross out the misspelled word and write it correctly.

Frequently Misspelled Words

outside
through
house

7. a trawt stream   7. _____
8. a raised eybrow   8. _____
9. a state's boundry line   9. _____
10. a broken flourpot   10. _____
11. a big cowerd   11. _____
12. a nose like a hawnd 12. _____

© Pearson Education, Inc., 4

School + Home **Home Activity** Your child identified misspelled words with *ou* and *ow*. Spell some of the list words aloud. Make some mistakes so your child can correct them.

Subject-Verb Agreement

Directions Read the passage. Then read each question. Circle the letter of the correct answer.

The Myth of the Bear

(1) The Native Americans tells this story. (2) Bear was very hungry. (3) He trys to catch a fish with his tail. (4) Bear dangles his tail in the water. (5) He caught nothing. (6) The ice pulled off Bear's tail. (7) The other animals laughs at Bear's stumpy tail.

1 What change, if any, should be made in sentence 1?

  A Change *tells* to **tell.**

  B Change *tells* to **are telling.**

  C Change *tells* to *are.*

  D Make no change.

2 What change, if any, should be made in sentence 2?

  A Change *was* to **are.**

  B Change *was* to **were.**

  C Change *was* to **am.**

  D Make no change.

3 What change, if any, should be made in sentence 3?

  A Change *trys* to **tryd.**

  B Change *trys* to **tried.**

  C Change *catch* to **caught.**

  D Make no change.

4 What change, if any, should be made in sentence 4?

  A Change *dangles* to **dangled.**

  B Change *dangles* to **is dangled.**

  C Change *dangles* to **dangle.**

  D Make no change.

5 What change, if any, should be made in sentence 7?

  A Change *laughs* to **laught.**

  B Change *laughs* to **laughed.**

  C Change *laughs* to **laughes.**

  D Make no change.

© Pearson Education, Inc., 4

Home Activity Your child prepared for taking tests on subject-verb agreement. Have your child explain the rules he or she has learned about how verbs change when the subject is singular or plural. Ask your child to give examples of these rules.

Cause and Effect

- A **cause** is *why* something happens.
- An **effect** is *what* happens.
- Look for clue words such as *because, so,* and *cause.*
- When there are no clue words, you must figure out if one thing causes another.
- A cause can have more than one effect.

Directions Read the following passage.

Most tornadoes and thunderstorms occur in spring, when cold, dry air meets warm, moist air. The colliding air masses cause updrafts that pull air upward, creating tall "chimneys" of rotating air. The spinning of a large tornado can cause winds up to 300 miles per hour.

Tornadoes and other strong windstorms can destroy buildings and create widespread damage. Sometimes water particles freeze and grow while moving inside a tornado. As the pieces of ice build up layers, hailstones result. Some can grow as big as softballs. Hailstones can damage roofs and cars.

Directions Complete the graphic organizer for cause–and–effect relationships.

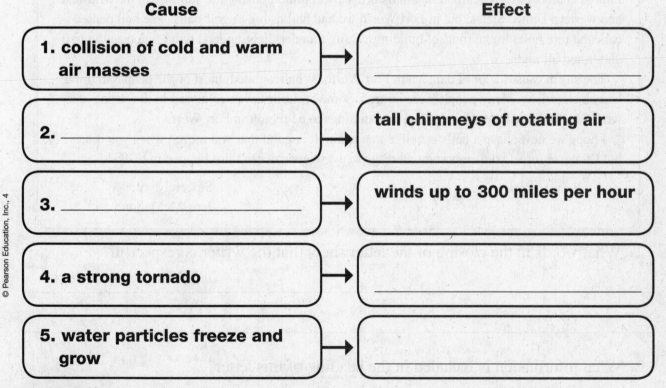

Cause

1. collision of cold and warm air masses

2. _____

3. _____

4. a strong tornado

5. water particles freeze and grow

Effect

_____

tall chimneys of rotating air

winds up to 300 miles per hour

_____

_____

School + Home **Home Activity** Your child identified cause and effect relationships from a short passage about tornadoes. Talk with your child about what to do to prevent the harmful effects of storms. Discuss both good and bad effects of weather. Then ask your child if one effect can become the cause of another effect.

© Pearson Education, Inc., 4

Writing • Formal Letter

Key Features of Formal Letters

• includes a heading, address, salutation, body, closing, and signature

• stays focused on one idea

• uses a business-like tone and is polite and respectful

1400 South Spring Street
Fort Worth, TX 76123
May 20, 20__

Ms. Laura Ramirez
555 Grove Street
Chicago, IL 60617

Dear Ms. Ramirez,

   Last week, something terrible happened, but it made me think of you and the unit on weather we started to study right before you moved. On the evening of May 5, we had a horrible storm. We are okay, but we had to move to an apartment until the holes in our roof can be fixed.

   Luckily, our school was not hit by the storm. This week I learned more about what happened. Most of the damage was caused by balls of ice called hail. Hail is a form of precipitation that falls as chunks of ice. I learned that hailstorms are common during the summer in the Midwest and western United States, but in Fort Worth we had hail as big as golf balls. The hail dented cars and tore holes in the roofs of buildings. Rain, thunder, lighting, and wind followed the hail and lasted all night.

   The storm caused a lot of damage in Fort Worth. When it ended, most of the people in town had no electricity. Many people were injured. Some buildings even collapsed in the strong winds. I think it will take a long time for buildings to be rebuilt in Fort Worth.

   I hope we never have a hailstorm like that again. It is good that you moved when you did, but I'll never forget your important message to us: science doesn't just happen in books!

Sincerely,
Jane McMahon

© Pearson Education, Inc., 4

1. What words in the closing of the letter show that the writer is respectful?

_____

_____

2. What information is included in the heading of this letter?

_____

_____

_____

Vocabulary

Directions Choose the word from the box that best matches each definition. Write the word on the line to the left.

_____ 1. a swelling motion

_____ 2. in or toward the interior

_____ 3. statements of what is coming; predictions

_____ 4. great damage; ruin

Check the Words You Know

___destruction
___expected
___forecasts
___inland
___shatter
___surge

Directions Solve the following puzzle by writing the word that matches each definition. The circled letters will spell a secret word.

5. the land away from the border of a coast _____○_____

6. to break into pieces suddenly _____○_____

7. devastation _____○_____

8. sweep or rush, especially of waves _____○_____

9. descriptions of the future _____○_____

10. thought something would probably come or happen _____○_____

Write a Business Letter

On a separate sheet of paper, write a business letter asking for aid after a hurricane. Decide to whom you would write this letter and what you would say. Use as many vocabulary words as you can.

© Pearson Education, Inc., 4

Home Activity Your child identified and used vocabulary words from *Eye of the Storm*. Together, read an encyclopedia entry about hurricanes. Then have your child write a few descriptive sentences about hurricanes, using the vocabulary words.

Name _____

Past, Present, and Future Tenses

The **tense** of a verb tells when an action happens. A verb in the **present tense** tells about action that is happening now. A verb in the **past tense** tells about action that has already happened. Many past tense verbs end in *-ed*. A verb in the **future tense** tells about action that will happen in the future. The helping verb *will* is added to a verb to form the future tense.

   Present Tense She <u>enjoys</u> winter. They <u>skate</u> on the pond.
   Past Tense   It <u>snowed</u> many times last year. We <u>played</u> in the snow.
   Future Tense Tomorrow it <u>will rain</u>.

• When a verb ends with *e*, drop the *e* before adding *-ed: hope   hoped*

• When a one-syllable verb ends with one vowel followed by one consonant, double the final consonant before adding *-ed: stop   stopped*

• When a verb ends with a consonant followed by *y*, change the *y* to *i* before adding *-ed: worry   worried*

Directions Write *present, past,* or *future* to identify the tense of each underlined verb.

1. My family <u>lives</u> in Massachusetts.   _____

2. We <u>moved</u> here from Florida last year.   _____

3. We <u>will miss</u> Florida's warm winters.   _____

4. I even <u>liked</u> the hurricanes in Florida.   _____

Directions Write the verb in each sentence. Circle the past tense verbs. Underline the future tense verbs.

5. It never snows in Florida.   _____

6. She really wants a snowy winter.   _____

7. In school we learned about blizzards.   _____

8. This year I will play in the snow.   _____

Home Activity Your child learned about past, present, and future tenses. Ask your child to use verbs in these three tenses. If necessary, prompt him or her with questions: *What did you do yesterday? What do you do every day? What will you do tomorrow?*

© Pearson Education, Inc., 4

Compound Words

Spelling Words				
watermelon	homemade	understand	sometimes	shoelace
highway	upstairs	thunderstorm	shortcut	doorbell
jellyfish	touchdown	campfire	skateboard	anyway
fireworks	haircut	loudspeaker	laptop	flashlight

Definitions Write the correct list word beside its definition.

1. portable light powered by batteries
2. hairstyle; trim
3. display of exploding chemicals
4. more direct route; easier way of performing a task
5. occasionally; not in every case
6. main road
7. device to signal that a visitor has arrived
8. clear, transparent marine animal with tentacles
9. outdoor stack of burning wood
10. nevertheless; no matter what

1. _____
2. _____
3. _____
4. _____
5. _____
6. _____
7. _____
8. _____
9. _____
10. _____

Complete the Sentence Write a list word to complete each sentence.

11. A cold, juicy slice of ____ tastes great on a hot summer day.
12. Tie that ____ so you don't trip!
13. Mom bakes the most delicious ____ apple pies.
14. Did you hear the announcement that just came over the ____?
15. My ____ computer has a very small screen.
16. I wish I could ride a ____ like my older brother.
17. The team is on the three-yard line and going for a ____.
18. Do you ____ all the rules of the new game?
19. The fourth-grade classroom is ____ on the fourth floor.
20. High winds during the ____ shook the house.

11. _____
12. _____
13. _____
14. _____
15. _____
16. _____
17. _____
18. _____
19. _____
20. _____

Home Activity Your child wrote compound words. Have your child draw a vertical line through each word to separate the compound word into its parts.

© Pearson Education, Inc., 4

Outline Form A

Title _____

A. _____

   1. _____

   2. _____

   3. _____

B. _____

   1. _____

   2. _____

   3. _____

C. _____

   1. _____

   2. _____

   3. _____

© Pearson Education, Inc., 4

Vocabulary • Root Words

- When you come across a new word, look at the **root word** to figure out its meaning.
- The root *struct* means "to build."

Directions Read the following passage. Then answer the questions below.

> The winds were growing stronger than expected, and Dee looked out the window nervously. Weather forecasts on radio and television stations called for heavy rain. News programs instructed everyone to stay indoors.
>
> Dee knew that a storm like this could easily bring destruction. The last time there was a really bad storm, many roads flooded.
>
> Grass and leaves had obstructed the storm drains, leaving the rain no place to go.
>
> Suddenly, the lights went out. Her aunt's instructions were to use a flashlight if the power went out.
>
> Just as Dee's aunt handed her a flashlight, they heard a loud boom. A tree branch hit the front door! Wow! This was going to be some storm.

1. How does the root *struct* in *destruction* help you understand the word?

_____

_____

2. What do you think the root *struct* has to do with *instructed*, meaning "taught" or "gave information"?

_____

3. The word part *con-* in *construct* can mean with or together. What do you think *obstruct* means?

_____

4. What is the meaning of *instructions*?

_____

5. What is a possible connection between *instructions* and the root *struct?*

_____

_____

Home Activity Your child used knowledge of roots to identify the meanings of words. Together, use a dictionary to find other words that contain the root *struct* and discuss their meanings.

© Pearson Education, Inc., 4

Online Telephone Directory

- An **online telephone directory** lists phone numbers and addresses for individual people and businesses.
- The white pages lists entries for individuals and businesses in alphabetical order.
- The yellow pages lists entries for businesses (as well as advertisements) by category, or type of business.

Directions Examine the online yellow pages screen. For each of the five businesses listed below, write words that define the category of business you wish to search.

Yellow Pages   Hotels   Restaurants   Movies   About Us

Powered by Software Source

Quick Search—The quickest way to find the business you're looking for. Either type in the business name or enter the category of business you would like to find.

Business name or type

> Insurance companies

○ Business name   [   ] city

◉ Category of business   [   ] state

Search!

_____ **1.** a business that sells raincoats

_____ **2.** a business that sells storm shutters for windows

_____ **3.** a business that sells hurricane safety kits

_____ **4.** a business that sells homeowners' insurance

_____ **5.** a business that repairs storm-damaged roofs

© Pearson Education, Inc., 4

Directions Use the online yellow pages screen to answer the following questions.

6. Why is it important to include the city and state for the business you are searching for online?

_____

_____

7. If you knew the type—but not the name—of a business, would it best to use the white pages or yellow pages to find it? Why?

_____

_____

8. What might be the result if your search keywords were spelled incorrectly?

_____

_____

9. If you remembered only part of the name of a local business, how would you search for its telephone number?

_____

_____

_____

10. Why might a person choose to use an online telephone directory instead of a regular telephone book?

_____

_____

© Pearson Education, Inc., 4

Home Activity Your child learned about locating and collecting information using various sources, including an online telephone directory. Together, search for three businesses using the white and yellow pages of an online directory and of a print telephone book.

Name _____

Compound Words

Spelling Words

watermelon	homemade	understand	sometimes	shoelace
highway	upstairs	thunderstorm	shortcut	doorbell
jellyfish	touchdown	campfire	skateboard	anyway
fireworks	haircut	loudspeaker	laptop	flashlight

Proofread a Schedule Circle six misspelled words in the camp schedule and write them on the lines. Find the word with a capitalization error and write it correctly.

Monday	Tuesday	Wednesday	thursday	Friday
Noon Monkey Walk: Cross a rope highway to get over a stream	**11 A.M.** All About Knots: Bring a long shoe lace	**10 A.M.** Fun with Sound: Sing over the loud speaker	**9 A.M.** Baking: Learn a shortcut for making a shortcake	**10 A.M.** Shave and a Harecut, Two Bits: Fun with shaving cream
5 P.M. Homade Fudge Tasting	**2 P.M.** Candy Making: Gummy jellyfish	**3 P.M.** Skateboard Contest: Meet on the basketball court	**Noon** Watermelon Seed-Spitting Contest	**Noon** Upload Camp Pictures to the School Laptop
9 P.M. Flashy Flickers: Bring your flashlite	**5 P.M.** Weather Watch: How to predict a thunderstorm	**9 P.M.** Group Meeting: Meet everywon at the campfire	**9 P.M.** Fireworks	

1. _____   2. _____

3. _____   4. _____

5. _____   6. _____   7. _____

Frequently Misspelled Words

sometimes
basketball
everyone
everybody

© Pearson Education, Inc., 4

Proofread Words Circle the list word that is spelled correctly. Write the word.

8. high way	highway	hiway	**8.** _____
9. understand	under stand	undestand	**9.** _____
10. somtimes	some times	sometimes	**10.** _____
11. doorbell	door bell	dorbell	**11.** _____
12. upstairs	upstares	up stares	**12.** _____

School + Home

Home Activity Your child identified misspelled compound words. Say and spell the first word in a compound list word. Have your child complete the word.

Past, Present, and Future Tenses

Directions Read the passage. Then read each question. Circle the letter of the correct answer.

Wild Weather

(1) Tornadoes often forming in the spring. (2) Warm oceans creates hurricanes. (3) Every summer the desert heats the cool air. (4) Then thunderstorms appear the next September. (5) A big storm rolls through here last summer. (6) When I grow up, I want to study weather.

1 What change, if any, should be made in sentence 1?

A Change *forming* to **form.**

B Change *forming* to **will forming.**

C Change *forming* to **have forming.**

D Make no change.

2 What change, if any, should be made in sentence 2?

A Change *creates* to **was creating.**

B Change *creates* to **creating.**

C Change *creates* to **create.**

D Make no change.

3 What change, if any, should be made in sentence 3?

A Change *heats* to **was heated.**

B Change *heats* to **heat.**

C Change *heat* to **is heating.**

D Make no change.

4 What change, if any, should be made in sentence 5?

A Change *rolls* to **rolled.**

B Change *rolls* to **roll.**

C Change *rolls* to **will roll.**

D Make no change.

5 What change, if any, should be made in sentence 6?

A Change *grow* to **grown.**

B Change *grow* to **grew.**

C Change *study* to **will study.**

D Make no change.

Home Activity Your child prepared for taking tests on the past, present, and future tenses of verbs. Have your child prepare flash cards that say *past, present,* and *future.* Have him or her choose a card and name a verb you say in the tense shown.

© Pearson Education, Inc., 4

Conventions Past, Present, and Future Tenses **221**

Generalize

- A **generalization** is a type of conclusion in which a broad statement is made based on several examples.
- Clue words such as *all, most, always, usually,* or *generally* signal generalizations.
- A generalization can be valid (logical) or faulty (wrong) depending on the number of examples on which it is based and how logical the thinking is.

Directions Read the following passage. Then complete the diagram below by finding a generalization and its support.

In the past several years, winters in my part of the country have become warmer and warmer. As a result, there is less snow at the mountain ski resorts. This has been a dramatic change for my family, because for years we have gone skiing every winter vacation. We have always enjoyed the cold, crisp mountain air and the solid snow pack.

Three years ago, everything changed. That winter, the temperature in the mountains never went below fifty degrees.

We were still able to ski, because the ski resort blew artificial snow over the trails. Skiing in a T-shirt, however, isn't quite the same as skiing in my fleece-lined parka. Two years ago, it snowed before vacation, but then it got really warm. The snow melted in two days. Last year, it rained and temperatures were in the sixties until February. I didn't ski once. Now it's October again, and it's eighty degrees. My family is looking for a new way to spend winter vacations. Tennis, anyone?

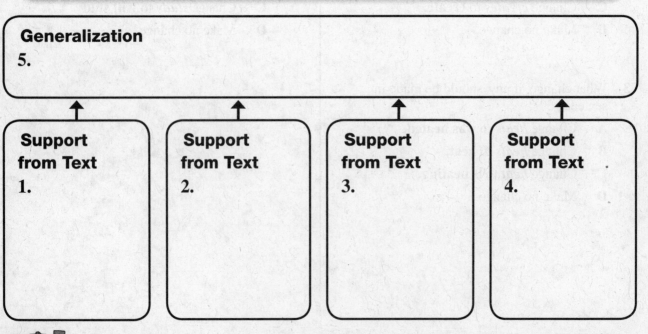

Generalization

5.

Support from Text

1.

Support from Text

2.

Support from Text

3.

Support from Text

4.

© Pearson Education, Inc., 4

School + Home

Home Activity Your child used a graphic organizer to find a generalization and the support for it. Together, read a short passage from a fiction or nonfiction text. Have your child make two generalizations about the events in the story—one valid and one faulty. Have him or her explain the difference between the two.

Writing • Summary

Key Features of an Summary

- includes key events or main ideas
- is written in the writer's own words
- tells the events in chronological order

Summary of *How Night Came from the Sea* by Mary-Joan Gerson

How Night Came from the Sea is a myth from Brazil, retold by Mary-Joan Gerson. The story tells about Iemanjá, the African goddess of the sea and her daughter who marries an earthling.

At the beginning of time, there was no night, only sunlight on the earth. The daughter of Iemanjá happened to fall in love and marry an earth person. The two of them lived a happy life on the earth until the daughter began to miss the darkness she had grown up with in the depths of the sea.

Seeing his wife's sadness, the earth husband ordered his servants to get a bag of night from Iemanjá. When the scared servants arrived in the depths of the sea, Iemanja gave them a bag of night with clear instructions to not open up the bag until they were near her daughter, who could calm the night spirits. But the curious servants came back to the earth and opened the bag by themselves. All of the night beings exploded out of the bag, and night swiftly came to the earth. But the daughter of Iemangá was able to tame the night beings, and she was again happy to have night.

Once the daughter was happy again, she celebrated by giving three gifts to the earth: the morning star to announce the birth of a new day, the rooster to remind us that day has begun, and singing birds to announce when dawn will come. In Brazil this kind of morning is called the *madruggada*.

1. Reread the summary. Write one sentence that tells the main idea of the second paragraph.

_____

_____

2. What key events does the summary explain?

_____

_____

© Pearson Education, Inc., 4

Vocabulary

Directions Choose the word from the box that best matches each definition. Write the word on the line to the left.

> ### Check the Words You Know
>
> ___announcement ___requirements
> ___feature ___thaw
> ___harness ___unnatural
> ___lumberjacks ___untamed

_____ 1. wild, natural, not cultivated

_____ 2. melt, release from a frozen state

_____ 3. distinguishing trait or characteristic

_____ 4. necessities, conditions, or qualifications that must be met

_____ 5. combination of straps and hardware used to attach an animal to a cart or object to be moved

Directions Choose the word from the Words to Know box that best replaces the underlined word or words. Write the word on the line to the left.

_____ 6. The geese made the <u>unusual</u> choice not to migrate because people kept feeding them.

_____ 7. The coach's <u>statement</u> that practice would increase by one hour made the players groan.

_____ 8. The <u>forest workers</u> took their lunch breaks sitting on logs.

_____ 9. The jungle was wild and <u>savage</u>, full of strange sounds at night.

_____ 10. Marilyn's most memorable <u>trait</u> was the birthmark at the corner of her mouth.

Write a Narrative

On a separate sheet of paper, write a narrative about the changes that occur in nature as your favorite season approaches. Use as many vocabulary words as you can.

Home Activity Your child identified and used vocabulary words from the tall tale *Paul Bunyan*. With your child, read a children's book or comic book and discuss any features it shares with tall tales.

© Pearson Education, Inc., 4

Name _____

Irregular Verbs

Usually you add *-ed* to a verb to show past tense. **Irregular verbs** do not follow this rule. Irregular verbs change to other words to show past tense.

Present Tense   He <u>makes</u> a huge logging camp.

Past Tense   He <u>made</u> a huge logging camp.

Past with *has, have,* or *had*   He <u>has made</u> a huge logging camp.

Irregular verbs have a special form when they are used with *has, have,* or *had.* Below are some irregular verbs and their past forms.

Present Tense	Past Tense	Past with *has, have,* or *had*
bring	brought	(*has, have, had*) brought
choose	chose	(*has, have, had*) chosen
come	came	(*has, have, had*) come
do	did	(*has, have, had*) done
feel	felt	(*has, have, had*) felt
get	got	(*has, have, had*) gotten
give	gave	(*has, have, had*) given
go	went	(*has, have, had*) gone
make	made	(*has, have, had*) made
say	said	(*has, have, had*) said
speak	spoke	(*has, have, had*) spoken
teach	taught	(*has, have, had*) taught

Directions Write the past tense form of the irregular verb in ( ).

1. Paul Bunyan (go) to the Maine woods.   _____

2. He (bring) an ax and a fishing pole.   _____

3. He (make) a new friend.   _____

4. He (teach) his friend how to cut down trees.   _____

5. He (say) he would start a logging camp.   _____

© Pearson Education, Inc., 4

Home Activity Your child learned about irregular verbs. Have your child tell you what happened this morning using a past tense form of the words *feel, make, say, get,* and *give.*

Possessives

Spelling Words

its	ours	mine	yours	family's
families'	man's	men's	girl's	girls'
hers	theirs	brother's	brothers'	teacher's
teachers'	aunt's	aunts'	boy's	boys'

Words in Context Complete each pair of sentences by writing the singular or plural possessive form of the word that is to the left of the sentences.

girl   1. Both ____ coats were new.   1. _____

2. That ____ coat looks very warm.   2. _____

teacher   3. I borrowed my ____ pen.   3. _____

4. The ____ workroom is off-limits to students.   4. _____

brother   5. This is my oldest ____ room.   5. _____

6. These are my twin ____ rooms.   6. _____

family   7. The party is at the Jackson ____ house.   7. _____

8. Their driveway is full of other ____ cars.   8. _____

aunt   9. My favorite ____ dog follows her everywhere.   9. _____

10. My ____ husbands are my uncles.   10. _____

boy   11. The little ____ toy sailboat drifted across the pond.   11. _____

12. The ____ baseball team plays this afternoon.   12. _____

Word Meanings Write the list word that fits each meaning.

13. belonging to that adult male   13. _____

14. belonging to an adult female   14. _____

15. belonging to us   15. _____

16. belonging to an object   16. _____

17. belonging to several adult males   17. _____

18. belonging to me   18. _____

19. belonging to the person spoken to   19. _____

20. belonging to those people   20. _____

Home Activity Your child wrote possessive nouns and pronouns. Have your child tell whether each possessive noun names one person or more than one person.

© Pearson Education, Inc., 4

Scoring Rubric: Summary

	4	3	2	1
Focus/Ideas	Strong summary; only uses important information	Good summary; mostly uses important information	Summary has some main ideas and main details	Does not understand summary form
Organization	Important ideas are in correct sequence	Sequence of events is generally correct	Sequence isn't always clear	Unorganized
Voice	Shows understanding of the main ideas	Shows understanding of topic	Lacks understanding of the topic	Does not understand topic
Word Choice	Uses descriptive adjectives, verbs, and time-order words	Uses some descriptive adjectives, verbs, and time-order words	Few or no descriptive adjectives or time-order words	Poor word choice
Sentences	Uses simple and compound sentences	Some varied sentence structures	Sentences are not varied	Fragments or run-on sentences
Conventions	Excellent control, few or no errors	Good control; few errors	Little control; many errors	Many serious errors

© Pearson Education, Inc., 4

Vocabulary • Suffixes

- A **suffix** is a word part added to the end of a base word to change its meaning or the way it is used in a sentence. For example, the suffix *-ous* can make a noun mean "full of _____." The suffix *-ment* means "the action, process, or result of _____."
- In dictionaries, the definition of a base word with the suffix added is usually found near that of the base word. The base word's definition is helpful in understanding a word's meaning.

Directions Read the following passage. Then answer the questions below.

The announcement was finally made: Jones's Maple Barn was open for the maple syrup season! In addition to the wondrous, sweet pancake topping, Jones's Maple Barn also sold breakfast. Of course, their pancakes were simply marvelous.

Sugar maple trees have a liquid that runs inside their trunks and branches called sap. In the winter, the sap doesn't move much through the tree. In the spring, however, the sap flows quickly as the weather turns warmer. People collect the sap by inserting tubes into the trees' trunks. Then the sap is cooked. The requirement for making one gallon of syrup is 40 gallons of sap. That's a lot of work, but nothing is more delicious than pure maple syrup!

1. What is the suffix in the word *announcement?*

_____

2. How does the suffix help you understand the meaning of *announcement?*

_____

_____

3. How does the suffix in *wondrous* help you figure out the meaning of the word?

_____

_____

4. How does the suffix in *requirement* help you figure out the meaning of the word?

_____

_____

Home Activity Your child identified and used suffixes to understand new words in a passage. Work together to identify meanings of words with *-ous* and *-ment* in an article. Help your child come up with a way to remember the meanings of these suffixes.

© Pearson Education, Inc., 4

Schedule

- A **schedule** is a special chart that lists events and when they take place, side by side.
- Bus, train, and other travel schedules often present information in boxes. They usually contain both rows and columns, each of which may have a label or heading.

Directions Paul Bunyan used a ship full of Hawaiian sugar docked in Lake Superior to outsmart the bee-squitoes. Read this sugar-shipping schedule to answer the questions below.

Hawaiian Sugar Shipments to Lake Superior via Gulf of Saint Lawrence				
Ship	Depart Honolulu, Hawaii	Arrive Portland, Maine	Load Lumber and Coal in Portland	Arrive Lake Superior (Duluth, Minnesota)
Puako	June 1	July 31	August 4–8	September 1
KoKo	July 5	September 8	September 12–16	October 5
Lahina	August 10	October 15	October 19–23	November 10
Puako	December 15	February 21	February 24–28	March 15
KoKo	January 20	March 28	April 2–6	April 20
Lahina	February 27	May 1	May 5–9	May 27

1. How many months is each journey? How can you tell?

_____

_____

2. How many ships travel this route? How can you tell?

_____

3. If you traveled with the shipping crew on the second sailing of the *KoKo*, during which days would you help load lumber and coal in Portland?

_____

4. On which ship would you travel to be in Portland on October 18?

_____

5. If you wanted to sail with the crew of the *Puako*, what would be your choice of departure dates from Honolulu?

_____

© Pearson Education, Inc., 4

Directions Use the schedule of events to answer the questions below.

Big Onion Lumber Company Schedule of Activities for April 1							
Activity	**7–8 A.M.**	**8–9 A.M.**	**9–10 A.M.**	**11–12 P.M.**	**12–1 P.M.**	**1–2 P.M.**	**2–3 P.M.**
Skate on the griddle	+						
Eat breakfast		+					
Haul water from the Great Lakes			+				
Eat lunch				+			
Log					+		
Stoke the griddle fire					+		
Eat dinner						+	
Knit beards to make socks							+
Make umbrella shoes							+
Listen to Shot's melted words		+	+	+	+	+	+
+ = Activity is available.							

1. What do the plus signs on the schedule represent? How do you know?

_____

_____

2. Between which hours might the men hear Shot's words?

_____

3. Which activities occur at the same time as making umbrella shoes?

_____

4. If some men are hauling water, what are the other men doing?

_____

5. How does the schedule assist the loggers in planning their day?

_____

_____

Home Activity Your child learned about reading a schedule. Together, look at the schedule for a sporting event or for a form of travel. Have your child read and explain the schedule to you.

© Pearson Education, Inc., 4

Possessives

Proofread a Newspaper Feature Proofread the article. Circle six misspelled words and a word with a capitalization error. Write the words correctly on the lines.

Spelling Words

its
ours
mine
yours
family's
families'
man's
men's
girl's
girls'

hers
theirs
brother's
brothers'
teacher's
teachers'
aunt's
aunts'
boy's
boys'

The Smith Family and It's Reunion

Today was the Smith family's reunion. Seven brothers' families grew to more than one Thousand people in 100 years. The families' cars were parked in a field. The  mens group made special T-shirts for the children. All the girl's shirts had flowers, and the boys' shirts were striped. Everyone laughed and asked, "Yours, ours, or their?" when they looked at the group pictures. The aunt's tent had fifty tables filled with a variety of food. When family members asked who made each dish, the women laughed, pointed at each other, and said, "It's hers." At the end of the day, everyone said, "That's enouf! I can't eat another thing!"

1. _____   2. _____
3. _____   4. _____
5. _____   6. _____
7. _____

Frequently Misspelled Words

friend's
enough

Possessives Add apostrophes to the underlined words. Write the possessives correctly on the lines.

8. the <u>families</u> yards   8. _____
9. my <u>teachers</u> desk   9. _____
10. the <u>mans</u> hat   10. _____
11. my <u>brothers</u> toothbrushes 11. _____
12. the <u>girls</u> bicycle   12. _____

Home Activity Your child identified misspelled possessive nouns and pronouns. Have your child use the possessive pronouns in sentences.

© Pearson Education, Inc., 4

Irregular Verbs

Directions Read the passage. Then read each question. Circle the letter of the correct answer.

Paul Bunyan's Feats

(1) Paul feel lonely in the woods. (2) He chosen Babe the ox to be his helper.
(3) Paul Bunyan do amazing feats. (4) He made the Grand Canyon with a pickax.
(5) Then Paul go to Big Onion, Minnesota. (6) He hired a thousand lumberjacks.

1 What change, if any, should be made in sentence 1?

  A Change *feel* to **feeling.**

  B Change *feel* to **felt.**

  C Change *feel* to **felled.**

  D Make no change.

4 What change, if any, should be made in sentence 5?

  A Change *go* to **gone.**

  B Change *go* to **is gone.**

  C Change *go* to **went.**

  D Make no change.

2 What change, if any, should be made in sentence 2?

  A Change *chosen* to **was chosen.**

  B Change *chosen* to **choose.**

  C Change *chosen* to **chose.**

  D Make no change.

5 What change, if any, should be made in sentence 6?

  A Change *hired* to **hire.**

  B Change *hired* to **hiring.**

  C Change *hired* to **will hired.**

  D Make no change.

3 What change, if any, should be made in sentence 3?

  A Change *do* to **done.**

  B Change *do* to **did.**

  C Change *do* to **is done.**

  D Make no change.

Home Activity Your child prepared for taking tests on irregular verbs. Help your child prepare flash cards with an irregular verb on one side and its forms on the other side. Quiz your child using the flash cards.

© Pearson Education, Inc., 4

Adding -ed and -ing

Spelling Words				
watched	watching	danced	dancing	studied
studying	stopped	stopping	dried	drying
happened	happening	noticed	noticing	robbed
robbing	slipped	slipping	hurried	hurrying

Watch the Changes Write the *-ed* and the *-ing* form for each word. Circle the list words that change the spelling of the base form.

dance   1. _____   2. _____

dry   3. _____   4. _____

happen   5. _____   6. _____

hurry   7. _____   8. _____

notice   9. _____   10. _____

rob   11. _____   12. _____

stop   13. _____   14. _____

slip   15. _____   16. _____

study   17. _____   18. _____

watch   19. _____   20. _____

© Pearson Education, Inc., 4

 Home Activity Your child learned to spell words with *-ed* and *-ing* endings. Ask your child to spell list words and explain what ending was added.

Name _____

Action and Linking Verbs

Directions Write the verb in each sentence.

1. Some people look at clouds for fun. _____

2. Different clouds have different shapes and heights. _____

3. People still wonder about the weather. _____

4. Some people watch clouds for weather information. _____

5. Storm chasers follow cumulonimbus clouds. _____

6. All ten kinds of clouds appeared in one sky. _____

7. Luke published his observations nearly two hundred years ago. _____

8. Luke owned a chemist's shop. _____

9. People argued about Luke's names. _____

10. Most of Luke's names are still popular. _____

Directions Underline action verbs. Circle linking verbs.

11. Luke Howard became famous because of his hobby.

12. Many people write about the weather in their journals.

13. Cumulonimbus clouds are associated with heavy rain.

14. Luke used Latin names.

15. Each name describes the cloud's shape and height.

16. A stratus cloud is often wide and flat.

17. The weather forecast tells if a day will be clear or cloudy.

18. Today people know what clouds are made of.

19. Clouds form when warm, moist air, and cool air come together.

20. Some people feel gloomy on a cloudy day.

© Pearson Education, Inc., 4

Name _____

Homophones

Spelling Words				
two	to	too	piece	peace
break	brake	there	their	they're
threw	through	by	bye	beat
beet	thrown	throne	aloud	allowed

Words in Context Write the list word whose meaning best fits each sentence.

1. The _____ is a remarkable vegetable.
2. The children handed in _____ papers.
3. After working an hour, we were ready for a _____.
4. I would like a _____ of pumpkin pie.
5. The queen rested on her _____.
6. The class likes it when Mr. Fox reads _____.
7. You should be home _____ 5 p.m.
8. Tara _____ us all in the race.
9. The ball crashed _____ the window.
10. The shortstop has _____ the ball to the catcher.

1. _____
2. _____
3. _____
4. _____
5. _____
6. _____
7. _____
8. _____
9. _____
10. _____

Definitions Circle the word that fits each definition. Then write the word.

11. in that place	their	there	11. _____
12. permitted	allowed	aloud	12. _____
13. calm silence	peace	piece	13. _____
14. used for stopping	brake	break	14. _____
15. farewell	by	bye	15. _____
16. also	two	too	16. _____
17. they are	their	they're	17. _____
18. rhythm of music	beat	beet	18. _____
19. tossed	threw	through	19. _____
20. monarch's seat	throne	thrown	20. _____

Home Activity Your child has learned word pairs that sound the same but have different spellings and meanings. Challenge your child to use each pair of homophones in a single sentence.

© Pearson Education, Inc., 4

Main and Helping Verbs

Directions Write the verb phrase in each sentence.

1. The killer whales are swimming in a group.

   _____

2. Yesterday people were watching them from a boat.

   _____

3. The whales have caught squid and other fish.

   _____

4. This group of whales has stayed together for years.

   _____

5. I am hoping for more whale viewing today.

   _____

Directions Underline the main verb and circle the helping verb in each sentence.

6. Humpback whales were hunted for many years.

7. The number of humpbacks was falling.

8. Now the whale population is growing again.

9. People have seen humpbacks in all the world's oceans.

10. That whale is slapping the water with its tail.

11. Those two are rolling on their sides.

12. They have fed all summer in the north.

13. Now they are migrating south.

14. That baby has followed its mother all the way.

15. It is swimming to the warm waters of the Caribbean.

© Pearson Education, Inc., 4

Vowel Sound in *shout*

Spelling Words				
however	mountain	mound	scout	shout
couch	towel	ounce	coward	outdoors
flowerpot	scowl	browse	announce	hound
trout	drowsy	grouch	eyebrow	boundary

Match Up Draw a line connecting two word parts that form a list word.

1. moun   brow
2. flower   tain
3. eye   nounce
4. out   sy
5. boun   ever
6. how   dary
7. drow   doors
8. an   pot

Word Search Find the list words from the box hidden in the puzzle. Words are down, across, and diagonal.

```
B Z S C O U T K M C B G
X R H N I V R P O O S R
A H O U N D O A U W I O
C O U W B C U E N A V U
V W T I S D T Q D R U C
K N M P C E K O K D M H
Z D I Q O O X U I Y N E
E H F C W Z U N A T R R
T O W E L Y O C J T S X
J K L Z Q Y I E H P A E
```

scout
towel
hound
grouch
mound
trout
ounce
shout
scowl
couch
browse
coward

 Home Activity Your child learned words with /ou/ spelled *ou* and *ow*. Write each list word leaving blanks where the *ou* or *ow* belong. Ask your child to complete each word.

© Pearson Education, Inc., 4

Subject-Verb Agreement

Directions Write *Yes* if the subject and the verb in the sentence agree. Write *No* if the subject and the verb do not agree.

1. Brazilians tell many folktales. _____

2. These stories often includes strange creatures. _____

3. One forest creature is the caipora. _____

4. It ride a large boar. _____

5. I like these stories. _____

Directions Write the verb in ( ) that correctly completes each sentence.

6. Another myth (describes, describe) the curupira. _____

7. Its toes (point, points) backwards. _____

8. Hunters (is, are) confused by its footprints. _____

9. The curupira (protect, protects) Brazil's animals and trees. _____

10. Brazil's animals (need, needs) the curupira. _____

11. The negrinho (are, is) an invisible little boy. _____

12. People (believe, believes) in the negrinho. _____

13. Brazilians (ask, asks) the negrinho for help. _____

14. Some folk creatures (frightens, frighten) people. _____

15. One big snake (lives, live) in the water. _____

16. It (scares, scare) away fishers. _____

17. A fisher (is, are) afraid of this snake. _____

18. We (finds, find) these stories very interesting. _____

19. A society (create, creates) its own myths. _____

20. Myths (answer, answers) questions about the world. _____

© Pearson Education, Inc., 4

Compound Words

Spelling Words				
watermelon	homemade	understand	sometimes	shoelace
highway	upstairs	thunderstorm	shortcut	doorbell
jellyfish	touchdown	campfire	skateboard	anyway
fireworks	haircut	loudspeaker	laptop	flashlight

Double Clues Each item gives two clues for small words. Write the list word made by adding the smaller words together.

1. for your foot + string   1. _____
2. put on toast + swims in water   2. _____
3. on your head + snip with scissors   3. _____
4. not down + passage to second story   4. _____
5. sleep outdoors + light with a match   5. _____
6. opening into house + ringer   6. _____
7. not low + route   7. _____
8. liquid to drink + large fruit   8. _____
9. not quiet + one who talks   9. _____
10. booming noise + big wind   10. _____

Proofread Words Circle the misspelled list word in each sentence. Write the word correctly.

11. The park sets off firewurks on July 4th.   11. _____
12. We had a flaslight in our tent.   12. _____
13. If you do not unnerstand, ask questions.   13. _____
14. These pies are homade by Uncle Tim.   14. _____
15. It rained, but we went for a walk enyway.   15. _____
16. Do you have a laptope or a desktop computer?   16. _____
17. The football team scored a tuchdown.   17. _____
18. I sumtimes eat dessert before dinner.   18. _____
19. Damien can do tricks on his scatboard.   19. _____
20. We took a shortkut through the woods.   20. _____

School + Home **Home Activity** Your child learned compound words. Write each list word on a paper strip. Have your child cut the two words apart. Mix strips and have your child reform the words.

© Pearson Education, Inc., 4

Past, Present, and Future Tenses

Directions Write *present*, *past*, or *future* to identify the tense of each underlined verb.

1. Winds in a tornado <u>whirl</u> with great power. _____

2. Many tornadoes <u>formed</u> in the Midwest last year. _____

3. They <u>destroyed</u> houses, cars, and businesses. _____

4. Hail sometimes <u>falls</u> before a tornado strikes. _____

5. Tomorrow we <u>will inspect</u> the damage. _____

6. That car <u>landed</u> on a supermarket roof. _____

7. The driver <u>escaped</u> without injury. _____

8. People often <u>hide</u> from a tornado in their basements. _____

9. Scientists <u>will learn</u> more about these storms. _____

10. We <u>will feel</u> safer with better weather forecasts. _____

Directions Write the verb in each sentence. Circle the past tense verbs. Underline the future tense verbs.

11. Some people chase tornadoes. _____

12. They like the excitement. _____

13. I followed a tornado last year with my friend Bill. _____

14. At first, the sky darkened. _____

15. A huge twister approached us at high speed. _____

16. Luckily, the tornado hopped over our car. _____

17. Then the winds quickly died. _____

18. Bill loved the adventure. _____

19. Next time, I will stay at home. _____

20. However, Bill will go again. _____

© Pearson Education, Inc., 4

Possessives

Spelling Words				
its	ours	mine	yours	family's
families'	man's	men's	girl's	girls'
hers	theirs	brother's	brothers'	teacher's
teachers'	aunt's	aunts'	boy's	boys'

Who Owns It? Write the list word pronoun that fits in each box.

BELONGING TO	ONE OWNER	TWO OR MORE OWNERS
AN OBJECT	1.	
A FEMALE	2.	
PERSON/PEOPLE SPOKEN TO	3.	3.
YOU AND ME		4.
ME	5.	
THOSE PEOPLE		6.

Singular or Plural? Write the possessive forms of each noun.

NOUN	SINGULAR POSSESSIVE	PLURAL POSSESSIVE
family	7.	8.
teacher	9.	10.
man	11.	12.
girl	13.	14.
brother	15.	16.
aunt	17.	18.
boy	19.	20.

Home Activity Your child learned to spell singular and plural possessives. Use each word in a sentence and have your child spell it correctly.

© Pearson Education, Inc., 4

Name _____

Irregular Verbs

Directions Write the past tense of the irregular verb in ( ).

1. Our teacher (bring) a book of tall tales to class. _____

2. She (choose) a story about Paul Bunyan to read. _____

3. The story (make) everyone smile. _____

4. Paul Bunyan (do) amazing feats. _____

5. He (come) to the Midwest to make farmland. _____

6. Our teacher (give) us an interesting assignment. _____

7. She (say) we should find some more American tall tales. _____

8. Roberto and I (go) to the library after school. _____

9. Roberto (get) a book about Johnny Appleseed. _____

10. I (speak) to the class about Pecos Bill. _____

Directions Write the correct past form of the verb in ( ) that goes with *has, have,* or *had*.

11. Johnny Appleseed had (give) people seeds to plant trees. _____

12. Jamal has (choose) to read about John Henry. _____

13. John Henry had (go) to join a railroad crew. _____

14. He had (bring) a hammer in each hand. _____

15. We have (feel) excited about reading tall tales. _____

© Pearson Education, Inc., 4

Venn Diagram

Directions Fill in the Venn diagram with similarities and differences about the two things you are comparing.

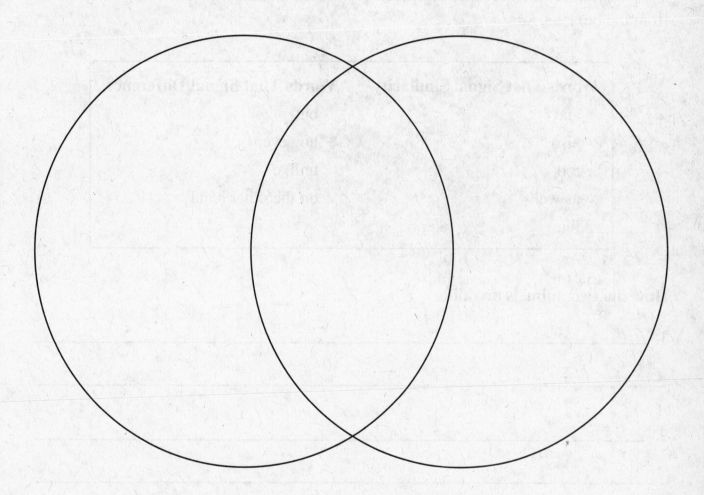

© Pearson Education, Inc., 4

Name _____

Words That Compare and Contrast

Directions The words in the box signal that two things are alike or different. Write two sentences that explain how your two animals are alike, using words from the box. Then write two sentences that explain how your two animals are different, using words from the box.

Words That Signal Similarity	Words That Signal Difference
and	but
also	however
too	unlike
as well	on the other hand
like	

How the two animals are alike

1. _____

_____

2. _____

_____

How the two animals are different

1. _____

_____

2. _____

_____

© Pearson Education, Inc., 4

Strong Verbs

Directions Replace each underlined verb with a strong verb from the box.
Write each new sentence.

barks	adopt	romp	grow
own	scamper	buy	

1. Many people <u>have</u> a dog or gerbil as a family pet.

_____

_____

2. Dogs need more space for exercise. They <u>move around</u> in a yard or park, but gerbils usually <u>are</u> in their cage.

_____

_____

3. A dog <u>knows</u> when strangers approach. However, a gerbil does not provide a warning.

_____

_____

4. Generally, dogs <u>are</u> much larger than gerbils.

_____

5. You can <u>get</u> both dogs and gerbils at a pet store. However, you might choose to <u>get</u> a dog from a local shelter.

_____

_____

© Pearson Education, Inc., 4

Editing 2

Directions Edit these sentences. Look for errors in spelling, grammar, and mechanics. Use proofreading marks to show the corrections.

Proofreading Marks		
Delete (Take out)		⟋ ˀ
Add		∧
Spelling		⬭
Uppercase letter		≡
Lowercase letter		/

1. How are frogs and toads alike and diferent.

2. Because they are amphibians they lived partly in water and partly on land.

3. both frogs and toad hatch from eggs that are laid in water.

4. Toads and frogs also hibirnate during the Winter.

5. Frogs hide in the mud in a lake, while toads dug deep into the dry grownd.

6. A toad have dry skin with many little bumps on them.

7. A frogs skin is ususally smooth and moist.

8. Both toads and frogs are exsellent jumpers they use their strong back legs.

Now you'll edit the draft of your compare and contrast essay. Then you'll use your revised and edited draft to make a final copy of your essay. Finally, you'll share your written work with your audience.

© Pearson Education, Inc., 4

Name _____

Compare and Contrast

- To **compare and contrast** means to tell how two or more things are alike and different.
- Clue words such as *like* and *as* can show similarities. Clue words such as *however* and *instead* can show differences.

Directions Read the following passage. Then complete the diagram by comparing and contrasting magic tricks with special effects.

Have you seen strange creatures and amazing superheroes in movies? Today's special effects are like the stage magic performed for years and years, but they're even harder to figure out. For years, magicians have used quick hands and distraction to make something seem to appear or disappear. In a similar way, special effects make you think you're seeing something that doesn't really exist. To create movie magic, special-effects artists use computers to create moving pictures that fool the eye. When you see them unfolding in front of you, both magic tricks and special effects seem real. They both work because of the hard work of people who love to entertain us.

Special Effects and Magic Tricks	
Alike	**Different**
Both seem real.	3.
1.	4.
2.	5.

© Pearson Education, Inc., 4

Home Activity Your child compared and contrasted two kinds of illusions in a nonfiction passage. Take turns with your child pointing out similarities and differences between two pieces of furniture.

Name _____

Writing • Mystery

Key Features of a Mystery

- describes a problem or puzzling situation
- characters may include detectives, suspects, and witnesses
- plot keeps readers in suspense
- setting may be in an ordinary or an unusual place

The Case of the Missing Crayons

"Huh!" Erika grunted to herself, puzzled. She looked again into the big box of crayons in her hands. All the red and yellow ones were missing! Why would anyone take those two colors of crayons from the box? Frowning in annoyance, she looked around the sunny family room, but she could see no sign of the missing crayons. How could she make a birthday card for Grandpa without using his favorite colors?

"I'll bet Emma took the crayons! She's always making trouble for me," Erika murmured. Quickly, she walked down the hall to her older sister's room. There, on the desk, she noticed a pile of little paper scraps. Coming closer, she saw they were crayon wrappers. "Aha! She did take the crayons! Now where is she?"

Next, Erika tried the dining room. The table was covered in newspaper, and on the paper she could see tiny, brightly colored crumbs. Erika picked up some of the waxy crumbs. They were shavings from yellow and red crayons. Emma was destroying the crayons! Why would she do that? Now Erika was confused as well as angry.

"Now be very careful!" That was her mother's voice coming from the kitchen. Erika sniffed and realized there was an odd smell in the air. Walking into the kitchen, she saw her mother and Emma standing next to the stove. Emma was stirring something in a pot.

"Erika, you're just in time to help us out," said her mother happily when she noticed Erika in the doorway. "We're making candles for Grandpa out of crayons! We're using red and yellow because those are his favorite colors. We scraped down the crayons and we're melting them now. Next, we're going to pour the wax into some molds."

Erika smiled. She had solved the mystery of the missing crayons, and she was going to help make a birthday present for Grandpa.

© Pearson Education, Inc., 4

1. Reread the selection. What is the mystery that must be solved?

_____

_____

2. Underline the name of the detective. Draw two lines under the name of the suspect.

Vocabulary

Directions Choose the word from the box that best matches each definition. Write the word on the line. Use the dictionary to look up words you do not know.

_____ **1.** a thin glass or metal container used in laboratories

_____ **2.** a planned talk on a chosen subject given before an audience

_____ **3.** not lessening in strength or pace; unyielding

_____ **4.** very exact; completely in agreement with a fact or standard

_____ **5.** the fact of being the same thing or person as claimed

Check the Words You Know

___analysis
___beaker
___hollow
___identity
___lecture
___microscope
___precise
___relentless

Directions To solve this puzzle, write the word that matches each definition. The circled letters will spell a secret word.

6. ___ ___ ___ ___ (○) ___ ___ ___

7. ___ ___ ___ ___ (○) ___ ___

8. ___ ___ (○) ___ ___ ___ ___ ___

9. ___ ___ ___ ___ ___ (○) ___ ___ ___ ___

10. (○) ___ ___ ___ ___ ___

6. the fact of being the same person as claimed
7. a type of speech
8. an examination of details
9. a device used to make small things look larger
10. empty inside

Write a Note

Think of something that puzzled you. On a separate sheet of paper, write a note to a friend describing it. Be sure to tell why it puzzled you. Use as many vocabulary words as you can.

Home Activity Your child identified and used words from the story *The Case of the Gasping Garbage.* Review the definitions of each of the vocabulary words with your child and work together to use the words in sentences.

© Pearson Education, Inc., 4

Name _____

Singular and Plural Pronouns

Pronouns are words that take the place of nouns. Pronouns that take the place of singular nouns are **singular pronouns**. *I, me, he, she, him, her, it, myself, himself,* and *herself* are singular pronouns. Pronouns that take the place of plural nouns are **plural pronouns**. *We, us, they, them, ourselves,* and *themselves* are plural pronouns.

Directions Circle the pronoun in each sentence.

1. He worked alone in the homemade laboratory.

2. Drake's glasses made him look scientific indeed.

3. They were in business together.

4. She was nice, even if she talked a lot.

5. I don't want to be someone's dinner.

Directions Choose a pronoun in ( ) to replace each underlined noun or noun phrase. Write the pronoun on the line.

6. <u>Doyle and Fossey</u> never had a monster assignment before. (He, They)

_____

7. <u>Nell</u> was the fastest runner in the fifth grade. (She, Her)

_____

8. What made <u>Gabby</u> think there was a monster? (she, her)

_____

Home Activity Your child learned about singular and plural pronouns. Have your child tell you what he or she did today. Ask your child to identify any singular or plural pronouns he or she uses.

© Pearson Education, Inc., 4

Name _____

Contractions

Spelling Words				
don't	won't	wouldn't	there's	we're
you're	doesn't	I've	here's	wasn't
shouldn't	couldn't	where's	hadn't	aren't
they're	it's	we've	when's	haven't

Familiar Sayings Write the contraction that correctly completes each saying.

1. _____ count your chickens before they hatch.   1. _____

2. People in glass houses _____ throw stones.   2. _____

3. _____ no time like the present.   3. _____

4. _____ as alike as two peas in a pod.   4. _____

5. _____ the time gone?   5. _____

6. _____ the thought that counts.   6. _____

Contractions Write the contraction that can be made from the underlined words.

7. The band was so loud I <u>could not</u> hear you.   7. _____

8. The kindergartners <u>have not</u> visited the zoo yet.   8. _____

9. Carrie <u>will not</u> be here today because she is sick.   9. _____

10. <u>When is</u> our next club meeting?   10. _____

11. <u>You are</u> right on time!   11. _____

12. <u>Here is</u> my homework assignment.   12. _____

13. Lisa was so angry she <u>would not</u> speak to me all day.   13. _____

14. We <u>are not</u> old enough to drive.   14. _____

15. The actor <u>was not</u> sure he knew his lines.   15. _____

16. Before today, Kim <u>had not</u> played softball.   16. _____

17. <u>I have</u> been taking dancing lessons for five years.   17. _____

18. Do you know when <u>we are</u> leaving?   18. _____

19. Jennifer <u>does not</u> have any pets.   19. _____

20. Do you want to know where <u>we have</u> been?   20. _____

Home Activity Your child wrote contractions. Have your child tell which letters were replaced by the apostrophe in each contraction.

© Pearson Education, Inc., 4

Story Sequence C

Title _____

Characters

Setting

Problem

Events

_____
_____
_____
_____
_____
_____
_____
_____
_____

Solution

© Pearson Education, Inc., 4

Vocabulary: Context Clues

- When you see an unfamiliar word in your reading, use **context clues** to figure out the meaning.
- Sometimes an author will use a synonym or an antonym as a context clue.
- **Synonyms** are words that mean almost the same thing.
- **Antonyms** are words with opposite meanings.

Directions Read the following passage about the apprentice and the street magician. Then complete the analogies below. Think about synonyms and antonyms as you read.

At the village square, the apprentice was relentless as she pushed her way through the quickly yielding crowd. She wanted to see the street magician. No one knew his identity and it was this lack of familiarity that made him a mystery. The girl got to inspect the magic hat. He claimed it was empty. Indeed, it looked hollow to her. But then he pulled out a dove from the hat. He claimed to read minds, but most of the time he was more inaccurate than precise. The little girl believed that an investigation and analysis of his process would reveal the magician's secrets.

1. _____ is to *empty* as *untamed* is to *wild*.

2. *Damage* is to *destruction* as *investigation* is to _____.

3. *Heroic* is to *cowardly* as _____ is to *yielding*.

4. *Familiarity* is to _____ as *biologist* is to *scientist*.

5. *Dull* is to *brilliant* as *inaccurate* is to _____.

Home Activity Your child identified synonyms (words with the same meaning) and antonyms (words that are opposite in meaning) in a short passage. Read a magazine or newspaper article with your child. Take turns finding synonyms and antonyms for words in the article.

© Pearson Education, Inc., 4

Procedures and Instructions/Manual

- **Procedures and instructions** are directions for doing or making something.
- Instructions are given in order. They usually include numbered steps.
- Read through all the instructions before you begin. Then follow the directions, one step at a time.
- A **manual** usually takes the form of a small book. It has instructions to help the reader understand how to use or build something.
- Look at illustrations and diagrams. Watch out for warnings about special hazards.

Directions Read the directions in the chart below. Then answer the questions.

Quick White Bread Recipe

1	Prepare the bread batter. In a large bowl, mix 2 cups hot water, 5 cups flour. Then mix in 2 tbsp. each of the following: yeast, salt, sugar, oil.
2	Knead the dough. This is done by mashing and squeezing the dough in your hands.
3	Let the dough rise at room temperature for 1 hour. Dough should double in size.
4	Mash the dough down into a smaller size and divide into three equal parts. Place each part in a bread pan.
5	Bake loaves in preheated oven at 350 degrees for 25 minutes.

1. What is the purpose of these instructions?

_____

2. What do the numbers in the left column represent?

_____

3. Which step in this procedure involves measuring?

_____

4. Why is it important that you follow the instructions in order?

_____

5. To follow these instructions successfully, what are three skills that you need?

_____

Home Activity Your child learned about procedures and instructions. Read a favorite recipe with your child. Review aloud the steps you would have to follow to make the recipe. Ask your child questions about the sequence of steps.

© Pearson Education, Inc., 4

Directions Read over this section from the index of a cookbook. Then answer the questions below.

Dish/Ingredient	Page
Biscuits	43–45
Bread	24–29, 32, 34, 40–42
Brussels Sprouts	180
Butternut Squash	151, 206
Cakes	73–76
Carrots	76, 159, 164, 166
Cauliflower	172
Cookies	80–101
Corn	157, 161, 163
Crepes	121
Deep Dish Pizza	303–304

6. What is the purpose of this index?

_____

7. On how many pages will you find recipes using corn?

_____

8. On which pages would you look to find a recipe for angel food cake?

_____

9. Where would you look to find how to make pizza dough?

_____

10. On what page would you most likely find a recipe for carrot cake? Why do you think so?

_____

_____

© Pearson Education, Inc., 4

Home Activity Your child learned about using the index of a cookbook. Together, look through a cookbook. Invite your child to find favorite foods in the index.

Contractions

Proofread Riddles Circle six spelling errors in Vicki's list of riddles. Write the words correctly on the lines. Rewrite the sentence that ends with the wrong punctuation mark.

Why don't rivers go out of style?
Because theyr'e always current!

When'is fishing not a good way to relax?
When you're a worm!

Wheres' the ocean the deepest?
At the bottom.

What driver does't need a license.
A screwdriver!

Why should you wear a watch in the desert?
Because there's a spring inside.

Why woudn't the letter E spend any money?
Because its always in debt.

1. _____   2. _____

3. _____   4. _____

5. _____   6. _____

7. _____

Missing Words Circle the contraction that is spelled correctly. Write it.

8. **We've We'ev** chosen you for our team.   8. _____

9. There **ar'nt aren't** any more books on the shelf.   9. _____

10. The puppy **wouldn't woodn't** come when I called. 10. _____

11. **Hear's Here's** my missing shoe!   11. _____

12. Nick **doesn't dosen't** like ice cream.   12. _____

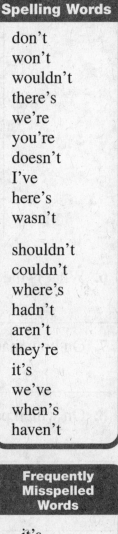

Spelling Words

don't
won't
wouldn't
there's
we're
you're
doesn't
I've
here's
wasn't

shouldn't
couldn't
where's
hadn't
aren't
they're
it's
we've
when's
haven't

Frequently Misspelled Words

it's
we're
you're

© Pearson Education, Inc., 4

Home Activity Your child identified misspelled contractions. Write each contraction, omitting the apostrophes. Have your child add the missing apostrophe to each word.

Name _____

Singular and Plural Pronouns

Directions Read the passage. Then read each question. Circle the letter of the correct answer.

Mystery Muddle

(1) Drake and Nell walked, dragging the garbage can between they. (2) Drake slipped and nearly fell but her helped Drake up. (3) Drake thought to themselves, "We have to simulate the same environment." (4) They poked in the garbage can for a clue. (5) "Have you ever seen they?" Nell asked. (6) This mystery was not going to solve itself!

1 What change, if any, should be made in sentence 1?

  A Change *they* to **you.**

  B Change *they* to **her.**

  C Change *they* to **them.**

  D Make no change.

2 What change, if any, should be made in sentence 2?

  A Change *her* to **Drake.**

  B Change *her* to **him.**

  C Change *her* to **she.**

  D Make no change.

3 What change, if any, should be made in sentence 3?

  A Change *themselves* to **ourself.**

  B Change *themselves* to **himself.**

  C Change *themselves* to **myself.**

  D Make no change.

4 What change, if any, should be made in sentence 5?

  A Change *they* to **this.**

  B Change *they* to **we.**

  C Change *they* to **I.**

  D Make no change.

5 What change, if any, should be made in sentence 6?

  A Change *itself* to **herself.**

  B Change *itself* to **themselves.**

  C Change *itself* to **himself.**

  D Make no change.

© Pearson Education, Inc., 4

Home Activity Your child prepared for taking tests on singular and plural pronouns. Have your child write a list of pronouns. Ask your child to tell a story using as many of the pronouns as possible.

Compare and Contrast

- To **compare** and **contrast** two or more things is to show how the things are alike and different.
- Some clue words are as, *like, but, instead,* and *however.*
- Sometimes writers do not use clue words when they compare and contrast things.

Directions Read the following passage.

As twilight approaches, many different flying animals become active. Insects are the first to appear. Moths flutter around streetlights. Some regions have fireflies that can "light up" their bodies. Mosquitoes, however, are real pests. They feed on the blood of animals, as well as humans.

Fortunately, bats hunt at night. As they flap through the air, bats eat mosquitoes and other insects. Like bats, owls wake up at dusk to hunt. Some owls hunt bats. Some owls nest in barns and tall trees. Others nest inside cacti or burrow into the ground.

Directions Answer the questions and complete the graphic organizer.

1. How are moths and fireflies similar to mosquitoes? Is there a clue word that tells you they are similar?

_____

2. How are mosquitoes different from the other flying insects? Which word suggests a contrast?

_____

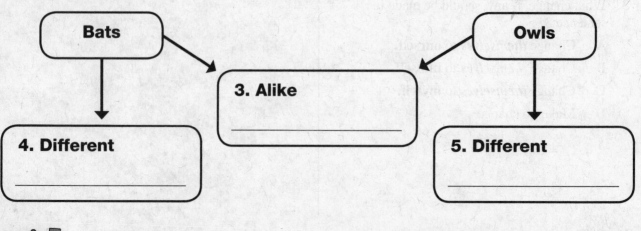

Bats

3. Alike
_____

Owls

4. Different
_____

5. Different
_____

© Pearson Education, Inc., 4

School + Home **Home Activity** Your child compared and contrasted details from a short passage. With your child, compare and contrast favorite animals. Ask your child to tell you some differences among owls.

Name _____

Writing • Song

Key Features of a song

- has words that are set to a melody
- is divided into lines
- often uses rhyme

That's a Blue Jay

(to the tune of "London Bridge")

Bright blue wings reflect the sun,
Blue like sky,
Catch my eye.
Bright blue wings reflect the sun,
That's a blue jay.

Shrieking call sounds through the trees,
Harsh and fierce,
Hurts my ears!
Shrieking call sounds through the trees,
That's a blue jay.

Chasing smaller birds away,
Black eyes shine,
"This yard's mine!"
Chasing smaller birds away,
That's a blue jay.

Feeding hungry fluff-topped chicks,
Babies fear,
But Mom is near.
Feeding hungry fluff-topped chicks,
That's a blue jay.

1. Reread the song. Underline the refrain each time you see it. Where does it appear?

_____

2. Look for rhyming words in the song and circle them.

© Pearson Education, Inc., 4

Writing Song **259**

Name _____

Vocabulary

Directions Choose the word from the box that best matches each definition.
Write the word on the line.

_____ 1. regular, measured beats

_____ 2. easily bent

_____ 3. greatly delighted, charmed

_____ 4. short, quick views or looks

_____ 5. the top of the ground or soil,
or of a body of water

**Check the Words
You Know**

___aquarium
___dolphins
___enchanted
___flexible
___glimpses
___pulses
___surface

Directions Choose the word from the box that best completes
each sentence. Write the word on the line shown to the left.

_____ 6. The show at the ___ features dolphins and sharks.

_____ 7. ___ are mammals that live in the sea.

_____ 8. In one trick, a baby dolphin jumps above the ___ of the
water.

_____ 9. The crowd is ___ by the magic of the dolphins' tricks.

_____ 10. Through portholes, visitors can catch ___ of the
creatures underwater.

Write an Advertisement

Imagine that you run an aquarium and want people to attend your dolphin show. On a separate
sheet of paper, write an advertisement that will persuade people to come. Use colorful words to
make the show sound like fun. Use as many vocabulary words as you can.

© Pearson Education, Inc., 4

Home Activity Your child identified and used vocabulary words from *Encantado: Pink Dolphin of the
Amazon*. Together, write your own short story that takes place at the ocean, a lake, or a river. Try to use all of
the vocabulary words in the story.

Name _____

Kinds of Pronouns

A **subject pronoun** is used in the subject of a sentence. Singular subject pronouns are *I, you, he she,* and *it*. Plural subject pronouns are *we, you,* and *they*.

An **object pronoun** is used as the direct object of a sentence or the object of a preposition. Some object pronouns are *them, him, her,* and *me*.

A **demonstrative** pronoun demonstrates the position of an object. *This, that, these,* and *those* are demonstrative pronouns.

A **reflexive** pronoun reflects the action of the verb back on the subject. *Himself, herself, myself,* and *themselves* are reflexive pronouns.

Directions Circle each subject pronoun.

1. We were studying the rain forests in class.

2. I would love to learn more about them.

3. Sarah, Maria, and she are showing us a forest model.

Directions Circle each object pronoun.

4. Next week you and Jaime will tell them about dolphins.

5. It looks really interesting to me.

6. They are doing more research with Karl and her.

Directions Circle each demonstrative pronoun.

7. I want to do that.

8. We can read this next.

9. Do you have any more of those?

Directions Circle each reflexive pronoun.

10. I will write a report myself.

11. He wanted to write one himself too.

12. The scientists themselves will give a talk.

 Home Activity Your child studied kinds of pronouns. Ask your child to tell you something that happened today. Have your child identify the kinds of pronouns in his or her account.

© Pearson Education, Inc., 4

Final Syllable Patterns

Spelling Words				
chicken	natural	several	paddle	oval
eleven	together	summer	animal	frighten
brother	calendar	threaten	pitcher	mumble
jungle	needle	caterpillar	shelter	deliver

Word Groups Write the list word that best completes each word group.

1. turkey, goose, ____

2. murmur, mutter, ____

3. joined, with, ____

4. winter, spring, ____

5. elliptical, egg-shaped, ____

6. cocoon, butterfly, ____

7. usual, normal, ____

8. many, numerous, ____

9. row, oar, ____

10. startle, scare, ____

1. _____

2. _____

3. _____

4. _____

5. _____

6. _____

7. _____

8. _____

9. _____

10. _____

Missing Words Write a list word to complete the sentence.

11. Turn to a new page on the ____.

12. When the rain came, we took ____ in the library.

13. My little sister will ____ to run away if she gets angry.

14. Please fill the ____ with water.

15. The number ____ is one more than ten.

16. The driver will ____ the packages to the airport.

17. A domestic ____ lives with people.

18. It takes some skill to get thread through the eye of a ____.

19. My baby ____ will cry out when he is hungry.

20. Monkeys swing from tree to tree in the ____.

11. _____

12. _____

13. _____

14. _____

15. _____

16. _____

17. _____

18. _____

19. _____

20. _____

© Pearson Education, Inc., 4

Home Activity Your child wrote words that end with *le, al, en, ar,* and *er.* Have your child identify the five list words that are most difficult for him or her, spell the words, and use them in sentences.

Web B

© Pearson Education, Inc., 4

Vocabulary • Multiple-Meaning Words

- **Multiple-meaning words** are words with the same spelling but different meanings.
- If you read a word that you recognize, but it is used in an unfamiliar way, look for clues about its meaning in the words nearby. Then use a dictionary to help you understand its meaning.

Directions Read the following passage. Then answer the questions below.

> Kerry was enchanted by his visit to this delightful place, the rain forest. Just beneath the surface of the water, he saw fish unlike any of those in his aquarium at home. The trees grew so large that their branches reached out into the water, like flexible arms bending out to his boat.
>
> He was surprised when he caught quick glimpses of dolphins making their way down the long river. Kerry knew he would not have enough time to absorb everything that he saw. He knew he would return to learn more about this amazing world so different from where he lives.

1. After looking up *enchanted* in a dictionary, what words in the sentence do you recognize as clues?

_____

2. *Glimpses* can mean "sees" or "brief views." How is it used in the passage? How can you tell? _____

_____

3. *Surface* can mean "the outside or top" or "to rise up." How is it used here? How can you tell? _____

_____

4. *Branches* are "streams flowing off a main river" or "limbs of a tree." Which meaning is used here? How can you tell?

_____

5. *Absorb* can mean "to soak up" or "to learn." How is it used in the passage? How can you tell?

_____

Home Activity Your child identified words that are spelled the same, but have different meanings in a passage. Discuss the multiple meanings of the words for many ordinary objects around the house. Challenge your child to find ten things in the home whose names have more than one meaning. Have him or her use a dictionary to look up the meanings.

© Pearson Education, Inc., 4

Poster/Announcement

- A **poster** is an **announcement** for an event. Posters are large in size. Usually they use color and large type to attract attention.

- Posters answer these questions about an event: Who? What? When? Where? How? Why?

Directions Read this poster. Then complete the chart by telling how the poster answers the questions.

See the Top Trainers in America!

All–New Dolphin Show

Springfield City Aquarium
Saturday, March 8
11:00 A.M.
Only $1 per person

Proceeds Benefit the Red Cross

Who?	top trainers in America
What?	1.
When?	2.
Where?	3.
Why?	4.

5. On a large sheet of paper, make a colorful poster for a school event. Choose the most important information. Make sure your poster tells who, what, when, why, how, and where.

© Pearson Education, Inc., 4

Directions Read over this announcement. Then answer the questions below.

HELP SAVE THE RAIN FOREST!

Come hear
Manuel Ortega,
Costa Rican Biologist

"What Kids Can Do to Save the Rain Forest"

Don't miss this multimedia presentation for children ages 8–11. Enjoy activities, animals, and rain forest snacks. Bring your questions.

January 12, 5 P.M.
Santa Fe Public Library
2100 S. Rio Grande Way

6. What is the purpose of this announcement?

_____

7. What is the event? Who is featured?

_____

_____

8. When and where is the event taking place?

_____

9. Why do you think the event is taking place?

_____

10. What does this announcement emphasize? How?

_____

_____

Home Activity Your child learned about announcements. With your child, think of a school or community activity that is coming up. Work with your child to write an announcement to post. Make sure your child includes answers to these questions: who, what, when, why, how, and where?

© Pearson Education, Inc., 4

Final Syllable Patterns

Proofread a Story Melissa is writing a story. Proofread her first paragraph. Circle six spelling errors. Write the words correctly. Find a run-on sentence and write it correctly.

© Pearson Education, Inc., 4

Spelling Words

chicken
eleven
brother
jungle
natural
together
calendar
needle
several
summer

threaten
caterpillar
paddle
animal
pitcher
shelter
oval
frighten
mumble
deliver

The Mysterious Path

All elevin students zigzagged in a path across the wet field. Then they entered a forest that was as dark as a jungal the students had to walk through the tangle of bushes in a single line. Every thorn scratched like a needel. Even though the students tried to hold their voices to a soft mumbel, they couldn't help but frightan some of the animals. An aminal ran across their path and snarled, trying to threaten these strange people.

1. _____   2. _____

3. _____   4. _____

5. _____   6. _____

7. _____

_____

_____

Frequently Misspelled Words

people
hospital
another

Proofread Words Fill in the circle beside the word that is spelled correctly. Write the word.

8. ○ ovel   ○ oval   ○ ovle   8. _____

9. ○ naturall   ○ naturale   ○ natural   9. _____

10. ○ deliver   ○ dilever   ○ diliver   10. _____

11. ○ pither   ○ pitcher   ○ pitcer   11. _____

12. ○ frigten   ○ frighten   ○ frightten   12. _____

Home Activity Your child identified misspelled words that end with *le*, *al*, *ar*, *er*, and *en*. Say list words that end with the schwa-*l* sound and have your child tell whether the final syllable is spelled with an *le* or *al*.

Kinds of Pronouns

Directions Read the passage. Then read each question. Circle the letter of the correct answer.

The Enormous Spider

(1) "Look at the giant spider!" Jesse said to I. (2) The giant spider looked at we and waved a hairy leg. (3) Us didn't wait to see what it would do. (4) We took myself back to camp as fast as we could. (5) "What's going on?" Jaime asked. (6) "A spider out there scared us," we told him. (7) "I'll never go near that again!" I said.

1 What change, if any, should be made in sentence 1?

  A   Change *I* to **me.**

  B   Change *Jesse* to **I.**

  C   Change *I* to **she.**

  D   Make no change.

2 What change, if any, should be made in sentence 2?

  A   Change *we* to **you.**

  B   Change *we* to **them.**

  C   Change *we* to **us.**

  D   Make no change.

3 What change, if any, should be made in sentence 3?

  A   Change *Us* to **It.**

  B   Change *Us* to **We.**

  C   Change *Us* to **Me.**

  D   Make no change.

4 What change, if any, should be made in sentence 4?

  A   Change *myself* to **ourselves.**

  B   Change *myself* to **themselves.**

  C   Change *myself* to **himself.**

  D   Make no change.

5 What change, if any, should be made in sentence 7?

  A   Change *that* to **this.**

  B   Change *that* to **them.**

  C   Change *that* to **these.**

  D   Make no change.

© Pearson Education, Inc., 4

Home Activity Your child prepared for taking tests on subject, object, demonstrative, and reflexive pronouns. Have your child write a list of pronouns. Ask him or her to use the pronouns in sentences as you say them.

Name _____

Sequence

- **Sequence** is the order in which events happen in a story or article.
- The clue words *first, then, next, after,* and *last* tell you the order of events when the sequence is explicit.
- If the sequence is implicit, there may be no clue words. You have to figure out how the ideas relate to each other without clue words.
- The clue words *while, meanwhile,* and *during* tell you that events are happening at the same time.

Directions Read the following passage. Then write the correct letters on the lines to show the sequence of events.

> During World War II, the German military used a special machine, the *Enigma,* to send and receive coded messages. The *Enigma* was so effective, that it wasn't until 1941 that the Poles, French, and British, working together, were able to crack its code.
>
> Because it feared an invasion from their neighbor, Poland was the first country to begin trying to decode the *Enigma.* The French and British joined the effort later.
>
> When Germany did invade Poland in 1939, most of the Polish cryptologists—people who study secret codes—fled to France in order to continue their work. Later, when Germany invaded France, some of these same people fled to England's Bletchley Park, a top-secret school for code breakers.

1. First Event _____   **a.** German troops invaded France.

2. Second Event _____   **b.** Germany began using the *Enigma* to send messages.

3. Third Event _____   **c.** France, Poland, and Britain broke the *Enigma's* code.

4. Fourth Event _____   **d.** German troops invaded Poland.

5. Fifth Event _____   **e.** The Poles tried to decode the *Enigma.*

© Pearson Education, Inc., 4

Home Activity Your child read a short passage and identified a sequence of events. Talk with your child about what you both did today. Then make a short list, in random order, of those events. Take turns recalling the correct sequence of events.

Writing • Instructions

Key Features of Instructions

- explain each step in a process
- often use sequence words such as *first, next,* and *last*.
- are often written in list form

The Name Code

Last year, my friends and I made up a code. It's great for sending short messages that we don't want anyone else to read. We call it the Name Code. Here's how you can create a Name Code of your own:

1. First, make a list of first names that start with each letter of the alphabet. For example, you could use Ann for A, Beth for B, Carlos for C, Darius for D, and so on. Give copies of the list to your friends so that they can use the code to send messages, too.

2. To write a message in Name Code, write a name from your list for each letter in your message. For example, imagine you want to say "Meet me at the park." You might use "Maria Emma Emma Thomas" for the letters M-E-E-T in "Meet."

3. Next, give your message to a friend, and make sure he or she knows how to decode it. You don't have to go back to the name list to figure out the message. Just circle the first letter in each name, then read the circled letters.

Try making up your own Name Code, or see if you can make up something similar, like an Animal Code. You and your friends will amaze and amuse yourselves as you communicate your secret messages!

1. Reread the selection. Circle the sequence words.

2. What other clue tells you that the selection is a set of instructions?

_____

_____

© Pearson Education, Inc., 4

Vocabulary

Directions Choose the word from the box that best matches each definition. Write the word on the line.

_____ 1. tiring, wearying

_____ 2. early, ahead of time

_____ 3. uncover, make known

_____ 4. created, invented

_____ 5. extreme, severe, to a
great degree

Check the Words You Know
___advance
___developed
___exhausting
___headquarters
___impossible
___intense
___messages
___reveal

Directions Choose the word from the box that best completes each sentence. Write the word on the line.

_____ 6. The lieutenant called _____ on the radio to warn
his commander of the attack.

_____ 7. The _____ contained information that was
important to the troops.

_____ 8. Once believed _____, people travel at the speed of
sound daily.

Write a Secret Message

On a separate sheet of paper, write a secret message to a friend. Replace important words, such as colors, animals, and foods. Include a key on the back of the paper to remind you which words you replaced. Use as many vocabulary words as you can.

© Pearson Education, Inc., 4

Home Activity Your child identified and used vocabulary words from *Navajo Code Talkers*. With your child, write a message that you need to get to troops in battle. Discuss how you might come up with code words for the people, places, and events in the message.

Pronouns and Antecedents

A **pronoun** takes the place of a noun or nouns. An **antecedent**, or referent, is the noun or nouns to which the pronoun refers. A pronoun and its antecedent must agree in number and gender.

Before you use a pronoun, ask yourself whether the antecedent is singular or plural. If the antecedent is singular, decide whether it is masculine, feminine, or neuter. Then choose a pronoun that agrees. In the following sentences, the antecedents are underlined once; the pronouns are underlined twice.

The man had an idea, so he told the Marines about it.

The Navajos knew an unusual language, and they made a code with it.

Directions Write the letter of the pronoun next to the noun or noun phrase that could be its antecedent.

_____ **1.** language   **A** he

_____ **2.** a Navajo code talker   **B** she

_____ **3.** an officer and a recruit   **C** them

_____ **4.** Chester and me   **D** it

_____ **5.** Chester's wife   **E** us

Directions Write the correct pronoun in ( ) to complete each sentence. The antecedents of the pronouns have been underlined to help you.

6. Johnston and Jones agreed (they, he) should create a Navajo code. _____

7. The men knew the language, so the Marines recruited (they, them). _____

8. The Navajo code was difficult, and (he, it) worked well. _____

9. Chester Nez said the code was not easy for (him, he). _____

10. Hawthorne spoke Navajo, and (him, he) became a code talker. _____

Home Activity Your child learned about pronouns and antecedents. Ask your child to explain to you how a pronoun can change with a different antecedent.

© Pearson Education, Inc., 4

Consonant Digraph /sh/

Spelling Words				
nation	special	lotion	mansion	precious
creation	vacation	tension	especially	motion
tradition	gracious	extension	addition	caution
official	solution	suspension	politician	portion

Missing Words Write the list word that completes the sentence.

1. The telephone was a very helpful ____.

2. I have devised a ____ to our problem.

3. The wealthy surgeon lives in the ____ on the hill.

4. Please bring an extra bottle of ____ to the beach.

5. You have certainly earned your ____ of the prize.

6. We are studying the laws of ____ in physics class.

7. There are fifty states in our ____.

8. The Golden Gate Bridge is a huge ____ bridge.

9. In ____ to his speech, he presented a demonstration.

10. My family once took a ____ to Hawaii.

1. _____

2. _____

3. _____

4. _____

5. _____

6. _____

7. _____

8. _____

9. _____

10. _____

Categorizing Write the list word that completes each word group.

11. unusual, unique, ____

12. valuable, prized, ____

13. stress, pressure, ____

14. mainly, particularly, ____

15. custom, ritual, ____

16. senator, president, ____

17. concern, care, ____

18. executive, representative, ____

19. expansion, addition, ____

20. sociable, cordial, ____

11. _____

12. _____

13. _____

14. _____

15. _____

16. _____

17. _____

18. _____

19. _____

20. _____

© Pearson Education, Inc., 4

Home Activity Your child wrote words with the sound /sh/. Say the /sh/ words, and ask your child to spell them.

Steps in a Process

Process _____

```
┌─────────────────────────────────────────────────┐
│ Step 1                                           │
│                                                  │
│                                                  │
└─────────────────────────────────────────────────┘
                        │
                        ▼
┌─────────────────────────────────────────────────┐
│ Step 2                                           │
│                                                  │
│                                                  │
└─────────────────────────────────────────────────┘
                        │
                        ▼
┌─────────────────────────────────────────────────┐
│ Step 3                                           │
│                                                  │
│                                                  │
└─────────────────────────────────────────────────┘
                        │
                        ▼
┌─────────────────────────────────────────────────┐
│ Step 4                                           │
│                                                  │
│                                                  │
└─────────────────────────────────────────────────┘
                        │
                        ▼
┌─────────────────────────────────────────────────┐
│ Step 5                                           │
│                                                  │
│                                                  │
└─────────────────────────────────────────────────┘
```

© Pearson Education, Inc., 4

Vocabulary • Unknown Words

- **Dictionaries** and **glossaries** provide alphabetical lists of words and their meanings. A dictionary is its own book, but a glossary is part of another book.

- Sometimes using context clues won't help you figure out the meaning of an unknown word. When this happens, you can use a dictionary or glossary to find the word's meaning.

Directions Read the following passage. Look for the context clues as you read to help you define each word in the table. Use a dictionary or glossary if necessary. Complete the chart below, with definitions in your own words.

The pets in the Johnsons' house weren't getting along. As usual, it was the cats against the dogs. The cats had gone too far this time! They decided that the new dog food, "Gravy Boat," tasted better than their food, "FrouFrou Feast." Because the cats walked so quietly, it was impossible for the dogs to hear the cats sneak into the kitchen to steal the dog food. The dogs needed a way to give each other advance warning that the cats were about to snatch their precious kibble.

Dixon, the Dalmatian, developed a secret code that all the dogs learned. If none of the cats were upstairs, one dog would wag its tail, thumping it against the wall three times. If a dog saw a cat heading for the kitchen, it would scratch with intense energy. If the cats were actually eating the dog food, another dog would reveal this fact to the people of the house by running back and forth across the downstairs at an exhausting pace. This system of messages worked so well, that the cats were defeated! The cats decided that "FrouFrou Feast" wasn't so bad after all.

Word	Definition
froufrou	1.
advance	2.
intense	3.
reveal	4.
exhausting	5.

Home Activity Your child learned to understand unknown words after looking them up in a dictionary or glossary. Work with your child to identify unknown words in a story. Have him or her look them up in a dictionary and see which meaning best fits in the sentence.

© Pearson Education, Inc., 4

Follow and Clarify Directions

- **Directions** tell you how to get somewhere or how to do something.
- Do what the first step says before going on to the next step.
- Try to visualize the end result of the directions to see where you are headed.

Directions Follow the directions to decode the message Joanie gave to Mary. Then answer the questions below.

1. Look for spellings you don't understand.
2. Take notes as needed.
3. Study the decoder to see what the unusual spellings mean.
4. Use the information to find the way to your friend's party.

When u leave your house tk a lft & wok 2 the crnr. Tk a rt & go 3 blks to Carpenter Street. Tk a rt on Carpenter & wok to Washington. My house is on the crnr of Carpenter & Washington, btwn a large yellow house and a supermarket. The party starts at 2 PM. I can't wait 2 c u.

Decoder

tk = take   lft = left   2 = to   u = you   crnr = corner   rt = right   blks = blocks

wok = walk   btwn = between   c = see

1. What should Mary do when she leaves her house? What part of the message tells her this?

_____

_____

2. What direction should she take when she gets to the corner? What code does Joanie use for the word *right*?

_____

3. How many blocks should she walk to get to Carpenter Street?

_____

4. Which buildings will Mary use to find Joanie's house?

_____

_____

© Pearson Education, Inc., 4

Name _____

Directions Read over these directions. Then answer the questions below.

You may have seen sand castles on the beach or watched the results of a sand castle building contest live or on television. Here's the best way to build your own sand castle.

1. Choose sand that is moist enough to stick together. Fine, flat-grained sand is best. This sand is often found near the high-water line.

2. Start by making a pile of sand about 1 foot to 1 1/2 feet high. Its height and width will depend on what you want your castle to look like. Work from the top down to the base for the best results.

3. Pack down the sand pile and make a smooth, flat top.

4. Use a shovel edge or ruler to carve the castle's tower and walls. You can also use pails, shovels, cans, spoons, melon ballers, and so on.

5. Move down the pile in a stairstep fashion. Be creative, creating towers and walls.

6. Remember that sand castles have a very short life. Don't spend a long time trying to make a single perfect window on one tower. Instead, have fun and remember what you might try differently on your next attempt.

1. What is the purpose of these directions?

_____

2. How high should your pile of sand be?

_____

3. Should you work from the bottom up or from the top down?

_____

4. Name some items you might use in building your sand castle.

_____

_____

5. Why shouldn't you worry much about your first attempt at building a sand castle?

_____

_____

_____

© Pearson Education, Inc., 4

Home Activity Your child learned about following directions. With your child, read the directions for a card or board game. Try to follow them, step by step. Help your child to clarify each step in the directions.

Consonant Digraph /sh/

Proofread a Speech Circle six misspelled words in the speech. Write the words correctly. Write the sentence with a verb in the incorrect tense correctly.

> Holiday Vacasion Packages!
>
> Fly anywhere in the nashion. We have the best rates! Book your flight now and get a free 2-night extention at America's offishal hotel of choice. Our gratious flight attendants will make you feel at home. Call now and a porshion of your cost will be donates to Charity.

1. _____   2. _____   3. _____

4. _____   5. _____   6. _____

7. _____

Proofread Words Circle the list word in each sentence that is spelled correctly.

8. My mother is a very **speshial** **special** person.

9. We made an interesting **creation** **creacion** in science class.

10. Mr. Buck is building an **addishion** **addition** to the school.

11. Always use **caution** **causion** when swimming at the lake.

12. My mountain bike is my most **pretious** **precious** belonging.

Spelling Words

nation
special
lotion
mansion
precious
creation
vacation
tension
especially
motion

tradition
gracious
extension
addition
caution
official
solution
suspension
politician
portion

Frequently Misspelled Words

let's
that's

Home Activity Your child identified misspelled words with the sound /sh/. Misspell the list words your child did not use on this page, and have your child correct them.

© Pearson Education, Inc., 4

Pronouns and Antecedents

Directions Read the passage. Then read each question. Circle the letter of the correct answer.

The Trouble with Speaking Navajo

(1) Roy got in trouble because they spoke Navajo. (2) American soldiers needed a code to help him. (3) "I have an idea," said Johnston, "and she can't fail." (4) Navajos joined the Marines and he made up a code. (5) The code was simple, but he was unbreakable.

1 What change, if any, should be made in sentence 1?

  A Change *they* to **we.**

  B Change *they* to **it.**

  C Change *they* to **he.**

  D Make no change.

2 What change, if any, should be made in sentence 2?

  A Change *him* to **her.**

  B Change *him* to **their.**

  C Change *him* to **them.**

  D Make no change.

3 What change, if any, should be made in sentence 3?

  A Change *she* to **he.**

  B Change *she* to **its.**

  C Change *she* to **it.**

  D Make no change.

4 What change, if any, should be made in sentence 4?

  A Change *he* to **them.**

  B Change *he* to **him.**

  C Change *he* to **they.**

  D Make no change.

5 What change, if any, should be made in sentence 5?

  A Change *he* to **they.**

  B Change *he* to **it.**

  C Change *he* to **she.**

  D Make no change.

© Pearson Education, Inc., 4

Home Activity Your child prepared for taking tests on pronouns and antecedents. Read an article with your child and have him or her name the pronouns and point out their antecedents.

Graphic Sources

- A **graphic source,** such as a picture, a map, a time line, or a chart, organizes information and makes it easy to see.

Directions Study the map and the caption below it. Answer the questions that follow.

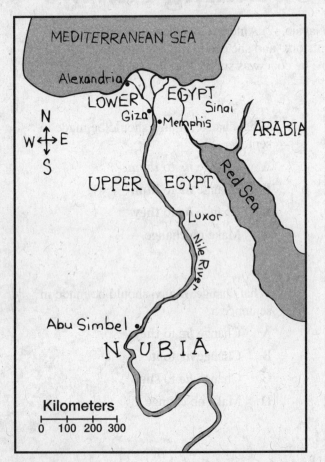

Egyptian history dates back eight thousand years to about 6000 B.C. Ancient Egypt consisted of two parts: Lower Egypt and Upper Egypt. The southern boundary of modern Egypt is about 50 kilometers south of Abu Simbel.

1. What does this map show?

_____

_____

2. Where is Alexandria located? In what part of Egypt is it?

_____

_____

_____

3. How close were the cities of ancient Egypt to the Nile River?

_____

_____

4. About how far is Alexandria from Giza, the home of the pyramids?

_____

5. How does this map help you better understand ancient Egypt?

_____

_____

_____

© Pearson Education, Inc., 4

Home Activity Your child used information on a map to answer questions. Look at a map with your child. Talk about the information you can learn from the map, such as key locations and distances between the places shown.

Writing • Problem-Solution Essay

Key Features of Problem-Solution Essay

- clearly establishes the problem
- uses opinions supported by facts and details
- uses solutions supported by facts and details

Let's Clean Up the Sidewalks!

Every morning, five kids from our neighborhood walk to Central School. Most days, we love our walk. But in the winter after it snows, walking to school turns into a chore. It's especially bad when people shovel their driveways and toss the snow onto the sidewalks. Slogging through the deep snow and scrambling up and down snow hills is hard work! Even wearing boots and snow pants, we still get to school with wet socks. Walking in the street is not a good solution because it is dangerous and against the law.

There is a simple solution to this problem. If every family in the neighborhood shoveled the sidewalk in front of their house, we would have a nice, clean, and safe path to school. It doesn't take very much work to shovel a few feet of sidewalk, and if everyone does his or her part, the whole walk will be clear in no time. We do understand that some people have a hard time doing physical work such as shoveling. Maybe more-able neighbors could help these people out. We kids would be happy to lend a hand sometimes, too.

Friends and neighbors, please join us in making our walk to school safer and more comfortable this winter. Let's all start shoveling!

1. Reread the selection. Underline the sentence that states the problem.

2. List two facts that support the writer's opinion about the problem.

_____

_____

3. Circle the sentence that states the solution to the problem.

© Pearson Education, Inc., 4

Vocabulary

Directions Choose the word from the box that best matches each definition. Write the word on the line.

_____ 1. anything that joins or connects

_____ 2. victory, success

_____ 3. to make known; to reveal

_____ 4. of times long past

_____ 5. people who have much
knowledge

<table>
<tr><td>

**Check the Words
You Know**

___ancient
___link
___scholars
___seeker
___temple
___translate
___triumph
___uncover

</td></tr>
</table>

Directions Choose the word from the box that best fits in each sentence. Write the word on the line.

Always on a quest, the knight was a **6.** _____ of a holy vessel. After

many years, he found the object of his search in a sacred **7.** _____.

After his discovery, his next task was to **8.** _____ the writing

inscribed on it. The writing was in an **9.** _____ language used

thousands of years earlier. The knight's discovery was hailed throughout the kingdom

as a **10.** _____.

Write a News Report

On a separate sheet of paper, write a news report announcing the discovery of a new language. You will need research to help you tell how, when, where, and by whom the discovery was made. Use as many vocabulary words as possible.

Home Activity Your child identified and used vocabulary words from *Seeker of Knowledge*. Have your child create a story about finding a secret treasure. Ask your child to use the vocabulary from the lesson in the story.

© Pearson Education, Inc., 4

Name _____

Possessive Pronouns

Possessive pronouns show who or what owns, or possesses, something. *My, mine, your, yours, her, hers, his, its, our, ours, their,* and *theirs* are possessive pronouns.

- Use *my, your, her, our,* and *their* before nouns.
  I study <u>my</u> notes. Marie looked at <u>her</u> drawing. Let us show you <u>our</u> alphabet.
- Use *mine, yours, hers, ours,* and *theirs* alone.
  These notes are <u>mine</u>. The drawing was <u>hers</u>. This alphabet is <u>ours</u>.
- *His* and *its* can be used both before nouns and alone.
  Jean-François followed <u>his</u> plan. The plan was <u>his</u>.
  The tomb guarded <u>its</u> secrets. The secrets were <u>its</u>.
- Do not use an apostrophe with a possessive pronoun.

Directions Circle the possessive pronoun in each sentence.

1. Justine and I are preparing our report on hieroglyphs.

2. We are learning how Jean-François Champollion made his discoveries.

3. You can see examples in your book of how the Egyptians wrote.

4. Modern writing is very different from theirs.

5. Justine will focus on their use of pictures.

Directions Write the possessive pronoun in ( ) that correctly completes each sentence.

6. The Raymonds went to Egypt, but their trip was different from (our, ours).

_____

7. She has shown us (hers, her) photographs and videos. _____

8. You should show the class (your, yours) drawings of Egypt. _____

9. Ms. Raymond's pictures were better than (my, mine)! _____

10. Can you help me make my pictures as good as (yours, your)?

_____

School + Home **Home Activity** Your child learned about possessive pronouns. Ask your child to use possessive pronouns in sentences about friends or family members and their belongings.

© Pearson Education, Inc., 4

Consonants /j/, /ks/, and /kw/

Spelling Words				
village	except	explain	quick	charge
bridge	knowledge	question	equal	queen
excited	expect	Texas	fudge	excellent
exercise	quart	liquid	quilt	expert

Missing Words Write the list word that completes the sentence.

1. The capital of ____ is Austin.

2. Some books are full of information, learning, and ____.

3. Stores and places of business are found in the ____.

4. The royal subjects bowed before the ____.

5. A good rainy day activity is making chocolate ____.

6. Two pints are equal to one ____.

7. A lot of work goes into making a handmade ____.

8. Water is a colorless, odorless, tasteless ____.

9. A healthy diet and ____ is the path to good health.

10. Four quarts are ____ to one gallon.

11. The ____ was built over the sparkling river.

12. We were ____ to go to the amusement park.

1. _____
2. _____
3. _____
4. _____
5. _____
6. _____
7. _____
8. _____
9. _____
10. _____
11. _____
12. _____

Categorizing Write the list word that completes each word group.

13. outstanding, superb, ____

14. but, excluding, ____

15. ask, query, ____

16. cost, fee, ____

17. describe, clarify, ____

18. fast, speedy, ____

19. specialist, authority, ____

20. demand, await, ____

13. _____
14. _____
15. _____
16. _____
17. _____
18. _____
19. _____
20. _____

© Pearson Education, Inc., 4

School + Home **Home Activity** Your child wrote words spelled with with consonants /j/, /ks/, and /kw/. Say those words and ask your child to spell them.

Name _____

Problem and Solution A

Problem

↓

Solution

© Pearson Education, Inc., 4

Vocabulary • Greek and Latin Roots

- When you see an unknown word, you can use what you know about **Greek and Latin roots** to help you figure out the word's meaning.

- The Latin word *ante* means "before," as in the word *antechamber*. The word *scholarly* comes from the Latin word *scholaris*, meaning "of a school." The word *celebrity* comes from the Latin word *celebrare*, which means "to honor."

Directions Read the following passage. Look for Latin roots as you read. Then answer the questions below. Use a dictionary to help you.

> Since ancient times, breaking an enemy's code has been very important. During World War II, Allied code breakers worked hard to uncover the secrets found in German codes. From 1939 to 1945, these scholars used their knowledge of math and technology to crack the codes of German communications. If code breakers could translate a message, spies might be caught and lives could be saved. Breaking a code was a triumph to celebrate!

1. How is the meaning of *ancient* similar to the meaning of the Latin word *ante*?

_____

2. How is the meaning of *scholars* related to the meaning of the Latin word *scholaris*?

_____

3. *Translate* comes from the Latin word *translatus,* meaning "carried across or transferred." How is the meaning of *translate* similar to the meaning of *translatus*?

_____

_____

4. Which word above comes from the Latin word *triumphus,* meaning "victory"?

_____

5. How does knowing the meaning of the Latin word *celebrare* help you understand the meaning of *celebrate?*

_____

Home Activity Your child identified and used Latin roots to understand unfamiliar words. Work with your child to identify words with Latin or Greek roots in an article. Use a dictionary to confirm meanings.

© Pearson Education, Inc., 4

Thesaurus

- A **thesaurus** is a kind of dictionary that lists **synonyms** (words with the same or similar meanings), **antonyms** (words with opposite meanings), and other related words. Parts of speech are listed to show how a word is used. If a word has multiple meanings, synonyms for each meaning are given.
- You can use a thesaurus to help you find new and interesting words so you don't repeat the same words too often in your writing.

Directions If you opened a page in a student thesaurus, you might find these listings. Use them to answer the questions below.

soundless (adj) still, mute, quiet. See SILENT.

spark (n) **1. flash:** flicker, flare, sparkle, glow, glint, glimmer; **2. stimulus:** goad, spur, motivation, inspiration.

spark (v) **1. flash:** flicker, flare, sparkle, glint; **2. stimulate:** goad, spur, motivate, inspire, ignite, start, activate. (ant) extinguish, douse.

sparkle (v) **1. with light:** glitter, shine, flicker, glint, glimmer, glow, dazzle, shimmer: *The silver ornaments sparkle in the firelight.* **2. with intelligence:** be lively, be vivacious, be the life of the party, shine, dazzle: *Her stories sparkle with clever humor.*

sparse (adj) scanty, meager, slight, scarce, thin, poor, spare, skimpy, few and far between. (ant) thick, abundant, plentiful.

1. How many synonyms are there for *sparse* on this thesaurus page? What part of speech are they?

_____

2. Which numbered list of synonyms would you use for *sparkle* as it is used in this sentence: "The crystal candlesticks sparkle brightly with light on the mantle." Why?

_____

3. Look at this sentence: "A spark of understanding appeared in Jeff's eyes as he read the explanation." Would you look at the entries for the noun or the verb *spark* to replace *spark* with a synonym?

_____

_____

© Pearson Education, Inc., 4

4. Rewrite the following sentence using a synonym for the verb *spark*. "The teacher's goal was to *spark* the students' interest in chemistry."

_____

_____

5. Give an antonym for *sparse*.

_____

6. Use an antonym for the verb *spark* in this sentence: "A thick, dull-looking textbook will probably _____ a student's interest in any subject."

_____

7. Give three synonyms for *soundless*. Do they have exactly the same meaning?

_____

_____

8. Where does the entry for *soundless* indicate you might find more synonyms for the word?

_____

_____

9. How are the two meanings for the verb *spark* like the two meanings for the noun *spark*?

_____

_____

_____

10. Why would you use a thesaurus when you write? Explain your answer.

_____

_____

 Home Activity Your child learned about using a thesaurus as a resource. Ask your child to use a thesaurus to find synonyms for a word picked at random from a newspaper article.

© Pearson Education, Inc., 4

Name _____

Consonants /j/, /ks/, and /kw/

Proofread an Ad Ed wants the newspaper ad about his gas station to be perfect. Circle the six misspelled words and write them correctly. Circle the word with a capitalization error and write it correctly.

> Drive into Ed's Gas Station!
>
> We have the lowest gas prices in the village.
>
> Try us for a qwick oil change or tire repair.
>
> We offer eggscellent repair and exspert service.
>
> Ask us any question about your car.
>
> We have knowledge about every make and model car.
>
> We explane the problem to you before we fix it.
>
> Your car will be fit for a king or qween.
>
> Open everyday exsept sunday.

village		
except		
explain		
quick		
charge		
bridge		
knowledge		
question		
equal		
queen		
excited		
expect		
Texas		
fudge		
excellent		
exercise		
quart		
liquid		
quilt		
expert		

1. _____ 2. _____ 3. _____

4. _____ 5. _____ 6. _____

7. _____

Frequently Misspelled Words

except
off
something

Proofread Words Circle the misspelled list word. Write it correctly.

8. Everyone was ekscited when the circus came to town.

8. _____

9. The class will expand their knowlej about other countries.

9. _____

10. The brige was closed for construction.

10. _____

11. There was no admission chardge for students.

11. _____

12. All team members get equel playing time.

12. _____

Home Activity Your child identified misspelled words with the sound /j/, /ks/, and /kw/. Misspell the list words your child did not use on this page, and have your child correct them.

© Pearson Education, Inc., 4

Possessive Pronouns

Directions Read the passage. Then read each question. Circle the letter of the correct answer.

Egypt's Mummies

(1) Ours class went to the museum and learned about ancient Egypt. (2) The Egyptians preserved the bodies of there dead. (3) When a king died, its body was placed in a great tomb. (4) When I do mine report, it will be about mummies. (5) What will you report be about?

1 What change, if any, should be made in sentence 1?

   A   Change *Ours* to **Yours.**

   B   Change *Ours* to **Are.**

   C   Change *Ours* to **Our.**

   D   Make no change.

2 What change, if any, should be made in sentence 2?

   A   Change *there* to **their'.**

   B   Change *there* to **the're.**

   C   Change *there* to **their.**

   D   Make no change.

3 What change, if any, should be made in sentence 3?

   A   Change *its* to **it's.**

   B   Change *its* to **it.**

   C   Change *its* to **his.**

   D   Make no change.

4 What change, if any, should be made in sentence 4?

   A   Change *mine* to **our.**

   B   Change *mine* to **his.**

   C   Change *mine* to **my.**

   D   Make no change.

5 What change, if any, should be made in sentence 5?

   A   Change *you* to **ure.**

   B   Change *you* to **your.**

   C   Change *you* to **you's.**

   D   Make no change.

© Pearson Education, Inc., 4

Home Activity Your child prepared for taking tests on possessive pronouns. Have your child write a list of possessive pronouns. Then help your child come up with sentences using the words.

Literary Elements: Character and Plot

- A **character** is a person or an animal who takes part in a story. You can learn about a character through the character's words, actions, and thoughts.

- A **plot** is the series of related events in a story. The plot includes a problem or *conflict*, the *rising action,* the *climax,* and the *resolution,* or outcome.

- A story may be written in the first person, which is indicated by the narrator's use of the words *I, we,* or *our.* It may also be written in the third person, indicated by the words *he, she,* or *they.*

Directions Read the following passage. Complete the plot chart below. Then answer the question.

Becky burst into the kitchen. "Quick, there's a UFO!" she shouted. We hurried outside. "Where?" I asked. Becky pointed up. I saw nothing and was not convinced. "Really," she insisted, "I saw this bright, tiny light speed past. *Whoosh!* And it was gone!" Becky's claim was both silly and exciting.

Deciding to investigate, I went online to research the night sky where we lived. One Web page had a recent video clip of a meteor shower. We watched it together.

"That's the UFO!" Becky exclaimed.

"It's a *shooting star,*" I reminded her. She was disappointed. "Next time make a wish."

Conflict	1.
Rising Action	2.
Climax	3.
Resolution	4.

5. Is the story told in the first person or third person?

_____

Home Activity Your child read a short passage and identified whether it was written in first or third person and the elements of its plot. Read a story with your child. Afterward, ask your child to identify whether it was written in first person or third person and to name the elements of the plot: the conflict, rising action, climax, and resolution. What does the resolution tell you about the characters?

© Pearson Education, Inc., 4

Writing • Adventure Story

Key Features of an Adventure Story

- Often takes place in an interesting setting.
- The story is built around a quest or problem.
- Includes unusual and exciting situations.

The Mysterious Diary

"Oof!" Anne gasped as her chin slammed into the stair. The rotten step under her left foot had given way, pitching her forward onto the stairs above.

"Anne, are you OK?" came a frightened whisper. Emma was three steps behind Anne, anxiously pointing the beam of her flashlight up at her older sister.

"I think so," Anne managed. "Oooh, that hurt!" She recovered her own flashlight from the place it had fallen and shone it around. The light revealed dust, cobwebs, and peeling wallpaper. The mansion was even spookier on the inside than the outside.

"Are you OK to keep going?" Emma asked. "All the clues indicated that Great Grandma Catherine's diary is somewhere in this house. And we have to find that diary."

"I know," Anne replied. Taking a deep breath, Anne made herself ignore the bruises she felt forming as a result of her fall. "OK, let's go." Carefully, she climbed the rest of the stairs.

Anne paused at the top of the staircase to wait for Emma to finish her own cautious climb. Together, the girls shone their flashlights into the gloomy hallway at the top of the stairs. To their right, a doorway gaped open.

"I guess we'll start there," Anne said, pointing to the door.

Emma nodded. "You first."

Slowly, Anne walked to the doorway and looked in. The flashlight's beam showed ancient furniture covered with sheets. More cobwebs and dust decorated the room. "I don't see anyplace where someone would hide a diary. Do you see anything, Emma?"

Silence.

Anne turned swiftly. Nobody was behind her. "Emma?" she called in a quavering voice. "Emma!" Anne's shout was greeted with silence. Anne had never felt so alone in her life.

© Pearson Education, Inc., 4

1. Reread the selection. Write one sentence to describe the setting.

_____

2. Underline the two sentences that tell the quest at the heart of this adventure.

3. Circle words that help create the excitement in the story.

Vocabulary

Directions Choose the word from the box that best matches each definition. Write the word on the line.

_____ 1. cold-blooded animals with backbones and moist skins

_____ 2. confused because something is hard to understand or solve

_____ 3. a source used for information

_____ 4. reptiles with long bodies and tails and movable eyelids

_____ 5. animals shaped like lizards but related to frogs and toads

> **Check the Words You Know**
>
> ___ **amphibians**
> ___ **crime**
> ___ **exhibit**
> ___ **lizards**
> ___ **reference**
> ___ **reptiles**
> ___ **salamanders**
> ___ **stumped**

Directions Choose the word from the box that best completes each sentence. Write the word on the line.

David raced over to the new **6.** _____ at the zoo. Nothing was there! He was baffled and **7.** _____. Had there been a **8.** _____ in which the animals were stolen? Had they escaped? He checked the sign as a **9.** _____ about the animals that should be in the new exhibit. Suddenly he noticed where all of the rattlesnakes and other **10.** _____ were hiding! The large sign had hidden them from view.

Write a Description

On a separate sheet of paper, write a description of an imaginary animal. Use as many vocabulary words as you can.

Home Activity Your child identified and used vocabulary words from *Encyclopedia Brown and the Case of the Slippery Salamander.* Read an encyclopedia article with your child. Have your child point out unfamiliar words. Work together to try to define each word by using the synonyms or antonyms around it.

© Pearson Education, Inc., 4

Contractions and Negatives

A **contraction** is a shortened form of two words. An apostrophe takes the place of one or more letters. Some contractions are formed from a pronoun and a verb: *she is = she's*. Other contractions combine a verb and the word *not: would not = wouldn't*.

Contractions with Pronouns and Verbs				Contractions with Verbs and *not*	
I am	I'm	she will	she'll	is not	isn't
he is (has)	he's	you will	you'll	are not	aren't
she is (has)	she's	we will	we'll	was not	wasn't
it is (has)	it's	they will	they'll	were not	weren't
you are	you're	I had (would)	I'd	has not	hasn't
we are	we're	he had (would)	he'd	have not	haven't
they are	they're	she had (would)	she'd	did not	didn't
I have	I've	you had (would)	you'd	does not	doesn't
you have	you've			will not	won't
we have	we've			would not	wouldn't
they have	they've			could not	couldn't
I will	I'll			should not	shouldn't
he will	he'll			cannot	can't

Directions Choose the correct contraction in ( ) to complete each sentence. Write the contraction.

1. (She'll, She's) read all the *Encyclopedia Brown* stories later. _____

2. (I'd, I'm) like to borrow a book from her. _____

3. I hear that (there, they're) all interesting. _____

4. (Its, It's) hard to believe that anyone could be that smart! _____

5. I (don't, hasn't) think I could be a detective. _____

© Pearson Education, Inc., 4

School + Home **Home Activity** Your child learned about contractions and negatives. Ask your child to show you how an apostrophe can make two words become one word. Encourage him or her to use contractions in oral sentences.

Name _____

Prefixes un-, dis-, in-

Spelling Words				
distrust	uncertain	incomplete	unlikely	unfair
discontinue	unaware	disorder	discount	indirect
unopened	disrespect	unimportant	unlisted	disrepair
inability	disapprove	unsolved	disobey	unsuspecting

Add Prefixes Write the list word that can replace the underlined words.

1. The mystery of the missing book is still <u>not solved</u>. 1. _____

2. My best friend's phone number is <u>not listed</u>. 2. _____

3. We decided to <u>not continue</u> the newspaper delivery. 3. _____

4. We <u>do not trust</u> people who do not tell the truth. 4. _____

5. It's seven o'clock, and my homework is still <u>not complete</u>. 5. _____

6. It's <u>not likely</u> that we'll see a flying elephant anytime soon. 6. _____

7. The new box of cookies is <u>not opened</u>. 7. _____

8. The puppy does not mean to <u>not obey</u>. 8. _____

9. The outcome of the contest is still <u>not certain</u>. 9. _____

Synonyms Write a list word that has the same or almost the same meaning as the clues.

10. not suspicious 10. _____

11. ignorant 11. _____

12. mess 12. _____

13. rudeness 13. _____

14. roundabout 14. _____

15. unjust 15. _____

16. insignificant 16. _____

17. not in working order 17. _____

18. money off 18. _____

19. turn down 19. _____

20. lack of skill 20. _____

© Pearson Education, Inc., 4

School + Home **Home Activity** Your child wrote words with prefixes un-, dis-, and in-. Say base words. Ask your child to add a prefix to say the list word.

Scoring Rubric: Adventure Story

	4	3	2	1
Focus/Ideas	Quest is clearly stated; plot is tightly focused on resolving the quest	Quest is well stated; plot is mostly focused on resolving the quest	Quest is not entirely clear; plot wanders away from quest	Plot has no quest or direction
Organization	Events are in sequence and lead logically to plot's climax	Events are in sequence and generally lead to the climax	Events are poorly sequenced and not logically connected to the climax	No logical sequence
Voice	Voice is lively and interesting	Voice is generally engaging	Voice is sometimes dull	Voice is flat and dull
Word Choice	Uses strong verbs and a variety of descriptive words	Uses some strong verbs and descriptive words	Few or no strong verbs; few or no descriptive words	Poor word choice
Sentences	Uses simple and compound sentences	Some varied sentence structures	Sentences are not varied	Fragments or run-on sentences
Conventions	Few or no errors; correct use of contractions and negatives	Few errors; few or no errors in use of contractions and negatives	Many errors	Many serious errors

© Pearson Education, Inc., 4

Vocabulary • Synonyms and Antonyms

- **Synonyms** are words with the same or almost the same meaning.
- **Antonyms** are words with opposite meanings.
- When you read, you may come across a word you don't know. Look for synonyms or antonyms as clues to the unknown word's meaning. Use a dictionary or thesaurus to look up any words you are unsure of.

Directions Read the following passage. Then answer the questions below.

Tamika's science fair exhibit, or display, featuring rattlesnakes was amazing. She presented a rattlesnake's skin and explained that unlike amphibians, reptiles have scales. Tamika also included pictures of the rattlesnake's diet, which included rabbits, rats, and squirrels.

Her best friend, Ty, was stumped and confused. He asked, "How can a snake eat animals that are larger than itself?" Tamika had been baffled by this herself, but now she was enlightened. She showed Ty her encyclopedia. Together, they looked at pictures of the snake's jaws expanding.

1. What does *exhibit* mean? What synonym helps you determine its meaning?

_____

2. Explain why *reptile* and *amphibian* are not antonyms.

_____

_____

3. What does *baffled* mean? What synonym helps you determine its meaning?

_____

4. What does *enlightened* mean? What antonym helps you determine its meaning?

_____

5. Use a dictionary or thesaurus to find three synonyms for the word *expanded* as it is used in this story. Then write a sentence using the word and one synonym.

_____

_____

Home Activity Your child identified synonyms and antonyms using a dictionary or thesaurus. With your child, read an article about an animal and ask your child to identify unfamiliar words. Encourage your child to figure out the meanings using context clues such as synonyms and antonyms, and use a thesaurus to look up synonyms for words whose meanings are still unclear.

© Pearson Education, Inc., 4

Name _____

Card Catalog/Library Database

Card catalogs and **library databases** provide information you need to find a book in the library. The card catalog has drawers with cards in them. The cards provide information about a book including its **author, title, subject,** and **call number.** You can search a card catalog by author, title, or subject. A library database is the online version of a card catalog.

Directions Use this card from a card catalog to answer the questions below.

J597.9 PA

Reptiles and Amphibians
Kel, Serge, 1960–

Through its descriptions and breathtaking photographs, this book provides readers a safe, up-close look at the fascinating world of crocodiles, caimans, salamanders, caecilians, and others.

Publisher: Reptile Universe Press
Pub date: c2003.
Pages: 96

ISBN: 0739842434

1. The call number for this book is in the upper left corner. What is its call number?

_____

2. The title of this book is in boldface type. What is its title?

_____

3. The author's name is underneath the title. Who is the author? When was he born?

_____

4. When was the book published? How many pages does it have?

_____

5. How would you search the card catalog to find more books on the subject of reptiles and amphibians?

_____

_____

© Pearson Education, Inc., 4

Directions Look at the search results from a library database. Then answer the questions below.

| Community Library | Contact Us | Events | Story Time | Films and Videos | Library Hours |

Online Card Catalog

Search Results for Title ▽ containing Encyclopedia Brown

5 entries found   Results page 1 of 1

Number	Title	Year	Status
1	Encyclopedia Brown and the Case of the Dead Eagles	1975	on shelf
2	Encyclopedia Brown and the Case of the Jumping Frogs	2003	checked out
3	Encyclopedia Brown and the Case of the Slippery Salamander	1999	reserved
4	Encyclopedia Brown and the Case of the Treasure Hunt	1988	on shelf
5	Encyclopedia Brown Boy Detective	1963	on shelf

Order title ▽   Reserve title 5. Encyclopedia Brown Boy Detective

6. These results are from a search for titles containing *Encyclopedia Brown*. How can you tell?

_____

7. How many entries were found for this search? How many are shown on the screen?

_____

8. How many of these books could you check out today? How can you tell?

_____

_____

9. Which book is the newest? When was it published?

_____

10. Which book is the oldest? When was it published?

_____

Home Activity Your child learned about using a card catalog and library database to locate books. Go to the library or check online for a library database. Practice finding books together using the card catalog or the library database.

© Pearson Education, Inc., 4

Prefixes *un-*, *dis-*, *in-*

Proofread a Letter Circle seven misspelled words in the letter. Write the words correctly. Add the missing punctuation mark.

Dear Mayor

It seems that you are inaware of the state of the city playground. The workers seem to have discontined their work, even though the project is still uncomplete. There is inorder everywhere. It appears that you think the needs of children are immmportant. We think it is best that you keep this unsafe place to play disopened untill everything is fixed.

Yours truly,
The Fourth-Grade Class

1. _____ 2. _____ 3. _____

4. _____ 5. _____ 6. _____

7. _____

Spelling Words

distrust
uncertain
incomplete
unlikely
unfair
discontinue
unaware
disorder
discount
indirect

unopened
disrespect
unimportant
unlisted
disrepair
inability
disapprove
unsolved
disobey
unsuspecting

Missing Words Circle the letter of the word that is spelled correctly. Write the word.

8. I love finding bargains at the _____ store.
   A. discont   B. discount   C. miscount

9. I am _____ of the exact directions to the museum.
   A. uncertan   B. incertain   C. uncertain

10. In the _____ event of a flood, go up the hill.
   A. unlikly   B. unlikey   C. unlikely

11. Why does your dog always _____ your commands?
   A. disobey   B. disobay   C. diobey

12. I have an _____ to keep a knapsack neat and in order.
   A. unability   B. inability   C. inabilty

Frequently Misspelled Words

until
into
unfair
disappear
invisible

8. _____

9. _____

10. _____

11. _____

12. _____

Home Activity Your child identified misspelled words with prefixes *un-*, *dis-*, and *in-*. Say a prefix and have your child name list words that begin with the prefix.

© Pearson Education, Inc., 4

Contractions and Negatives

Directions Read the passage. Then read each question. Circle the letter of the correct answer.

Crime Solvers

(1) Were investigating a crime. (2) It willnt be difficult to solve. (3) Shes got a kit for testing blood to help us. (4) Criminals don't have a chance against us. (5) They'll all be behind bars. (6) Im going to be a detective.

1 What change, if any, should be made in sentence 1?

   A   Change *Were* to **We're**.

   B   Change *Were* to **We**.

   C   Change *Were* to **Wear**.

   D   Make no change.

2 What change, if any, should be made in sentence 2?

   A   Change *willnt* to **want**.

   B   Change *willnt* to **wont**.

   C   Change *willnt* to **won't**.

   D   Make no change.

3 What change, if any, should be made in sentence 3?

   A   Change *Shes* to **She**.

   B   Change *Shes* to **She'**.

   C   Change *Shes* to **She's**.

   D   Make no change.

4 What change, if any, should be made in sentence 5?

   A   Change *They'll* to **The'll**.

   B   Change *They'll* to **They**.

   C   Change *They'll* to **They'l**.

   D   Make no change.

5 What change, if any, should be made in sentence 6?

   A   Change *Im* to **Iam**.

   B   Change *Im* to **I'm**.

   C   Change *Im* to **Im'**.

   D   Make no change.

© Pearson Education, Inc., 4

Home Activity Your child prepared for taking tests on contractions and negatives. Have your child write a list of contractions and negatives. Have him or her name which kind each word is.

Name _____

Contractions

Spelling Words				
don't	won't	wouldn't	there's	we're
you're	doesn't	I've	here's	wasn't
shouldn't	couldn't	where's	hadn't	aren't
they're	it's	we've	when's	haven't

Proofread Contractions Circle the list word that is spelled incorrectly.

1. The clothes havn't dried.

2. They dont' know the answer.

3. Some campers are'nt prepared.

4. Your halfway up the mountain.

5. That noise wasnot' familiar.

6. Campers shuldn't wander off.

7. Were hoping to reach the top.

8. Tomorrow their going home.

9. Whens breakfast going to be served?

10. Its way too hot to climb.

Proofread Contractions The underlined word in each sentence is incorrect. Write the corrected list word.

11. They <u>had'nt</u> put out the fire.

12. <u>Her's</u> a bucket for water.

13. Max <u>culdn't</u> make the cocoa.

14. This stew <u>duzn't</u> look done.

15. <u>Theirs</u> a strong breeze off the lake.

16. The trail <u>wont</u> be open after a storm.

17. The wet wood <u>would'nt</u> catch fire.

18. After <u>we'ave</u> set up, we can rest.

19. <u>Ive</u> had a lot of fun on this trip.

20. <u>Were's</u> my backpack?

11. _____

12. _____

13. _____

14. _____

15. _____

16. _____

17. _____

18. _____

19. _____

20. _____

© Pearson Education, Inc., 4

Home Activity Your child learned to spell contractions. Read each sentence on this page and have your child spell the contraction in it correctly.

Singular and Plural Pronouns

Directions Underline the pronoun in the sentence if it is a singular pronoun. Circle the pronoun if it is a plural pronoun.

1. Gabby was frightened that a garbage monster would eat her.

2. They knew James Frisco was a ~~bad~~ mad scientist.

3. Nell dropped what she was doing and reported for duty.

4. You are not going to take the lid off the can, are you?

5. They observed the garbage can and wrote down notes about it.

6. Doyle and Nell enjoyed themselves when they were solving mysteries.

Directions Replace each underlined noun or noun phrase with one of the pronouns in the box. Write the new sentence and underline the pronoun you chose.

> he   him   his   her   they   she   we

7. Drake and Nell removed the gloves Drake and Nell were wearing.

   _____

   _____

8. Drake muttered as Drake recorded his findings in Drake's notebook.

   _____

   _____

9. Nell used Nell's magnifying glass.

   _____

   _____

10. What does my dad think you and I are going to do?

    _____

    _____

© Pearson Education, Inc., 4

Final Syllable Patterns

Spelling Words				
chicken	natural	several	paddle	oval
eleven	together	summer	animal	frighten
brother	calendar	threaten	pitcher	mumble
jungle	needle	caterpillar	shelter	deliver

Analogies Write the list word that best completes the comparison.

1. Horse is to foal as _____ is to chick.   1. _____
2. Help is to hurt as protect is to _____.   2. _____
3. Bike is to pedal as canoe is to _____.   3. _____
4. Bison is to prairie as monkey is to _____.   4. _____
5. One is to two as ten is to _____.   5. _____
6. Girl is to boy as sister is to _____.   6. _____
7. Teddy bear is to bear as fake is to _____.   7. _____
8. Hot is to cold as _____ is to winter.   8. _____
9. Square is to rectangle as circle is to _____.   9. _____
10. Delight is to please as scare is to _____.   10. _____

Definitions Write the list word that fits the definition.

11. a few; more than one   11. _____
12. joined; not separate   12. _____
13. to drop off an object at some location   13. _____
14. a chart showing days in a year   14. _____
15. a structure that protects from rain and snow   15. _____
16. an insect that becomes a butterfly   16. _____
17. a living being that is not a plant   17. _____
18. to speak in a low, unclear way   18. _____
19. a container from which a liquid is poured   19. _____
20. a thin metal rod with a hole in one end   20. _____

© Pearson Education, Inc., 4

Home Activity Your child spelled words that end with *le, al, en, ar,* and *er.* Use each list word in a sentence and have your child spell it aloud.

Name _____

Kinds of Pronouns

Directions Write each subject pronoun.

1. They played near us for several minutes. _____

2. First, we watched them high in the air. _____

3. Then, I saw a mother dolphin with a baby. _____

4. She was swimming very close by. _____

Directions Write each object pronoun.

5. The baby was right behind her. _____

6. You should have seen them. _____

7. I will go back with you next week. _____

8. It will be fun for us. _____

Directions Write each reflexive pronoun. Say them aloud.

9. Scientists, themselves, wonder how
   dolphins "talk." _____

10. I tried to teach myself how to imitate their clicks
    and whistles. _____

11. Professor James made a recording of them herself. _____

12. She sounds as good at dolphin language as the
    dolphins themselves. _____

Directions Write each demonstrative pronoun. Say them aloud.

13. Please teach me to do that. _____

14. Use these. _____

15. How can I find out more about this? _____

16. Would you be able to swim with these? _____

© Pearson Education, Inc., 4

Consonant Digraph /sh/

Spelling Words				
nation	special	lotion	mansion	precious
creation	vacation	tension	especially	motion
tradition	gracious	extension	addition	caution
official	solution	suspension	politician	portion

Word Meanings Write the list word that fits the definition.

1. something that is made   1. _____

2. cream for your skin   2. _____

3. person who runs for office   3. _____

4. important or valuable   4. _____

5. a segment or piece of something   5. _____

6. answer or resolution   6. _____

7. a part that makes something longer or larger   7. _____

8. representative or high-ranking person   8. _____

9. tightness or strain   9. _____

10. extraordinary or unusual   10. _____

11. a routine or ritual   11. _____

12. holiday or break from work   12. _____

Analogies Write the list word that best completes the comparison.

13. Village is to town as _____ is to country.   13. _____

14. Largely is to greatly as particularly is to _____.   14. _____

15. Unfriendly is to unsociable as friendly is to _____.   15. _____

16. Hurry is to rush as delay is to _____.   16. _____

17. Car is to limousine as house is to _____.   17. _____

18. Plus is to minus as _____ is to subtraction.   18. _____

19. Act is to action as move is to _____.   19. _____

20. Haste is to careless as _____ is to careful.   20. _____

© Pearson Education, Inc., 4

Home Activity Your child learned words with the sound /sh/. Have your child identify list words that give him or her trouble. Have a joke-writing contest using these words.

Pronouns and Antecedents

Directions Write the letter of the pronoun next to the noun or noun phrase that could be its antecedent.

_____ **1.** American plans   **A** we

_____ **2.** code talker   **B** they

_____ **3.** code   **C** it

_____ **4.** a code talker and I   **D** he

Directions Write a pronoun to replace each underlined noun or noun phrase.

5. <u>Amy, Michael, and I</u> went to Amy's house. _____

6. Amy's grandpa is Navajo, and we talked to <u>Amy's grandpa</u>. _____

7. Amy is proud of her grandpa, and <u>Amy</u> is interested in his stories. _____

8. He told <u>Amy, Michael, and me</u> about Navajo code talkers. _____

9. Japanese forces wanted to know American plans, so <u>Japanese forces</u> had code breakers. _____

10. A civilian thought of a code and told leaders about <u>the code</u>. _____

11. Navajo is a difficult language, so <u>Navajo</u> made a good code. _____

12. Roy Hawthorne was a Navajo, and <u>Hawthorne</u> joined the Marines. _____

13. <u>Roy Hawthorne and Chester Nez</u> helped devise the Navajo code. _____

14. The code talkers were honored, and a film was made about <u>the code talkers</u>. _____

Directions Write each sentence. Replace the underlined noun or noun phrase with the correct pronoun.

15. Amy likes history, and World War II especially interests <u>Amy</u>.

_____

16. Germany and Japan are allies now, but <u>those nations</u> were our enemies then.

_____

17. Navajo code talkers helped win the war, and our leaders thanked <u>the Navajo code talkers</u>.

_____

© Pearson Education, Inc., 4

Consonants /j/, /ks/, and /kw/

Spelling Words				
village	except	explain	quick	charge
bridge	knowledge	question	equal	queen
excited	expect	Texas	fudge	excellent
exercise	quart	liquid	quilt	expert

Word Meanings Write the list word that fits the definition.

1. royal female ruler of a country

2. one fourth of a gallon

3. something asked that needs an answer

4. having the same amount, size, elements

5. bed covering patterned from cloth pieces

6. rich chocolate candy

7. small town in the country

8. structure built over water

9. done in a short time

10. matter that pours

11. to ask for as a price

12. what a person knows or understands

1. _____

2. _____

3. _____

4. _____

5. _____

6. _____

7. _____

8. _____

9. _____

10. _____

11. _____

12. _____

The ex's Have It Write the list words with *ex* to complete each sentence.

13. That is an _____ idea you had.

14. Everyone will go _____ Harry. He will stay here.

15. The class was _____ to see a deer in the playground.

16. You can skate or swim to get _____.

17. Your teachers _____ you to do your best.

18. Mr. Washington is an _____ on snakes.

19. Bree asked the teacher to _____ how bees fly.

20. The largest southern state is _____.

13. _____

14. _____

15. _____

16. _____

17. _____

18. _____

19. _____

20. _____

Home Activity Your child learned words with consonants /j/, /ks/, and /kw/. Have your child identify list words that give him or her trouble. Have a joke-writing contest using these words.

© Pearson Education, Inc., 4

Possessive Pronouns

Directions Write the possessive pronoun in ( ) that correctly completes each sentence.

1. We have learned some interesting facts in (our, ours) study of ancient Egypt.

   _____

2. Bread was the Egyptians' staple food, and goat milk was one of (theirs, their) drinks.

   _____

3. A boy would shave (its, his) hair, except for one braid. _____

4. A girl might wear (her, hers) in a pigtail.   _____

5. The sun was bright, and people wore eye makeup to guard against (their, its) rays.

   _____

6. What have you learned from (your, yours) reading?   _____

Directions Write a possessive pronoun to replace the underlined word or phrase.

7. Amy and José dressed as ancient Egyptians for <u>Amy and José's</u> presentation.

   _____

8. Amy wore shiny copper anklets on <u>Amy's</u> legs. _____

9. José looked funny in <u>José's</u> short skirt!   _____

10. They served us Egyptian food, which was better than <u>this writer's</u> lunch.

    _____

11. Rina and I are both making model pyramids for <u>Rina's and my</u> projects.

    _____

12. My pyramid is smaller than <u>Rina's</u>.   _____

13. Rina's pyramid is taller than <u>my pyramid</u>.   _____

14. A pyramid has a wide base, and <u>a pyramid's</u> top comes to a point.

    _____

© Pearson Education, Inc., 4

Name _____

Prefixes *un-, dis-, in-*

Spelling Words

distrust	uncertain	incomplete	unlikely	unfair
discontinue	unaware	disorder	discount	indirect
unopened	disrespect	unimportant	unlisted	disrepair
inability	disapprove	unsolved	disobey	unsuspecting

Missing Words Write a list word with *un-* to complete each sentence.

1. It is _____ to snow in July.
2. There are _____ cans of food in the pantry.
3. It would be _____ to give everyone a trophy.
4. Marie was _____ which coat to buy.
5. Our family phone number is _____.
6. The star detective leaves no case _____.
7. An _____ homeowner was about to be robbed.
8. The robber was _____ that the police lay in wait.
9. No detail was _____ to the police.

1. _____
2. _____
3. _____
4. _____
5. _____
6. _____
7. _____
8. _____
9. _____

Antonyms Write a *dis-* list word that means the opposite, or nearly the opposite, of each word or phrase.

10. shipshape _____
11. carry on _____
12. do what you're told _____
13. have faith in _____
14. overcharge _____
15. admiration _____
16. neatness _____
17. give your support _____

Word Scramble Unscramble the list words and write the letters on the lines.

18. blainiiyt _____
19. moctleepin _____
20. nictreid _____

© Pearson Education, Inc., 4

Home Activity Your child learned words with prefixes *un-*, *dis*, and *in*. Write each word. Have your child divide it between the prefix and the base word.

Contractions and Negatives

Directions Write the correct contraction in ( ) to complete each sentence.

1. (We've, We'll) been reading about the famous Sherlock Holmes. _____

2. He (aren't, wasn't) a real person, but many people think he was. _____

3. If Holmes (couldn't, doesn't) solve a case, no one could. _____

4. (I'll, I've) heard about his partner, Dr. Watson. _____

5. Together (you'd, they'd) solve crimes all over England. _____

6. The police (won't, weren't) as effective as Holmes and Watson. _____

Directions Find two words in each sentence that can be written as a contraction. Write the sentence using the contraction.

7. I have always wanted to be a detective.

_____

8. It is interesting and challenging work.

_____

9. Most detectives are not like Sherlock Holmes.

_____

10. Solving crimes is not easy to do.

_____

11. I will study law enforcement.

_____

12. You will not get a good job without an education.

_____

© Pearson Education, Inc., 4

Story Chart

Directions Fill in the graphic organizer with information about your story.

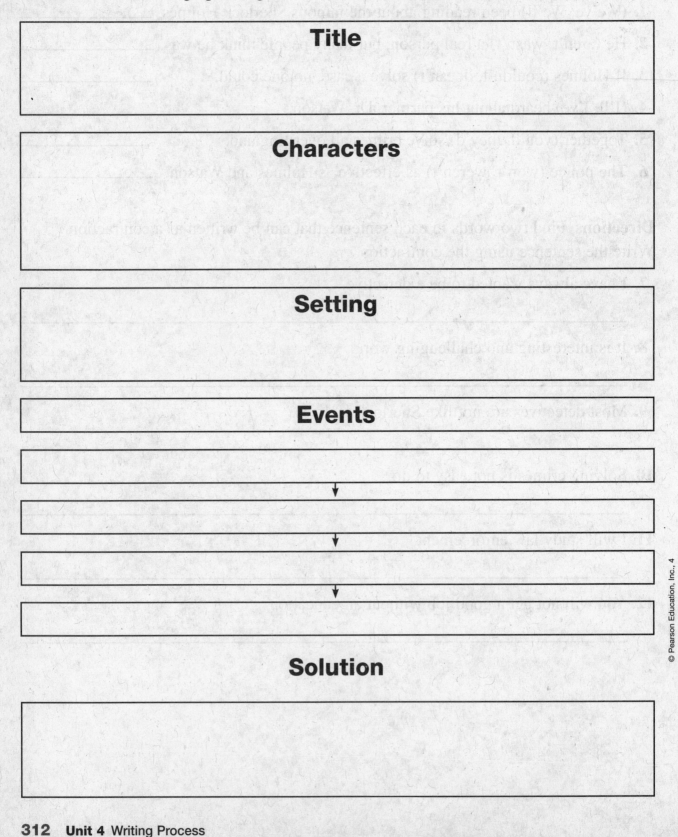

Title

Characters

Setting

Events

↓

↓

↓

Solution

© Pearson Education, Inc., 4

Good Beginnings

Make the beginning sentence of your story grab your readers' attention. Below are some different ways to write the beginning of a story.

Directions Write an attention-grabbing opening sentence (based on your characters, setting, and plot) using each idea. You can use one of the sentences you write to begin your story.

1. Ask a question. (What was that strange sound?)

_____

2. Use an exclamation. (Eek! I heard a strange sound.)

_____

3. Use a sound word. (Creeeaaak! The hair on the back of my neck stood up when I heard that strange sound.)

_____

4. Hint at the ending. (I had never heard a sound like that before, but who knew that I would hear it many times again.)

_____

5. Use alliteration. (The strange scraping sounded again, and I shivered.)

_____

6. Make a list. (Pounding heart, gasping breath, dropping stomach. Yes, I had all the signs of fear.)

_____

7. Set the scene. (The clouds blocked the moon's light. It was so dark I could not see where I was walking. Somewhere to my left I heard a strange scraping sound.)

_____

© Pearson Education, Inc., 4

Combining Sentences

When you write, you can combine short simple sentences to make compound or complex sentences. A compound sentence has two independent clauses—groups of words that can stand alone as sentences—joined by a word such as *and, but, or, nor, yet,* and *so.* A complex sentence has one independent clause and one dependent clause—a group of words that cannot stand alone as a sentence—joined by a word such as *if, when, because, although, since,* or *as.* Remember, the two sentences you combine must make sense together.

Directions Use the word in ( ) to combine the two sentences. Remember to use a comma when necessary.

1. I go on a trip. I like to travel by plane. (when)

_____

_____

2. Some people travel by train. Some people travel by car. (and)

_____

_____

3. Those people may be afraid to fly. Flying does not frighten me. (but)

_____

_____

4. I want to go to South America. I have relatives there. (because)

_____

_____

5. I may go this summer. I may wait until next fall. (or)

_____

_____

© Pearson Education, Inc., 4

Peer and Teacher Conferencing Story

Directions After exchanging drafts, read your partner's story. Refer to the Revising Checklist as you make notes about your partner's story. Write your comments or questions on the lines. Offer compliments as well as suggestions for revisions. Take turns talking about each other's draft using your notes. Give your partner your notes.

Revising Checklist

Focus/Ideas

☐ Is the story focused on one incident or event?

☐ Does the plot of the story include a problem and a solution?

Organization

☐ Does the story have a clear beginning, middle, and end?

☐ Does the beginning sentence grab the reader's attention?

Voice

☐ Does the narrator or main character have a distinct voice?

Word Choice

☐ Have vivid details been used to involve the reader in the story?

☐ Have time-order words been used to show the sequence of events?

Sentences

☐ Are there both simple and compound sentences? Have short, choppy sentences been combined to make compound or complex sentences?

Things I Thought Were Good _____

_____

_____

Things I Thought Could Be Improved _____

_____

_____

Teacher's Comments _____

_____

© Pearson Education, Inc., 4

Author's Purpose

- The **author's purpose** is the reason the author has for writing.
- An author may write to persuade, to inform, to entertain, or to express ideas or feelings.

Directions Read the following passage.

To learn more about people who respond in emergencies, please read the following passage.

The police and fire departments have teams of professionals who are trained to respond to emergencies. These local teams are often the first to arrive at the scene of an accident, a crisis, or a crime.

Depending on the size or location of an accident, the state police or fire marshals may also respond. For major disasters, such as flooding or plane crashes, the federal government gets involved. Its teams include the National Transportation Safety Board, the Federal Emergency Management Agency, and the Federal Bureau of Investigation.

Directions Answer the questions below.

1. For what purpose did the author write this passage?

_____

2. How do you know?

_____

3. What information does the author provide you with?

_____

4. Why did the author not use "I" in the passage?

_____

5. What words might the author have used to express his or her opinion?

_____

Home Activity Your child analyzed the author's purpose in a nonfiction passage. With your child, read aloud an article or a cartoon in a newspaper or magazine. Discuss the author's purpose.

© Pearson Education, Inc., 4

Writing • Fantasy

Key Features of Fantasy

• characters do things they cannot do in the real world

• describes events that couldn't happen in the real world

• may have a setting that does not exist in the real world

• may be written to seem almost real

• may have a tone of happiness, nostalgia, or danger

Hurricane Hunt

Roberto liked building models. He had just finished his latest model, a four-engine prop plane. On a warm summer afternoon, he admired its sleek, silver wings as it sat on the picnic table in his backyard. Suddenly, an icy wind blew across the table, knocking the plane to the ground. As it hit the grass, the model began to grow larger and larger. It became as large as a real airplane!

"Jump in and take off. There's a gigantic hurricane nearby and you have to investigate the eye!" a voice coming from the plane's radio boomed out.

Roberto jumped into the cockpit. As he settled into the pilot's seat, the plane took off. Roberto noticed that there was no equipment aboard. How would he locate the hurricane, and how would he investigate it if he found it?

Once again, the radio spouted directions. "Use your cell phone. Press 1 for radar. Press 2 for wind speed. Press 3 for wind direction. Press 4 to record information. Press 5 to transmit information to the Hurricane Center."

Roberto doubted his cell phone could do these things. But he followed the directions anyway. He pressed 1. The plane flew directly toward the hurricane's eye. Roberto punched the numbers to display the wind's speed and its direction. He pressed 4 to record the data and 5 to send it to the Hurricane Center.

The radio crackled on, "Job well done! Now you can head home."

With that, the plane changed direction. When it landed in Roberto's backyard, he hopped out. There on the picnic table stood his model. Astonished, Roberto turned back to look at the life-size plane that had taken him on his amazing adventure. It was nowhere to be seen.

© Pearson Education, Inc., 4

1. Reread the selection. Why is it a fantasy?

_____

_____

2. Underline the elements in the story that make it a fantasy.

Vocabulary

Directions Choose the word from the box that best matches each definition. Write the word on the line.

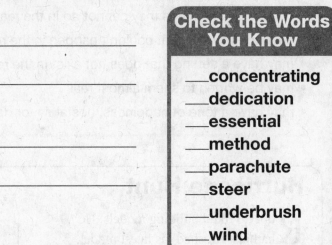

Check the Words You Know

___ concentrating
___ dedication
___ essential
___ method
___ parachute
___ steer
___ underbrush
___ wind

1. devotion, loyalty _____

2. air moving due to _____
   changing pressure

3. focusing mental attention _____

4. device shaped like _____
   an umbrella

5. control the direction of _____

Directions Choose words from the box that best replace the underlined words. Write the words on the lines.

_____ 6. The firefighters knew that the <u>bushes and small trees</u> would provide fuel to the fire that was already out of control.

_____ 7. The skydiver was thankful that the class knew the <u>way</u> to release the parachute with the push of one button.

_____ 8. Physical fitness is <u>necessary</u> to the work of fighting fires.

Write a Friendly Letter

Pretend that you are spending the summer fighting wildfires in Montana. On a separate sheet of paper, write a letter to your family describing the dangers of the work. Include words from the vocabulary list and details about fighting wildfires, training, and equipment. Use as many vocabulary words as you can.

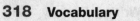

Home Activity Your child identified and used vocabulary words from the story *Smokejumpers: Life Fighting Fires*. With your child, write a short newspaper article about an imagined local firefighter who has been awarded a medal for bravery. Use as many vocabulary words as you can.

© Pearson Education, Inc., 4

Name _____

Adjectives and Articles

An **adjective** is a word that describes a noun or pronoun. An adjective usually comes before the word it describes, but it can also follow the noun or pronoun. Many adjectives answer the question *What kind?* They describe color, shape, size, sound, taste, touch, or smell. Other adjectives answer the question *How many?* or *Which one?*

What Kind?   A <u>new</u> fire was reported yesterday. It is <u>huge</u>.
How Many?   There were <u>three</u> forest fires last month.
Which One?   <u>That</u> fire was a big one.

A, an, and *the* are special adjectives called **articles.** *A* and *an* are used only with singular nouns. Use *a* before words that begin with a consonant sound. Use *an* before words that begin with a vowel sound or a silent *h. The* is used with both singular and plural nouns.

<u>A</u> fire started in <u>an</u> area nearby. <u>The</u> fire raged, and <u>the</u> trees burned.

- Proper adjectives are formed from proper nouns.

    Proper Nouns   Japan, Mexico
    Proper Adjectives   Japanese, Mexican

- Sometimes you can combine two sentences with adjectives.
  The plane took off. The plane was full. The full plane took off.

Directions Underline each adjective and circle each article.

1. Fighting fires is a difficult job.

2. A smokejumper uses the right equipment.

3. An orange jumpsuit can be seen easily.

Directions Decide what kind of question each underlined adjective answers. Write *What kind? How many?* or *Which one?*

4. The men saw the <u>smoky</u> air. _____

5. <u>Five</u> firefighters battled the blaze. _____

6. <u>This</u> fire was not too large. _____

School + Home **Home Activity** Your child learned about adjectives and articles. Ask your child to show you how adjectives answer the questions *What kind? How many?* and *Which one?*

© Pearson Education, Inc., 4

Multisyllabic Words

Antonyms Write a list word that has the opposite
or almost the opposite meaning.

1. pleasant   1. _____

2. joyfully   2. _____

3. inattentively   3. _____

4. unfairness   4. _____

5. certain   5. _____

6. unexceptionally 6. _____

Synonyms Write the list word that has the same or almost
the same meaning.

7. statement   7. _____

8. called the wrong number 8. _____

9. career's end   9. _____

10. relocation   10. _____

Definitions Replace the underlined words with list words that
mean the same thing.

11. You can call a number to listen to a <u>taped</u> message that   11. _____
    tells the movie schedule.

12. The <u>food</u> committee served cookies and lemonade.   12. _____

13. We sang the silly song <u>cheerfully</u>.   13. _____

14. The <u>naval cadet</u> mopped the deck.   14. _____

15. The figures in the painting are blurry and <u>vague</u>.   15. _____

16. My <u>response</u> to eating tomatoes is hives and puffy eyes.   16. _____

17. I <u>mistakenly</u> gave credit to the wrong person.   17. _____

18. Fortunately, the glass I dropped is <u>indestructible</u>!   18. _____

19. I returned the shoes, and I'm waiting for my <u>refund</u> check. 19. _____

20. Our <u>naughty</u> dog failed at puppy training school!   20. _____

Spelling Words
reaction
prerecorded
incorrectly
incredibly
disobedient
disagreeable
refreshment
unbreakable
declaration
retirement
misdialed
undefined
unhappily
watchfully
gleefully
sportsmanship
repayment
questionable
displacement
midshipman

© Pearson Education, Inc., 4

School + Home **Home Activity** Your child wrote multisyllabic words. Have your child spell the list words syllable by
syllable.

Story Sequence B

Title

Characters

Setting

Events
_____
_____
_____
_____
_____
_____
_____
_____

© Pearson Education, Inc., 4

Vocabulary • Homographs

- **Homographs** are words that are spelled the same but have different meanings and sometimes different pronunciations. *Steer* as a verb means "to guide the course of"; as a noun it means "a young cow."

  Wind as a verb means "to move this way and that"; as a noun it is "the air in motion."

- Use context clues, words and phrases near the homograph, to help you figure out the meaning of homographs.

Directions Read the following passage. Then answer the questions below.

The new Museum of Wildfire Prevention has exhibits that show how firefighting has evolved over the years. The first firefighter in the area was Byron Blick, back in 1885. At the first sign of smoke, he would hitch a steer or two up to a wagon. The big bulls would haul water to the edge of the fire so Byron could soak nearby grass and underbrush to prevent flames from spreading.

Nowadays, emergency workers are concentrating much of their effort on fire prevention. Hoping to harness the public support for the museum, firefighters are directing and using that enthusiasm toward programs focused on awareness of the human causes of wildfires. Officials know that the excitement generated by the museum will eventually wind down. For the safety of the public and the forests, the people's energy level for prevention has to be kept high, to keep fires from starting in the first place.

1. What does the word *steer* mean in the passage? How do you know?

_____

2. What does the word *concentrating* mean in this passage? How did you find out?

_____

3. What clue words tell you that *harness* means "to gather up and control"?

_____

4. What clue words tell you that the phrase, *wind down*, means "to slowly lose power"?

_____

Home Activity Your child identified the meanings of homographs by using context clues. Make a list of all the homographs you can think of. After each word, draw a picture that shows the different meanings of each word.

© Pearson Education, Inc., 4

Parts of a Book

- Learning the **parts of a book** helps you locate information. At the front of a book, the **title page** gives its title, author, and publisher. Then the **copyright page** tells the year a book was published. Finally, the **table of contents** lists titles and page numbers of chapters and sections. At the back of a book, an **appendix** contains graphs and charts. A **bibliography** lists books that an author used to research or write his or her own book. An **index** lists the page numbers where important words or ideas can be found. A **glossary** gives definitions of important words.

- A **chapter title** is the name of a chapter. A **section heading** is the name of a section within a chapter. **Captions** explain graphic sources and usually appear or below them. Numbered **footnotes** appear at the bottom of pages or at the back of a book. They provide additional information about a subject.

Directions Study the table of contents for the book *Lessons of the Spanish Flu* below.

Table of Contents

© Pearson Education, Inc., 4

Name _____

Directions Use the table of contents to answer the questions below.

1. Would you find the title page of this book before or after the table of contents?

   _____

2. The words in bold print are examples of which part of a book?

   _____

3. "The Black Death" is an example of what part of a book?

   _____

4. On what page can you begin to read about the connection between World War I and influenza?

   _____

5. Where in this book might you find a definition for the word *contagious*?

   _____

6. Given the topic of this book, what might you expect to find in the appendix?

   _____

7. Would this be a good book to use for a report on World War I? Why or why not?

   _____

8. If you wanted to read about prevention of the flu, in which chapter might you look?

   _____

9. How would it help you to study this table of contents before reading this book?

   _____

   _____

10. If you wanted to know if this book was more up-to-date than another book on infectious diseases, which part of the book would you consult?

   _____

   _____

Home Activity Your child learned about parts of a book and answered questions about how to use various parts. Together, open a reference book to any page. Take note of the section headings, graphic sources, and any captions. Name as many parts of the book you can find on several different pages.

© Pearson Education, Inc., 4

Multisyllabic Words

Proofread an Anecdote Read Amy's story. Circle six misspelled words. Write the words correctly. Circle a punctuation mistake and write the sentence correctly.

Spelling Words

reaction
prerecorded
incorrectly
incredibly
disobedient
disagreeable
refreshment
unbreakable
declaration
retirement

misdialed
undefined
unhappily
watchfully
gleefully
sportsmanship
repayment
questionable
displacement
midshipman

An Awful Day

My cousin was coming for a visit? I decided to order a pizza. I misdiled the number and got a precorded message from an insurance company. Then I dialed incorectly again! Finally, I placed my order. When my cousin saw the pizza, she made a startling declaration. She said she never eats pizza because she gets an allergic raction from tomatoes. We had an incredably awful dinner. Im going to go back to bed!

1. _____   2. _____   3. _____

4. _____   5. _____   6. _____

7. _____

Proofread Words Circle the letter of the word that is spelled correctly. Write the word.

Frequently Misspelled Words

I
I'm
off

8. My cat waited _____ as I prepared her meal.
   A. wachfully   B. watchfily   C. watchfully

9. Olympic athletes are expected to practice good _____.
   A. sportsmanship   B. sportsmenship   C. sportmanship

10. Adding ice cubes causes _____ of the liquid in the glass.
    A. displacmnt   B. displacement   C. displacemant

11. A villain's motives are always _____.
    A. questonable   B. questinible   C. questionable

12. His _____ behavior is usually punished.
    A. disobedient   B. disobediant   C. disobedint

8. _____

9. _____

10. _____

11. _____

12. _____

School + Home **Home Activity** Your child identified misspelled multisyllabic words. Have your child draw vertical lines to divide the list words into syllables.

© Pearson Education, Inc., 4

Adjectives and Articles

Directions Read the passage. Then read each question. Circle the letter of the correct answer.

Wildfire

  (1) An wildfire was far from the road. (2) Seven smokejumpers flew to the area. (3) The saw black smoke. (4) Some beautiful trees were burning. (5) Firefighters made many jumps into these area. (6) They wore white jumpsuits and carried useful equipment. (7) They pumped water on the fire.

1 What change, if any, should be made in sentence 1?

 A Change *An* to **These.**

 B Change *An* to **That.**

 C Change *An* to **Terrible.**

 D Make no change.

2 What change, if any, should be made in sentence 2?

 A Change *the* to **there.**

 B Change *the* to **these.**

 C Change *the* to **those.**

 D Make no change.

3 What change, if any, should be made in sentence 3?

 A Change *The* to **That.**

 B Change *The* to **This.**

 C Change *The* to **They.**

 D Make no change.

4 What change, if any, should be made in sentence 4?

 A Change been *Some* to **That.**

 B Change *Some* to **This**

 C Change the *Some* to **They.**

 D Make no change.

5 What change, if any, should be made in sentence 5?

 A Change *these* to **this.**

 B Change *these* to **those.**

 C Change *these* to **there.**

 D Make no change.

© Pearson Education, Inc., 4

Home Activity Your child prepared for taking tests on adjectives and articles. Have your child write a list of five adjectives and the words *a, an,* and *the.* Say each word on the list and ask your child to compose a paragraph using an adjective and an article in each sentence.

Compare and Contrast

- To **compare and contrast** means to tell how two or more things are alike and different.
- Clue words such as *like* and *as* can show similarities. Clue words such as *however* and *instead* can show differences.

Directions Read the following passage. Then complete the diagram below.

The ancient Greek and Roman cultures seem very similar on the surface. For instance, in both cultures, the people lived in areas with warm climates and wore similar clothing. Both societies also produced great poets and artists. However, they do have some major differences.

Greece was a series of small city-states. Rome, on the other hand, was a huge empire, ruled by an emperor. Greek buildings and Roman buildings were both grand, but Rome's were built using more advanced methods.

Greek and Roman Cultures	
Similarities	**Differences**
1.	3.
2.	4.

5. What did you visualize when you read the passage?

_____

_____

Home Activity Your child read a short passage and used a graphic organizer to compare and contrast two cultures. Have your child compare and contrast two people you both know well. Ask your child to be specific in naming their similarities and differences.

© Pearson Education, Inc., 4

Writing • Legends

Key Features of Legends

- may be based on historical characters or events
- invents or exaggerates the great deeds of a hero
- uses details to describe the fictional traits of the hero
- is often part fact and part fiction

The Legend of Pecos Bill and the Mountain Lion

As a young boy, Pecos Bill lived in Texas. When a neighbor moved in fifty miles away, his folks decided it was getting way too crowded. They hitched their cow and mule to their covered wagon and headed west. Bill, who was four, sat in the back of the wagon.

Crossing the Pecos River, the wagon's rear wheel hit a hole. Bill was thrown into the river. He shouted excitedly, "Wait for me!" but no one heard his cry. When his mom discovered he was missing, the family hastily turned back but, sadly, couldn't find him.

An old grandfather coyote found Bill and brought him up. Bill learned to talk to the coyotes. As he grew older, he ran so speedily that he could outrun an antelope. He grew so strong that he could catch a buffalo.

One day, many years later, Bill's brother Chuck came riding by. Chuck recognized Bill at once. Although Bill insisted he was a coyote, Chuck convinced him they were brothers. He persuaded Bill to journey with him to the ranch where Chuck was a cowboy.

Chuck suggested that Bill ride on the back of his pony, but Bill refused. Instead, he jumped on a snake sunning lazily in the grass and rode it until they met a mountain lion.

The lion jumped at Bill, but he fought back, vigorously pulling the lion's hair. After several hours, the lion begged Bill to stop. "Very well," said Bill. "But you must let me ride you like a pony." The lion agreed. Using the snake as a whip, Bill continued on his way.

At sunrise, several days later, Chuck and Bill rode up to the ranch. A man seven feet tall wearing a cowboy hat greeted them. He took one look at Bill and said, "I've been the boss of this ranch for many years. But you're boss from now on. Anyone who can ride a mountain lion and use a snake for a whip can be boss here for as long as he lives!"

1. What exaggerated deeds of Pecos Bill are included in the legend?

_____

_____

2. Circle a part of the story that may be based on fact.

© Pearson Education, Inc., 4

Vocabulary

Directions Choose the word from the box that best matches each definition. Write the word on the line.

_____ 1. a violent, rushing stream of water

_____ 2. magnificent; splendid

_____ 3. formed into flat, level land with steep sides

_____ 4. what is left after a building has fallen to pieces

_____ 5. an eager desire to know or learn

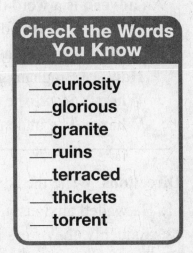

Check the Words You Know

___curiosity
___glorious
___granite
___ruins
___terraced
___thickets
___torrent

Directions Choose the word from the box that best completes each sentence. Write the word on the line shown to the left.

_____ 6. The ___ walls of the cave were cool to the touch.

_____ 7. The carvings were covered by overgrown ___ of berry bushes.

_____ 8. The ___ hill was planted with crops.

_____ 9. The archaeologists were thrilled to discover the ___ of an ancient city.

_____ 10. The ___ sunshine made the lake sparkle.

Write a Description

Pretend you are an archaeologist who has just discovered some ancient ruins. Write a description about what you have found. Use as many vocabulary words as you can.

Home Activity Your child identified and used vocabulary words from *Lost City: The Discovery of Machu Picchu*. With your child, make up a story about an ancient civilization. Use the vocabulary words from the selection.

© Pearson Education, Inc., 4

Name _____

Adverbs

An **adverb** is a word that tells how, when, or where something happens. Adverbs tell about verbs. An adverb can appear before or after a verb. Many adverbs that tell how something is done end in *-ly*.

How   Bingham gazed <u>thoughtfully</u>. He <u>repeatedly</u> asked about ruins.
When   <u>Slowly</u> he saw the city's outline. Travelers <u>seldom</u> stopped there.
Where   The mule train stopped <u>nearby</u>. The sun shone <u>overhead</u>.

Directions Write the adverb in each sentence.

1. He waited anxiously at the canteen.   _____
2. Suddenly, they were in the jungle.   _____
3. They traveled down the slippery bank.   _____
4. The river raged below.   _____
5. Finally, they reached the top of the mountain.   _____

Directions Write *how* if the underlined adverb tells how an action happens. Write *when* if it tells when an action happens. Write *where* if it tells where an action happens.

6. <u>Above</u> them was a snow-covered mountaintop.   _____
7. The boy <u>cheerfully</u> urged them forward.   _____
8. He looked <u>closer</u>.   _____
9. Bingham left the guide <u>behind</u>.   _____
10. It looked as though it had been cleared <u>recently</u>.   _____
11. There was more jungle <u>beyond</u> where they stood.   _____
12. <u>Wearily</u>, he walked through the jungle.   _____
13. <u>Immediately</u>, he took a picture of the boy.   _____
14. They <u>gently</u> pushed the vines out of the way.   _____
15. Bingham <u>honestly</u> thought he had found Vilcapampa.   _____

© Pearson Education, Inc., 4

Home Activity Your child learned about adverbs. Encourage your child to tell you about his or her day using adverbs telling *how, when,* or *where* things happened. Ask your child to identify the adverbs he or she used.

Words with Double Consonants

Spelling Words				
tomorrow	borrow	different	rabbit	matter
written	bottle	ridden	odd	bubble
offer	suffer	slippers	grasshopper	worry
current	lettuce	saddle	shudder	hobby

Word Groups Write the list word that best completes each word group.

1. yesterday, today, ___

2. raccoon, rat, ___

3. shake, tremble, ___

4. leafy, salad, ___

5. can, container, ___

6. give, present, ___

7. horse, stirrups, ___

8. etched, typed, ___

9. ladybug, butterfly, ___

10. shoes, sandals, ___

1. _____

2. _____

3. _____

4. _____

5. _____

6. _____

7. _____

8. _____

9. _____

10. _____

Missing Words Complete each sentence by writing a list word.

11. Please don't ____ about the spilled milk.

12. May I ____ your extra raincoat?

13. My cat was behaving in a rather ____ manner.

14. Do you have the ____ issue of this magazine?

15. Every person is ____ in his or her own way.

16. Building model cars is my grandfather's new ____.

17. My father continues to ____ with the flu.

18. Now we can get down to the heart of the ____.

19. I have never ____ such a tall horse.

20. My friends like to see who can blow the biggest ____.

11. _____

12. _____

13. _____

14. _____

15. _____

16. _____

17. _____

18. _____

19. _____

20. _____

Home Activity Your child wrote words with double consonants. Have your child explain how double consonants stand for one sound.

© Pearson Education, Inc., 4

Story Sequence B

Title

Characters

Setting

Events

© Pearson Education, Inc., 4

Vocabulary • Greek and Latin Roots

- Many English words are based on **Greek and Latin roots,** which are often included in their definitions in a dictionary. Your understanding of Greek and Latin roots may help you understand the meaning of unfamiliar words.

- The Latin word *terra,* meaning "earth, land," is in the words *terrain* and *territory.* The Latin word *gloria* means "praise," as in the word *glorify.*

Directions Read the following passage. Then answer the questions below.

The curiosity was getting the better of me. I had to know what was at the end of this path. We had been hiking on rugged terrain for hours. We had to change direction twice to avoid a very powerful torrent that could have knocked us to our feet if we had tried to cross it. At least it was a glorious day. The sun was shining bright and the sky was a beautiful light blue. Finally, we saw a terraced hill before us. Once we were completely out of the trees, I could see the top of the hill. There was a huge granite structure in all its glory.

1. What is the Latin root in *terraced?* How does the root help you understand the meaning of the word?

_____

2. How does the root in *glorious* help you understand its meaning?

_____

3. What do you think *terrain* means? How does the root help you understand the word's meaning? Use a dictionary to help you.

_____

4. How is the meaning of *glory* related to the meaning of the Latin root?

_____

5. Write a sentence using a new word with either the root *gloria* or *terra.*

_____

© Pearson Education, Inc., 4

Home Activity Your child read a short passage and identified the meanings of unfamiliar words using Latin roots. Look in a dictionary with your child to find other words that use the Latin roots, *gloria* and *terra.*

Outline

- An **outline** is a plan that shows how a story, article, report, or other text is organized. An outline includes a title, main topics, subtopics, and details. You can use an outline to better understand how a text is organized or as a way to organize your own thoughts before you write something of your own.

Directions Read the following outline. Then answer the questions below.

Ancient Civilizations

I. Aztecs
    A. Location and Size
       1. Mexico
       2. made up of hundreds
         of states
       3. 5 to 6 million people
    B. People
       1. priests and nobles
       2. warriors
       3. serfs or enslaved people

II. Incas
    A. Location and Size
       1. Peru, Ecuador, and Chile
       2. about 12 million people
    B. People
       1. emperor
       2. nobles
       3. farmers

1. What is the title of this outline?

_____

2. What two topics are under *Aztecs*?

_____

3. What types of Inca people will be included in this report?

_____

4. Why do you think the same two subtopics are used under *Aztecs* and *Incas?*

_____

_____

5. How would an outline help you to organize your thoughts before writing a report?

_____

© Pearson Education, Inc., 4

Name _____

Directions Read the following article. Then complete the outline below.

Even though the Incas lived long ago, they were highly civilized. Their system of farming was well planned. Their farming allowed them to feed themselves with enough left over to trade. Inca farmers grew cotton, potatoes, corn, and many other crops. Their irrigation system helped them water their crops. Incas kept animals on the farm too. They raised llamas, ducks, and alpacas.

Besides their farming system, the Incas also had buildings and roads. If you were to visit the Inca sites in South America today, you would be able to see the ruins of grand temples, palaces, and military forts. The Inca transportation system was based on two main roads that stretched for hundreds of miles. Minor roads connected the main roads. They also constructed bridges and tunnels.

Directions Complete the outline by writing the correct information on the line shown to the left.

Inca Civilization

6. **I.** _____

7. **I. A. 2.** _____

8. **I. B.** _____

9. **II. B.** _____

10. **III. A. 2.** _____

I. _____
    A. Crops
        1. cotton
        2. _____
        3. corn
    B. _____
        1. llamas
        2. ducks
        3. alpacas
II. Buildings
    A. Palaces
    B. _____
    C. Forts
III. Transportation
    A. Roads
        1. two main roads
        2. _____
    B. Bridges and Tunnels

© Pearson Education, Inc., 4

Home Activity Your child learned about outlines. Read an article and create an outline together based on the information in the article.

Words with Double Consonants

Proofread a Speech Circle six misspelled words in the speech. Write the words correctly. Write the sentence with a verb in the incorrect tense correctly.

Welcome, Friends of the Zoo! I'd like to thank all of you who kindly ofer your time to our local zoo. Tomorow is Family Education Day at the zoo. An expert will talk about the cicada, grasshoper, and beetle. Children can learn what makes them diferent. You can also feed letuce to a rabit in the petting zoo. Again, I want to thanks you all for your support.

Spelling Words

tomorrow
borrow
different
rabbit
matter
written
bottle
ridden
odd
bubble

offer
suffer
slippers
grasshopper
worry
current
lettuce
saddle
shudder
hobby

1. _____   2. _____

3. _____   4. _____

5. _____   6. _____

7. _____

_____

Proofread Words Circle the list word in each sentence that is spelled correctly.

8. What is the **matter mater** with Andy's parakeet?

9. Have you ever **ridden riden** in a hot air balloon?

10. At night, I like to wear my comfortable **slipers slippers**.

11. Please take an extra **bottle botle** of water.

12. My sister is letting me **borrow borow** her grey sweater.

Frequently Misspelled Words

again
different
were
want

© Pearson Education, Inc., 4

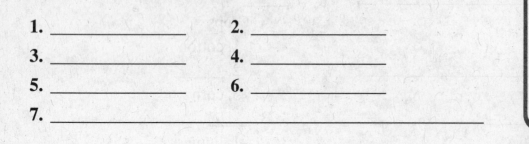

Home Activity Your child identified misspelled words with double consonants. Spell the first syllable of a list word and have your child spell the rest of the word.

Adverbs

Directions Read the passage. Then read each question. Circle the letter of the correct answer.

The Seekers

(1) Bingham careful started across the narrow, rickety bridge. (2) Bingham thought hard about the ruined lost city he hoped to find. (3) The travelers trod wary to a remote canyon. (4) Final, they broke through into the glaring sunlight. (5) The people whispered quietly that there were wonderful ruins on the mountain.

1 What change, if any, should be made in sentence 1?

   A Change *narrow* to **narrowly.**

   B Change *careful* to **caring.**

   C Change *careful* to **carefully.**

   D Make no change.

2. What change, if any, should be made in sentence 2?

   A Change *hoped* to **hopeful.**

   B Change *ruined* to **ruins.**

   C Change *hard* to **hardly.**

   D Make no change.

3 What change, if any, should be made in sentence 3?

   A Change *wary* to **careful.**

   B Change *wary* to **warily.**

   C Change *wary* to **warly.**

   D Make no change.

4 What change, if any, should be made in sentence 4?

   A Change *Final* to **Finally.**

   B Change *Final* to **Finale.**

   C Change *glaring* to **glareful.**

   D Make no change.

5 What change, if any, should be made in sentence 5?

   A Change *quietly* to **quiet.**

   B Change *wonderful* to **wonderfully.**

   C Change *quietly* to **quite.**

   D Make no change.

© Pearson Education, Inc., 4

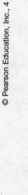

School + Home   **Home Activity** Your child prepared for taking tests on adverbs. Have your child look through a newspaper or magazine article. Ask him or her to highlight the adverbs and say whether they tell *how, when,* or *where* something happened.

Literary Elements: Character, Plot, and Theme

- **Characters** are the people and animals in a story.
- The **plot** is the sequence of events in a story.
- A story's **theme** is the most important idea.

Directions Read the following story. Use the graphic organizer to identify the characters, plot, and theme of the story and answer the questions below.

When her cat Whiskers did not show up for breakfast, Jasmine was worried.

"Whiskers is always here for food!" she cried to her mom. "What if she's lost?"

"Calm down, Jasmine," said her mom. "It's easier to solve a problem when you're calm."

So, Jasmine sat and thought. Then it came to her. Whiskers might be in the cellar.

She opened the cellar door. There was Whiskers, asleep on the stairs.

"Yesterday, Whiskers was very curious about the cellar," Jasmine explained.

Her mom smiled and said, "See what happens when you calm down and think about a problem?"

Characters	Plot	Theme
1.	2.	3.

4. How did Jasmine figure out where Whiskers was hiding?

_____

_____

5. Is the story's narrator first person or third person?

_____

© Pearson Education, Inc., 4

Home Activity Your child learned about a story's characters, plot, and theme. Discuss a problem your child recently solved as if it were a story. Ask your child to tell you the characters, plot, and theme.

Writing • Thank-You Note

Key Features of a Thank-you Note

- uses letter format
- has a friendly tone
- explains why the writer feels grateful

July 23, 20__

Dear Anna,

Flipping over in my sailboat as that storm began last week was the scariest thing that's ever happened to me. I panicked! I forgot everything I'd learned about righting the boat and climbing back on board. Then I saw you heading in my direction. I didn't think you'd reach me in time. The wind was blowing more strongly every second. The waves were getting higher and higher. Rescuing me was probably the hardest and most dangerous task you've ever done. But you're a great sailor! You reached me faster than I would have thought possible. Your calm voice helped me feel calmer, and your clear directions helped me climb safely onto your boat.

Anna, your sailing skill and courage saved me. I'll never forget what you did. You are truly amazing.

Your grateful friend,
Carol

---

1. Reread the selection. Why is it a Thank-you note?

_____

_____

2. Circle the body of the thank-you note.

© Pearson Education, Inc., 4

Vocabulary

Directions Choose the word from the box that best matches the word or words. Write the word on the line.

_____ **1.** path from top to bottom

_____ **2.** made a long and hard journey

_____ **3.** empty space

_____ **4.** loops wound into a spiral shape

_____ **5.** expected something to happen

Check the Words You Know

___coil
___descent
___foresaw
___rappel
___ridge
___shaft
___trekked
___void

Directions Circle the word that has the same or nearly the same meaning as the first word in each group.

6. ridge	tunnel	crest	bottom
7. rappel	descend	hike	rope
8. descent	end	boot	drop
9. shaft	light	rod	curve
10. foresaw	warned	predicted	worried

Write a Broadcast Report

Pretend you are a broadcast reporter who is delivering information about a young girl's daring climb up a dangerous mountain to save her sister. On a separate sheet of paper, write a broadcast report about the event. Use as many vocabulary words as you can.

© Pearson Education, Inc., 4

Home Activity Your child identified and used vocabulary words from the story *Cliff Hanger*. With your child, read an article about mountain climbing or rappelling. Help your child identify the meanings of unfamiliar words in the article.

Comparative and Superlative Adjectives and Adverbs

A **comparative adjective** compares two people, places, things, or groups. Add *-er* to most short adjectives to make the comparative form. Use *more* or *less* with longer adjectives. A **comparative adverb** compares two actions. Add *-er* to many adverbs to make them comparative. Use *more* or *less* with most adverbs that end in *-ly*.

Comparative Adjectives	This trail is shorter but more difficult than that one.
Comparative Adverbs	Grit climbed faster and less clumsily than Axel.

A **superlative adjective** compares three or more people, places, things, or groups. Add *-est* to most short adjectives to make the superlative form. Use *most* or *least* with longer adjectives. A **superlative adverb** compares three or more actions. Add *-est* to many adverbs to make them superlative. Use *most* or *least* with most adverbs that end in *-ly*.

Superlative Adjectives	It was the steepest and most neglected trail I've seen.
Superlative Adverbs	The wind blew hardest and most powerfully.

Directions Change the underlined adjective or adverb to its comparative form if the sentence is followed by *(C)*. Change it to the superlative form if the sentence is followed by *(S)*.

1. I had the tiny cabin. *(S)* _____

2. The weather is bad than last week. *(C)* _____

3. His gear was the messy of all the climbers. *(S)* _____

4. Trucks move slowly on wet roads than on dry roads. *(C)* _____

5. This mountain is steep than that one. *(C)* _____

6. Steering is easy over there. *(C)* _____

7. His is the fast truck of all. *(S)* _____

Home Activity Your child learned about comparative and superlative adjectives and adverbs. Ask your child to give you examples of how he or she feels about something or does something. Have your child identify the comparative and superlative adjectives or adverbs he or she uses.

© Pearson Education, Inc., 4

Name _____

Greek Word Parts

Word Groups Write the list word that best fits into each group.

Spelling Words

telephone
biography
telescope
photograph
microwave
diameter
barometer
microscope
headphones
microphone

autograph
microchip
telegraph
perimeter
paragraph
phonics
symphony
saxophone
periscope
megaphone

1. topic sentence, supporting sentences, ___   1. _____

2. life story, nonfiction, ___   2. _____

3. bacteria, lens, ___   3. _____

4. film, camera, ___   4. _____

5. oven, rapid, ___   5. _____

6. voice, record, ___   6. _____

7. instrument, woodwind, ___   7. _____

8. signature, celebrity, ___   8. _____

9. universe, lens, ___   9. _____

10. weather, air pressure, ___   10. _____

Missing Word Write the list word that best completes each sentence.

11. A ____ is shaped like a cone.

12. A ____ is a tiny processor inside a computer.

13. A ____ allows sailors in a submarine to see above water.

14. Measure across the center of a circle to find its ____.

15. Morse code, a series of dots and dashes, was sent by ____.

16. A full ____ orchestra has strings, woodwinds, brass, and percussion sections.

17. Wear ____ when you don't want to disturb others in the room.

18. To find the ____, measure the sides of a shape and add them together.

19. Beginning readers learn to use ____ to sound out new words.

20. Alexander Graham Bell invented the ____.

11. _____

12. _____

13. _____

14. _____

15. _____

16. _____

17. _____

18. _____

19. _____

20. _____

Home Activity Your child wrote words with Greek word parts. Ask your child to use the meanings of the Greek word parts to help define the words.

© Pearson Education, Inc., 4

Outline Form A

Title_____

A. _____

   1. _____

   2. _____

   3. _____

B. _____

   1. _____

   2. _____

   3. _____

C. _____

   1. _____

   2. _____

   3. _____

© Pearson Education, Inc., 4

Vocabulary • Unfamiliar Words

- **Context clues,** words and phrases near an **unfamiliar word** in a passage, can help you figure out the word's meaning.
- Context clues won't always help you figure out the meaning of an unfamiliar word. If this happens, use a dictionary, a book that lists words and their definitions, to find the word's meaning.

Directions Read the following passage. Then answer the questions below.

> Jack had never hiked so far before with his brothers. Today they had trekked seven miles to get to their wall. To Jack, the wall looked like a flat shaft, or pole, shooting straight up. When he blinked his eyes, he foresaw himself falling backward into the void, or emptiness, behind him, as if he expected to slip.
>
> "Let's go, Jack," called his oldest brother, Trev. Trev had been climbing for years, so Jack knew he was safe. Trev helped him with his equipment and showed him where to place his feet and hands. Before he knew it, they were at the top of the wall looking out over the ridge of hilltops in the distance. Trev then helped Jack rappel down the rock face. Gliding back down on ropes to make the descent was thrilling.

1. What does *trekked* mean? How do you know?

_____

_____

2. What context clue helps you to figure out the meaning of *shaft*?

_____

3. Why would a *descent* be easier than climbing up?

_____

4. Use a dictionary to look up the word *rappel*. Rewrite the sentence that uses the word so that you give context clues.

_____

_____

Home Activity Your child identified the meanings of unfamiliar words using context clues. Invent a few new words for common everyday items (for example: a hat could be a *tah*). Give clues as to their meanings in a conversation with your child. Have your child guess the real words. Switch roles and repeat the activity.

© Pearson Education, Inc., 4

Diagram/Scale Drawing

- A **diagram** is a special drawing with labels. Usually, a diagram shows how something is made, how an object's parts relate to one another, or how something works. Sometimes a diagram must be studied in a certain order to be understood—left to right, top to bottom, or bottom to top. Often diagrams contain text that explains something about the object being illustrated.

- A **scale drawing** is a diagram that uses a mathematical scale. For example, one inch on a scale drawing might be equal to one foot on the object in real life.

Directions Study the diagram of a rock climbing harness below.

Buckles   Waist Belt

Belay Loop

Gear Loop

Leg Loops

DEFINITIONS

belay loop: Place where the rope is fastened that is attached to another person or a rock as you climb.

buckles: These snap together to hold your harness on.

gear loop: Place for hanging other instruments for rock climbing.

leg loops: This is where your legs fit through.

waist belt: This part fastens around your waist.

© Pearson Education, Inc., 4

Name _____

Directions Use the diagram to answer the following questions.

1. What does this diagram show?

_____

2. What do the definitions tell you?

_____

3. Where is the belay loop located?

_____

4. Which parts fit around parts of your body?

_____

5. Which part would it be most important to check for a good fit? Why?

_____

6. When would someone refer to a diagram like this?

_____

_____

_____

© Pearson Education, Inc., 4

Home Activity Your child learned about diagrams and scale drawings. Together, use the Internet or a reference book to look up the actual measurements of a famous mountain. Then draw a scale drawing of it.

Greek Word Parts

Proofread an Assignment Sam quickly copied his teacher's assignment. Circle six misspelled words and one word with a capitalization error. Write the words correctly.

© Pearson Education, Inc., 4

> Class Assignment: Write a six-paragraph biografy of one of these famous people.
>
> Alexander Graham Bell, inventor of the telaphone
>
> Ludwig van Beethoven, Symphony composer
>
> Anton van Leeuwenhoek, inventor of the microscope
>
> Galileo and the telesope
>
> Charlie "Bird" Parker, great saxaphone player
>
> Jack Kilby, inventor of the microchip
>
> Percy Spencer, inventor of the micrawave oven
>
> Simon Lake, periscope inventor
>
> Teddy Roosevelt, President and frend of nature
>
> Evangelista Torricelli, inventor of the barometer

Spelling Words

telephone
biography
telescope
photograph
microwave
diameter
barometer
microscope
headphones
microphone

autograph
microchip
telegraph
perimeter
paragraph
phonics
symphony
saxophone
periscope
megaphone

1. _____   2. _____

3. _____   4. _____

5. _____   6. _____

7. _____

Frequently Misspelled Words

friend
then

Proofread Words Circle the list word that is spelled correctly.

8.	microphone	microfone	9.	phonics	phonicks
10.	peremeter	perimeter	11.	magaphone	megaphone
12.	autograff	autograph	13.	telegraph	teligraph
14.	diameter	diamiter	15.	perescope	periscope

Home Activity Your child identified misspelled words with Greek word parts. Have your child find and circle two letters that stand for the sound of *f* in the list words.

Comparative and Superlative Adjectives and Adverbs

Directions Read the passage. Then read each question. Circle the letter of the correct answer.

Climbing Cathedral Rock

(1) We took the most long route to the top of Cathedral Rock. (2) Climbing the rock should have been easier than it was. (3) Luckily, today's weather was much weller than yesterday's. (4) The weather had been stormy all week, but Monday was the most stormy. (5) I thought the most difficult part of the climb was the part near Monkey Ridge. (6) Getting back down in one piece would be my greater achievement of all.

1 What change, if any, should be made in sentence 1?

- **A** Change *most long* to **longer.**
- **B** Change *most long* to **longest.**
- **C** Change *top* to **topper.**
- **D** Make no change.

2 What change, if any, should be made in sentence 2?

- **A** Change *Climbing* to **climb.**
- **B** Change *it* to **climbing.**
- **C** Change *easyer* to **easier.**
- **D** Make no change.

3 What change, if any, should be made in sentence 3?

- **A** Change *weather* to **whether.**
- **B** Change *today's* to **todays.**
- **C** Change *weller* to **better.**
- **D** Make no change.

4 What change, if any, should be made in sentence 4?

- **A** Change *been stormy* to **been stormier.**
- **B** Change *most stormy* to **stormiest.**
- **C** Change *most stormy* to **most stormiest.**
- **D** Make no change.

5 What change, if any, should be made in sentence 6?

- **A** Change *greater* to **greatly.**
- **B** Change *greater* to **great.**
- **C** Change *greater* to **greatest.**
- **D** Make no change.

© Pearson Education, Inc., 4

Home Activity Your child prepared for taking tests on comparative and superlative adjectives and adverbs. Have your child write a list of five adjectives and five adverbs. Say each word on the list and ask your child to compose a sentence using the word in its comparative or superlative form.

Main Idea and Details

- The **main idea** tells the most important idea from a paragraph, passage, or article.
- **Details** are small pieces of information that tell more about the main idea.

Directions Read the following article. Then complete the diagram by finding the main idea and the details that support it.

Although Antarctica is far away from the rest of the world, scientists know a great deal about it. They have explored the continent and walked upon its ice. They have discovered mountain ranges and mapped them out. Scientists have even studied hidden features of Antarctica that exist underneath the ice. Now equipment that uses radio-echo sounding technology can determine what these features look like. The knowledge scientists have gained has encouraged tourists to see the continent for themselves.

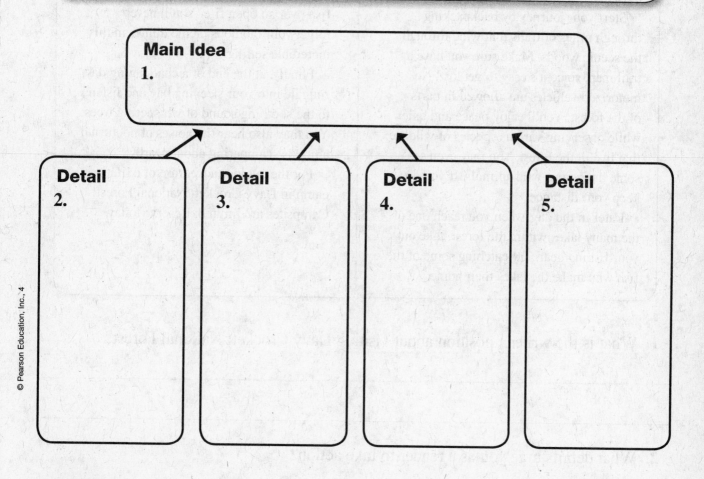

Main Idea

1.

Detail

2.

Detail

3.

Detail

4.

Detail

5.

© Pearson Education, Inc., 4

Home Activity Your child used a graphic organizer to determine the main idea and supporting details in an article. Discuss a place your child knows well. Have him or her write a paragraph about the place, including a main idea and details that support it.

Writing • Argument/Persuasive Ad

Key Features of an Argument/Persuasive Advertisement

- grabs reader's attention
- takes a position, or makes a claim about a product, service, or idea
- provides reasons that are supported by evidence, such as facts and details
- develops an argument to urge readers to take action or make a purchase

Visit Davy Crockett National Forest!

Do you love outdoor adventures? Would you like to backpack, hike, and fish in a wilderness area? Visit Davy Crockett National Forest in Texas for the most exciting trip you'll ever take!

Start your journey by backpacking through miles of trails that wind through the scenic woods. Make sure you have a trail map, since it's easy to get lost! No motorized vehicles are allowed in parts of the forest. You'll enjoy peace and quiet while observing various species of wildlife that live in the forest. You may even see some dangerous wild animals. If you do, keep your distance!

Later in the day, when you reach one of the many lakes within the forest, take out your fishing gear. Try catching some of the fish who make the lakes their home. You'll probably hook several largemouth bass or bowfin. However, catching a "big one" won't be easy! Expect a tough fight that tests your fishing skills.

Then, as the sun sets, cook your fresh fish over an open fire. You'll never forget your fabulous picnic dinner in this incredible setting.

Finally, at the end of a challenging day, snuggle into your sleeping bag and listen to the soothing sound of whispering trees. You may also hear the noises of nocturnal animals scampering about nearby!

For the outdoor adventure of a lifetime, camp in Davy Crockett National Forest! Campsites are limited. Reserve today.

© Pearson Education, Inc., 4

1. What is the writer's position about visiting Davy Crockett National Forest?

_____

_____

2. What details urge you as a reader to take action?

_____

_____

Vocabulary

Directions Choose the word from the box that best matches each definition. Write the word on the line.

_____ **1.** to go away

_____ **2.** large masses of ice floating in the sea

_____ **3.** expectation

_____ **4.** rises and falls alternately

_____ **5.** causing fear or dislike

Check the Words You Know

___anticipation
___forbidding
___continent
___heaves
___icebergs
___convergence
___depart

Directions Choose the word from the box that best completes each sentence. Write the word on the line shown to the left.

_____ **6.** Antarctica is a _____ on our planet.

_____ **7.** Scientists are studying the ___ of two large sheets of ice.

_____ **8.** I could barely stand the ___ of seeing my first whale.

_____ **9.** The ship had to make sure to avoid any floating ___.

_____ **10.** We have to___ from Antarctica tomorrow.

Write a Journal Entry

Write a journal entry you might make after sailing across icy waters to Antarctica. Use as many vocabulary words as you can.

Home Activity Your child identified and used vocabulary words from *Antarctic Journal: Four Months at the Bottom of the World.* Together, create a crossword puzzle using the words from the selection.

Vocabulary 351

© Pearson Education, Inc., 4

Time Order Words

> **Time order words and phrases** link related events and ideas together. They indicate a specific organization pattern. Time order words and phrases include words such as *meanwhile, first, before long, later on, soon, earlier, next,* and *as soon as*.
>
> First, we flew to Santiago; next, we flew to Punta Arenas.
>
> I began to set up camp, and meanwhile, the ice around me began to crack.

Directions Underline the time order word or words in each sentence.

1. After we received my clothing, we boarded our ship.

2. First, I explored my tiny cabin; later, I explored the ship's deck.

3. The whales have to pass before we turn the engines on again.

4. Monday afternoon, I watched the penguins; earlier, the sea was full of whales.

5. I listened to the loud cracking sounds, and meanwhile, the sky began to glow.

Directions Choose a time order word in ( ) which correctly completes each sentence. Write the word on the line.

6. I slipped on two pairs of socks, and _____, I put on the heavy boots. (next, first)

7. When I left, snow was beginning to fall, and _____, it turned into a blizzard. (later, earlier)

8. I knew that, _____, someone would come looking for me. (before long, as soon as)

© Pearson Education, Inc., 4

Home Activity Your child learned about time order words. Ask your child to give you examples of how he or she makes something. Have your child identify the time order words he or she uses.

Latin Roots

Spelling Words				
dictionary	abrupt	predict	import	locally
verdict	locate	portable	transport	bankrupt
dictate	location	erupt	passport	export
contradict	rupture	interrupt	disrupt	dislocate

Words in Context Write a list word to complete each sentence.

1. Please turn off your cell phone so it doesn't ____ the movie.   1. _____

2. Scientists say the volcano will ____ any day now.   2. _____

3. The explosion was caused by a ____ in the gas line.   3. _____

4. His ____ departure surprised everyone.   4. _____

5. It is not polite to ____ when someone is speaking.   5. _____

6. The company lost all its customers and went ____.   6. _____

7. We ____ tractors to Thailand.   7. _____

8. We ____ toys from China.   8. _____

9. The girls bought a ____ stove for their camping trip.   9. _____

10. The jumbo jet will ____ us across the ocean.   10. _____

11. You must have a ____ to visit a foreign country.   11. _____

12. Jason might ____ his shoulder if he lifts the heavy crate.   12. _____

13. Fresh fruits and vegetables were sold ____.   13. _____

14. The manager hopes moving to a new ____ will improve business.   14. _____

15. Were you able to ____ your missing shoe?   15. _____

Definitions Write the list word that matches each definition.

16. a book that tells how to say words   16. _____

17. to make a statement of disagreement   17. _____

18. a jury's statement of guilt or innocence   18. _____

19. to speak words aloud for someone to write down   19. _____

20. to say what will happen in the future   20. _____

© Pearson Education, Inc., 4

Home Activity Your child wrote words with Latin roots. Use the list words in sentences and have your child spell the words.

Outline Form A

Title _____

A. _____

    1. _____

    2. _____

    3. _____

B. _____

    1. _____

    2. _____

    3. _____

C. _____

    1. _____

    2. _____

    3. _____

© Pearson Education, Inc., 4

Vocabulary • Greek and Latin Affixes

- Many English words have **Greek or Latin parts**. When you see an unknown word, you can use what you know about Greek and Latin to help you figure out the word's meaning.

- The Latin prefix *com-* or *con-* means "with" or "together." The Latin prefix *de-* means "away from." The Latin prefix *anti-* means "against" or "before."

Directions Read the following passage. Then answer the questions below.

Never had the scientists felt such cold. Yesterday, they had departed from Christchurch, New Zealand. During the night, they felt the temperature drop, and their anticipation turned to tough reality. Antarctica, they knew, would show them the convergence between nature's beauty and its power to threaten life. They would be staying there for several months to compile information about the ecosystem. Something was destroying the natural food chain, and the scientists did not have much time to figure it out.

1. How does the prefix in *depart* help you to figure out its meaning?

_____

_____

2. What is the meaning of *convergence?*

_____

_____

3. Define the word *compile.*

_____

_____

4. *De-* and *con-* have nearly opposite meanings. Think about the meaning of *destroying*, and then write a word that means the opposite and uses the prefix *con-*.

_____

_____

5. What is the meaning of *anticipation?*

_____

_____

© Pearson Education, Inc., 4

Home Activity Your child used knowledge about Latin and Greek prefixes to identify the meanings of words. Together, use a dictionary to find other words that use the *con-, com-, anti-,* or *de-* prefix definitions mentioned above.

SQP3R

- **SQP3R** is a study skill that can help you when reading. Here's what it means:
- **Survey:** Look at the title, author, chapter headings, and illustrations to get an idea of what you are about to read.
- **Question:** Generate questions you want answered when reading the text.
- **Predict:** Try to imagine what the text you're going to read is about.
- **Read:** Read the text, keeping in mind your predictions and questions.
- **Recite:** Recite or write down what you learned from reading the text.
- **Review:** Look back at the text, the predictions you made, the questions you posed, the answers you found in the text, and the information you learned from your reading.

Directions Look at the illustration and read the information below. Follow the SQP3R method.

Glaciers: Wonders in Ice

Three layers make up what are called true glaciers. First, there is a layer of snow on top. The next layer is made of an ice and snow mixture. Finally, solid ice forms the bottom layer. There are also cracks called crevasses that appear while the glacier is moving. Some glaciers move very slowly, so slowly it is hard to tell, while others may move a few hundred feet in a day. It is this movement of the massive ice that makes the unique features of the land. Giant mountain peaks, lakes, and valleys are all results of glaciers that moved and eroded away the land years in the past.

You can visit glaciers but it is not recommended that you walk on them. Deep crevasses may be underneath the snow, making them hard to see. Trained people who have experience with climbing mountains and glaciers, and have special tools, like a rope, crampons, and an ice axe, are better equipped to do this kind of exploring. People who travel on glaciers should never go alone.

© Pearson Education, Inc., 4

Directions Use the information to answer the following questions.

1. After surveying the title and illustration, did you think the information would be fiction or nonfiction?

   _____

2. What are two questions you had before reading?

   _____

3. Before reading what did you predict the text would be about?

   _____

4. How far do some glaciers move in a day?

   _____

5. What is the middle layer in a glacier made up of?

   _____

6. What makes the unique features of the land?

   _____

7. Why is walking on a glacier dangerous?

   _____

8. What did you learn from this text that you did not know before?

   _____

9. How does making predictions before you read help you?

   _____

   _____

10. How does reviewing your questions and information help you?

    _____

    _____

© Pearson Education, Inc., 4

Home Activity Your child learned about the SQP3R study method. Choose a fictional story to read. Have your child apply the study method to the story. Ask your child to explain how the study method differed when using it with fiction instead of nonfiction.

Name _____

Latin Roots

Proofread a Sign The sign at the airport terminal has some errors. Circle six misspelled words and write them correctly on the lines. Find the sentence with a punctuation error and write it correctly.

> Transworld Transport
>
> Departing Passengers:
>
> Up on arrival please have your pass port and ticket ready.
>
> Airline rules ditate that all heavy luggage must be checked.
>
> Keep carry-on and portible luggage with you at all times.
>
> Locat your gate immediately.
>
> Stay in the proper location until your flight is called
>
> Do not desrupt other passengers with loud cell phone conversations or loud music.

Spelling Words

dictionary
abrupt
predict
import
locally
verdict
locate
portable
transport
bankrupt

dictate
location
erupt
passport
export
contradict
rupture
interrupt
disrupt
dislocate

1. _____   2. _____

3. _____   4. _____

5. _____   6. _____

7. _____

_____

Frequently Misspelled Words

didn't
upon

Proofread Words Circle the word that is spelled correctly. Write it.

8. The jury's _____ was not guilty.   8. _____
   verdik   verdict

9. The new evidence seemed to _____ the accepted theory.   9. _____
   contradict   contridict

10. Businesses that do not keep up with the times are likely   10. _____
    to go _____.
    bankrup   bankrupt

© Pearson Education, Inc., 4

Home Activity Your child identified misspelled list words. Have your child dictate list words as you spell them. Make some mistakes and have your child correct your misspellings.

Time Order Words

Directions Read the passage. Then read each question. Circle the letter of the correct answer.

Survival Snow Shelter

    (1) Antarctic weather can change from nice to dangerous, so last, learn how to build a snow shelter. (2) Throw everything you have, except the shovel, in a big pile. (3) After, shovel lots of snow on top of your gear. (4) Before you have completely buried your gear, climb up onto the pile and stamp the snow solid. (5) Then, build a tunnel into your gear. (6) Next, drag your gear piece by piece out of the tunnel. (7) Meanwhile, crawl into the tunnel and wait out the storm!

1 What change, if any, should be made in sentence 1?

  A Change *last* to **in an instant.**

  B Change *last* to **first.**

  C Change *last* to **later.**

  D Make no change.

2 What change, if any, should be made in sentence 3?

  A Change *After* to **Soon.**

  B Change *After* to **First.**

  C Change *After* to **Next.**

  D Make no change.

3 What change, if any, should be made in sentence 4?

  A Change *Before* to **After.**

  B Change *Before* to **First.**

  C Change *Before* to **Meanwhile.**

  D Make no change.

4 What change, if any, should be made in sentence 6?

  A Change the *Next* to **Third.**

  B Change *Next* to **Sometime.**

  C Change the *Next* to **Next to last.**

  D Make no change.

5 What change, if any, should be made in sentence 7?

  A Change *Meanwhile* to **Soon.**

  B Change *Meanwhile* to **Finally.**

  C Change *Meanwhile* to **In the meantime.**

  D Make no change.

© Pearson Education, Inc., 4

Home Activity Your child prepared for taking tests on time order words. Have your child write a list of five time order words. Then ask your child to write a paragraph using the words in the correct time order.

Draw Conclusions

- **Drawing a conclusion** is forming an opinion based on what you already know or on the facts and details in a text.

- Check an author's conclusions or your own conclusions by asking: Is this the only logical choice? Are the facts accurate?

Directions Read the following passage. Then answer the questions below.

Our basketball team, the Hawks, just finished the season. We had a record of 7 wins and 13 losses. Our season didn't start off too well. We lost our first six games. Coach told us we weren't playing like a team. After that, he put us through some tough practices. We worked on defense, passing, and helping each other out. Coach told us we had to play twice as hard as the other teams did to win.

After that, things improved. We started to win a few games. Other teams weren't shaking in their sneakers when we got to their gyms, but they knew they were going to have to play hard to beat us. And man, was it fun. When the season started I barely knew any of the other players on the team. Now that the season is over, I feel like I have twelve really good friends—thirteen if you count Coach.

1. Draw a conclusion about whether or not the Hawks were a good basketball team at first.

_____

2. What details support this conclusion?

_____

3. How do you think the coach made the Hawks better?

_____

4. Draw a conclusion about whether or not you think this was a successful season. Support your answer with facts.

_____

_____

Home Activity Your child read a short passage and drew conclusions using facts and details. Read an article with your child. Have your child draw conclusions from the article.

© Pearson Education, Inc., 4

Writing • Personal Narrative

Softball or Basketball?

It was time for team tryouts. I had to decide which team to try out for. It was a tough decision to make. I'm a really good softball player, so I was pretty sure I could make that team. But even though I'm not as good at playing basketball, I love the game.

After school, I spoke with my brother who had played on the basketball team. He didn't think I'd make the team. During dinner, my dad discouraged me, too. He said, "Stick with what you do really well." After dinner, I went into my room and thought and thought. I decided to take a risk.

Basketball tryouts were in the gym the next afternoon. Before they started, I felt as if butterflies were flitting around in my stomach. But when the coach threw out the ball, I forgot about everything but playing the best I knew how. I made some great shots and passes, and I guarded well.

When tryouts were over, I sat on the bench and waited to hear which players made the cut. After a few minutes, the coach walked onto the court. I could barely breathe as he began to read the names. Suddenly, I heard my name. I sat still but inside I was jumping up and down in excitement! My risk had paid off. I made the team!

1. Reread the selection. Why is this story a personal narrative?

_____

_____

2. Write what happens first, next, and last.

_____

_____

_____

_____

3. Circle an example of the author's thoughts and feelings.

© Pearson Education, Inc., 4

Name _____

Vocabulary

Directions Choose the word from the box that best replaces the underlined word or words. Write the word on the line.

_____ 1. The sun shone into the narrow valley on the moon.

_____ 2. Justin walked with effort as he grew tired in the hot sun.

_____ 3. My brother picked out the unusually small animal as his favorite of the litter.

_____ 4. Tina became unsteady when she tried to walk in the space suit.

_____ 5. Lisa mocked her brother at the dinner table.

_____ 6. The thunder cloud hung threateningly above them.

Check the Words You Know

__loomed
__rille
__runt
__staggered
__summoning
__taunted
__trench
__trudged

Directions Choose the word from the box that best matches each clue. Write the word on the line.

_____ 7. This is a ditch.

_____ 8. You are doing this when you call on your own courage.

_____ 9. You might have walked like this when you were tired.

_____ 10. You might have walked like this after becoming dizzy.

Write a Story

Write a story about an adventure on the moon. Use as many vocabulary words as you can.

Home Activity Your child identified and used vocabulary words from "Moonwalk." Together, try to act out the meanings of words such as *trudged, staggered, runt,* and *loomed.*

© Pearson Education, Inc., 4

Name _____

Prepositions and Prepositional Phrases

A **preposition** begins a group of words called a **prepositional phrase.** A prepositional phrase ends with a noun or pronoun called the **object of the preposition.** The preposition shows how the object of the preposition is related to other words in the sentence. A prepositional phrase can be used to tell *where, when, how,* or *which one.*

Preposition	We took a rocket <u>into</u> outer space.
Prepositional Phrase	<u>into outer space</u>
Object of the Preposition	<u>outer space</u>

Sometimes you can combine two sentences with prepositional phrases.
The astronauts studied the moon. They saw craters there.
The astronauts studied craters <u>on the moon.</u>

Common Prepositions
about, above, across, after, along, around, at, behind, below, beneath, between, by, for, from, in, into, of, on, over, through, to, under, upon, with, without

Directions Write the prepositional phrase in each sentence. Underline the preposition. Circle the object of the preposition.

1. Can you jump across that gully? _____

2. Don't trip over a rock. _____

3. Gravity on the moon is very weak. _____

4. At night the temperature here is very cold. _____

Directions Each sentence below contains two prepositional phrases. Underline the prepositional phrases.

5. The race to the moon ended in triumph.

6. Astronauts from the United States landed on the moon.

Home Activity Your child learned about prepositions and prepositional phrases. Ask your child to name some common prepositions and to show you how they combine with nouns or pronouns to make prepositional phrases.

© Pearson Education, Inc., 4

Related Words

Words in Context Write two related list words to complete each sentence.

Spelling Words

please
pleasant
breath
breathe
image
imagine
product
production
heal
health

triple
triplet
relate
relative
meter
metric
compose
composition
crumb
crumble

It would **(1)**____ me greatly if you were nicer
and more **(2)**____ to our neighbors.

1. _____   2. _____

My friend says being a **(3)**____ means she and her two
look-alike sisters have **(4)**____ the fun.

3. _____   4. _____

The company rushed to get the new **(5)**____ into **(6)**____ in
time for holiday sales.

5. _____   6. _____

Don't **(7)**____ on me with your bad **(8)**____!

7. _____   8. _____

A **(9)**____ is a basic unit of length in the **(10)**____ system.

9. _____   10. _____

The wound will **(11)**____, and then you will be the picture of
perfect **(12)**____.

11. _____   12. _____

At family gatherings, there's always at least one **(13)**____
who likes to **(14)**____ old family stories.

13. _____   14. _____

Mozart had the ability to **(15)**____ a lengthy musical
(16)____ in a short time.

15. _____   16. _____

Can you **(17)**____ what it would be like to be the exact
(18)____ of a famous person?

17. _____   18. _____

Even though the cake began to **(19)**____ when I picked it up,
I managed to eat every last **(20)**____.

19. _____   20. _____

© Pearson Education, Inc., 4

School + Home **Home Activity** Your child wrote related words to complete sentences. Name a list word and ask your child to say and spell the related word.

Scoring Rubric: Personal Narrative

	4	3	2	1
Focus/Ideas	Clear narrative with narrow topic	Mostly limited topic	Unclear account; topic rather broad	Confusing account, topic very broad
Organization	Organized in a time-order sequence	Organized in a mostly time-order sequence	Sequence isn't always clear	Unorganized
Voice	Sincere, first person account	Mostly sincere first person account	Writer expresses few feelings	Writer does not express feelings
Word Choice	Excellent use of describing words	Good use of describing words	Some use of describing words	No use of describing words
Sentences	Smooth sentence flow	Mostly smooth sentence flow	Many short sentences	Mostly short, choppy sentences
Conventions	Excellent use of prepositions and prepositional phrases	Good use of prepositions and prepositional phrases	Little or incorrect use of prepositions and prepositional phrases	Errors may prevent understanding

© Pearson Education, Inc., 4

Vocabulary • Synonyms

- **Synonyms** are words with the same or similar meanings.
- Sometimes a synonym can be a **context clue** to help you figure out the meaning of a word.
- An analogy compares two things to another pair of things. In an analogy the symbol : stands for "is to."

Directions Read the following passage about a vacation on the moon. Then complete the analogies below. Use context clues to help you find the answers.

Kiko and Val were excited about their vacation on the moon. Throughout their ride on the space shuttle, they were summoning, or rousing, their courage for their first moonwalk.

As they landed, they could make out some of the moon's various features. Val pointed out a rille, which is like a valley.

On their first day out, they both staggered and lurched from side to side. The moon's gravity felt so strange. When Kiko saw a deep ditch, or trench, she gave Val a challenging look and taunted her for being too scared to leap over it. Though Val didn't like being mocked by Kiko, she wasn't about to jump until she was perfectly ready.

1. Peak : mountaintop as valley : _____.

2. Summoning : _____ as dampening : deadening.

3. Hill : mound as _____ : ditch.

4. Taunted : _____ as praised : encouraged.

5. _____ : lurched as balanced : poised.

Home Activity Your child used synonyms and context clues in a short passage to complete analogies. With your child, reread the analogies above. For each numbered item, ask your child to point out the synonyms and antonyms.

© Pearson Education, Inc., 4

Order Form/Application

Order forms and **applications** are charts with columns and spaces in which you can write or type. An order form is the means by which a person can purchase merchandise by completing a form and e-mailing or sending it to a company. An application is a form by which a person can apply for a job. Application forms ask for identifying information such as name, address, and phone number, and also ask for the person's educational and job history.

Directions Answer the questions below about the following order form.

MOON BASE GAMMA ORDER FORM
Click SUBMIT when you have completed this form.

Item Number	Item	Quantity	Price
13715	Big Bracelet		$

+ $5 shipping and handling

TOTAL PRICE $

Billing Address	Shipping Address
	☐ Check this box if same as billing address
* Name	* Name
* Street Address	* Street Address
* City	* City
* State * ZIP	* State * ZIP
* Country	* Country
Phone	Phone
* E-mail address	

PAYMENT METHOD	Your comments and messages here.
* Type of Credit Card _____	
* Account Number _____	
* Expiration Date _____	

* REQUIRED FIELD   *Submit*

---

1. What is the difference between the two addresses on the form?

_____

2. When would you provide only one address?

_____

3. What does *quantity* mean?

_____

4. What boxes are you not required to fill in on this form?

_____

5. What do you do when you are finished filling out the form?

© Pearson Education, Inc., 4

Directions Use this online job application form to answer the questions below.

Lincoln Library Association		
SUMMER INTERNSHIP EMPLOYMENT APPLICATION		
1. **PERSONAL INFORMATION** Name Address Telephone Date You Can Start Working	2. **EDUCATION** Name and Location of School Grade You Will Complete This Year	
3. **JOB EXPERIENCE** Job Title Employer	4. **OTHER SKILLS**	
5. **REFERENCE** Name Telephone Relationship		
6. **WHY DO YOU WANT THIS JOB?**		

1. What is the purpose of this application?

_____

_____

2. Why would the library ask for a reference?

_____

_____

3. In what section would you say when you could start your internship?

_____

_____

4. In which of the six sections of the application would you give information about skills you would bring to a position at the library?

_____

5. What would be a good answer to the question in box number 6?

_____

Home Activity Your child learned about order forms and applications. Use the Internet to look up an online application. Have your child point out the different parts of an application.

© Pearson Education, Inc., 4

Name _____

Related Words

Proofread a Story Help Maggie edit her story about a family member. Circle six misspelled words and the capitalization error. Write them correctly.

© Pearson Education, Inc., 4

---

a family tale

I have a very pleasent and interesting elderly relative. He is ninety-five years old and is the imige of health. One of his daily health habits is to breath very deeply each morning. Then he starts exercising. Can you imagine someone who's ninety-five doing jumping jacks? I've even seen my relative do this in tripel time. Yesterday he went out and cought a fish that weighed 1,000 pounds. He reeled it in and ate the whole thing for breakfast. Maybe by now you've guessed that this compusition is a tall tale!

Spelling Words
please
pleasant
breath
breathe
image
imagine
product
production
heal
health
triple
triplet
relate
relative
meter
metric
compose
composition
crumb
crumble

1. _____   2. _____

3. _____   4. _____

5. _____   6. _____

7. _____

Frequently Misspelled Words
caught
bought

Proofread Words Circle the word that is spelled correctly. Write it.

8. breth   breath   breate   8. _____

9. health   helth   heathe   9. _____

10. tiplet   tripplet   triplet   10. _____

11. crumle   crumble   crumbel   11. _____

12. metric   metrik   metic   12. _____

Home Activity Your child identified misspelled list words. Make up sentences for some of the list words. Say the sentence, omitting the list word, and have your child write the missing word.

Prepositions and Prepositional Phrases

Directions Read the passage. Then read each question. Circle the letter of the correct answer.

Space Project

(1) Do you want to do a space project of me? (2) I want to learn more which the moon. (3) NASA has a good site behind the Internet. (4) Let's go beneath the library this afternoon. (5) People once thought there was life on the moon. (6) The moon's climate is too harsh for living things. (7) No creature could survive for those conditions.

1 What change, if any, should be made in sentence 1?

A   Change *of* to **at.**

B   Change *of* to **from.**

C   Change *of* to **with.**

D   Make no change.

2 What change, if any, should be made in sentence 2?

A   Change *which* to **about.**

B   Change *which* to **for.**

C   Change *which* to **between.**

D   Make no change.

3 What change, if any, should be made in sentence 3?

A   Change *behind* to **at.**

B   Change *behind* to **or.**

C   Change *behind* to **on.**

D   Make no change.

4 What change, if any, should be made in sentence 4?

A   Change *beneath* to **to.**

B   Change *beneath* to **at.**

C   Change the *beneath* to **on.**

D   Make no change.

5 What change, if any, should be made in sentence 7?

A   Change *for* to **under.**

B   Change *for* to **of.**

C   Change *for* to **at.**

D   Make no change.

© Pearson Education, Inc., 4

Home Activity Your child prepared for taking tests on prepositions and prepositional phrases. Have your child write a list of phrases to go with the prepositions *of, in, by, to, for,* and *with*. Take turns saying a sentence for each phrase.

Multisyllabic Words

Spelling Words				
reaction	prerecorded	incorrectly	incredibly	disobedient
disagreeable	refreshment	unbreakable	declaration	retirement
misdialed	undefined	unhappily	watchfully	gleefully
sportsmanship	repayment	questionable	displacement	midshipman

Word Sort Sort the list words by their number of syllables. Write every word.

Three-Syllable Words

1. _____
2. _____
3. _____
4. _____
5. _____
6. _____
7. _____
8. _____
9. _____
10. _____
11. _____

Four-Syllable Words

12. _____
13. _____
14. _____
15. _____
16. _____
17. _____
18. _____

Five-Syllable Words

19. _____
20. _____

© Pearson Education, Inc., 4

Home Activity Your child learned multisyllabic words. Say each word clearly. Have your child move a penny into a box for each syllable he or she hears.

Adjectives and Articles

Directions Each sentence has two adjectives. One adjective is underlined. Find and write the other adjective. (It may be an article.)

1. <u>Those</u> campers were careful with campfires. _____

2. Campfires are one cause of <u>harmful</u> fires. _____

3. We saw <u>a</u> bright flash of lightning. _____

4. Lightning can cause dangerous fires in <u>the</u> forest. _____

5. <u>That</u> fire burned for five days. _____

6. It threatened to destroy <u>several</u> large homes. _____

7. <u>Brave</u> firefighters fought the fire. _____

8. Smokejumpers did not fight that <u>particular</u> fire. _____

9. It was in an <u>open</u> area. _____

10. Fire trucks from nearby towns put out <u>the</u> blaze. _____

Directions Decide what kind of question each underlined adjective answers. Write *What kind? How many?* or *Which one?*

11. Would you like to be one of <u>those</u> smokejumpers? _____

12. A smokejumper carries <u>heavy</u> equipment. _____

13. Smokejumpers learn <u>many</u> parachuting methods. _____

14. <u>That</u> part of the job might scare some people. _____

15. The smokejumpers land in rough, <u>rocky</u> areas. _____

16. They must fight fires in <u>dense</u> mountain forests. _____

17. They must take <u>several</u> training courses. _____

18. Smokejumpers try to keep <u>green</u>, healthy forests. _____

19. Smokejumpers will fight many fires <u>this</u> year. _____

20. They are probably <u>proud</u> of their work. _____

© Pearson Education, Inc., 4

Words with Double Consonants

Spelling Words				
tomorrow	borrow	different	rabbit	matter
written	bottle	ridden	odd	bubble
offer	suffer	slippers	grasshopper	worry
current	lettuce	saddle	shudder	hobby

Word Groups Write the list word that best completes each word group.

1. One who is sick or hurt may do this.
2. This is to take on loan.
3. These will comfortably replace your shoes.
4. Everything on Earth is made of this.
5. Most salads are made of this.
6. This is something you do to pass the time.
7. When you wash the dishes, you might make this.
8. The day after today is this.
9. Something strange or awkward may also be this.
10. One who has pedaled a bicycle has done this.

1. _____
2. _____
3. _____
4. _____
5. _____
6. _____
7. _____
8. _____
9. _____
10. _____

Analogies Write the list word that best completes the comparison.

11. Smile is to relax as mope is to _____.
12. Road is to roadrunner as grass is to _____.
13. Kitty is to cat as bunny is to _____.
14. Tremor is to tremble as shake is to _____.
15. Light is to dark as same is to _____.
16. Seat is to bike as _____ is to horse.
17. Cereal is to box as milk is to _____.
18. Old is to past as new is to _____.
19. Type is to typed as wrote is to _____.
20. Want is to borrow as give is to _____.

11. _____
12. _____
13. _____
14. _____
15. _____
16. _____
17. _____
18. _____
19. _____
20. _____

© Pearson Education, Inc., 4

School + Home

Home Activity Your child learned words with double consonants. Use each list word in a sentence and have your child spell the word aloud.

Adverbs

Directions Write the adverb in each sentence.

1. "How quickly can you take us there?" _____

2. The guide agreed reluctantly. _____

3. The trail turned sharply toward the jungle. _____

4. The air was hot and very humid. _____

5. Eventually they met a local farmer. _____

6. He felt they were traveling slowly. _____

7. They had to stop repeatedly to rest. _____

8. He cautiously watched for snakes. _____

9. The wide river narrowed unexpectedly. _____

10. They wearily crept on all fours. _____

Directions Read each sentence. Circle the adverb in each sentence. Write *how* if the underlined adverb tells how an action happens. Write *when* if it tells when an action happens. Write *where* if it tells where an action happens.

11. Bingham asked about ruins everywhere. _____

12. Usually the answer was no. _____

13. The rain began noisily. _____

14. Beautifully carved stones caught his attention. _____

15. Earlier the Spanish had found gold and riches here. _____

16. He immediately carried on. _____

17. Bingham silently vowed to keep looking for Vilcapampa. _____

18. He instantly began to search some more. _____

© Pearson Education, Inc., 4

Greek Word Parts

Spelling Words				
telephone	biography	telescope	photograph	microwave
diameter	barometer	microscope	headphones	microphone
autograph	microchip	telegraph	perimeter	paragraph
phonics	symphony	saxophone	periscope	megaphone

What You Hear For each definition, write a list word containing *phon*.

1. a large orchestra
2. a device for sending sound by electricity
3. a funnel-shaped tube that magnifies the voice
4. a device that strengthens and broadcasts sound waves
5. a listening device fitted to the head
6. a curving musical instrument with a reed mouthpiece
7. use of sounds in words to teach beginning reading

1. _____
2. _____
3. _____
4. _____
5. _____
6. _____
7. _____

Proofread Sentences Circle the misspelled list word in each sentence. Write the word correctly on the line.

8. A baremoter measures air pressure.
9. I would like to get your autagraf.
10. I had to replace a computer mikrochep.
11. The perimmeter is the distance around a shape.
12. This circle has a daimeter of 3 inches.
13. Heat a cup of water in the microwav.
14. A parascope gives a submarine a view.

8. _____
9. _____
10. _____
11. _____
12. _____
13. _____
14. _____

Greek Pairs Use two list words with the same root to finish each sentence.

A good _____ of the subject helps you picture the subject of a _____. (*graph*)

15. _____   16. _____

You can use a _____ to see stars and a _____ to see cells (*scope*)

17. _____   18. _____

A complete _____ is a long _____ to send. (*graph*)

19. _____   20. _____

School + Home **Home Activity** Your child learned words formed from Greek word parts. Have your child look at words with *phon* and *graph*, and then tell what *phon* and *graph* probably mean.

© Pearson Education, Inc., 4

Comparative and Superlative Adjectives and Adverbs

Directions Fill in the chart. Write the comparative superlative forms of each adjective or adverb.

Adjective or Adverb	Comparative	Superlative
slow	1. _____	2. _____
hot	3. _____	4. _____
windy	5. _____	6. _____
bad	7. _____	8. _____
deep	9. _____	10. _____
heavily	11. _____	12. _____
rapidly	13. _____	14. _____
soon	15. _____	16. _____

Directions Write the correct form of the adjective or adverb in ( ) to complete each sentence.

17. Today's climbing gear is (safe) than the gear used only ten years ago.

_____

18. The wind near cliffs can be (dangerous) than the wind near the ground.

_____

19. The weather changes (quick) during spring.

_____

20. Axel let out the rope, sending Grits down (slowly) than usual.

_____

© Pearson Education, Inc., 4

Latin Roots

Spelling Words				
dictionary	abrupt	predict	import	locally
verdict	locate	portable	transport	bankrupt
dictate	location	erupt	passport	export
contradict	rupture	interrupt	disrupt	dislocate

Analogies Write the list word that best completes the sentence.

1. Thesaurus is to describe as _____ is to define.

2. Judge is to award as jury is to _____.

3. License is to drive as _____ is to travel.

4. Cloud is to storm as volcano is to _____.

5. Wealth is to rich as poverty is to _____.

6. Like is to dislike as lose is to _____.

1. _____

2. _____

3. _____

4. _____

5. _____

6. _____

Paragraph Completion Use list words with *port* to complete the paragraph.

Trains, ships, trucks, and airplanes **7.** _____ goods all over the world. Years ago, most materials were less **8.** _____ than they are now. The age of machines allows countries to **9.** _____ goods they have to sell and to **10.** _____ goods they need.

7. _____

8. _____

9. _____

10. _____

Word Scramble Unscramble the letters and write the list word.

11. pratub _____

12. pertcid _____

13. lalcoly _____

14. icedatt _____

15. notacoil _____

16. ratnodticc _____

17. puretur _____

18. pinetrrut _____

19. trupsid _____

20. etadiscol _____

Home Activity Your child learned words formed from Latin roots. Help your child brainstorm a list of additional words with *dic*, *rupt*, *port*, and *loc*.

© Pearson Education, Inc., 4

Time Order Words

Directions Write the time order word or phrase in each sentence.

1. As soon as we unpacked, we wanted to explore. _____

2. First on our list was Litchfield Island. _____

3. Before we left, we learned how to walk on moss. _____

4. We must not disturb the moss when we walk. _____

5. While on the island, we notice how quiet it is. _____

Directions Choose a time order word or phrase from the box to complete each sentence. Write the complete sentence.

> eventually   at first   once   instantly   suddenly

6. _____, a fierce storm raged for days.

_____

_____

7. _____ we tried to go outside.

_____

_____

_____

8. _____ we could not push the door open.

_____

_____

9. Then, _____, we were outside.

_____ ,

_____

10. I _____ felt the sting of wind-driven sleet.

_____

_____

© Pearson Education, Inc., 4

Name _____

Related Words

Spelling Words				
please	pleasant	breath	breathe	image
imagine	product	production	heal	health
triple	triplet	relate	relative	meter
metric	compose	composition	crumb	crumble

Adding Word Endings Base words may change when a word ending is added.
Write the pairs of list words in the correct column.

Drop *e*,
Add Word Ending

1. _____

2. _____

3. _____

4. _____

No Change,
Add Word Ending

5. _____

6. _____

7. _____

8. _____

9. _____

Change Base Word
Add Word Ending

10. _____

Home Activity Your child has learned pairs of related words. Challenge your child to use each pair of
words in a sentence. Listen for correct pronunciation.

© Pearson Education, Inc., 4

Prepositions and Prepositional Phrases

Directions Write the prepositional phrase in each sentence. Underline the preposition. Circle the object of the preposition.

1. Can you name the planet closest to Earth?

   _____

2. Mars is not far from us.

   _____

3. Venus is between Earth and Mercury.

   _____

4. There are beautiful rings around Saturn.

   _____

5. Let's focus on Jupiter.

   _____

6. That's Mars, just above the horizon.

   _____

7. After some practice, you'll recognize the planets.

   _____

Directions Each sentence below contains two prepositional phrases. Underline the prepositional phrases.

8. I enjoyed reading *The First Men in the Moon* by H. G. Wells.

9. It's about a scientist who creates a material that defies the force of gravity.

10. He flies from the Earth to the moon.

11. On the moon he discovers that there is a civilization beneath the moon's surface.

12. He goes into the moon's center and barely escapes with his life.

© Pearson Education, Inc., 4

Persuasion Chart

Directions Fill in the persuasion chart with the introduction to your position, supporting reasons, and a conclusion.

Introduction: State your position

↓

First reason

↓

Second reason

↓

Third reason (most important)

↓

Conclusion

© Pearson Education, Inc., 4

Persuasive Words

Directions Circle the persuasive word or words in each sentence. Write your own sentence using the same persuasive word or words. For number 5, write a sentence with one of the unused words from the box.

Persuasive Words					
better	worse	must	should	most important	need
best	worst	never	necessary	effective	

1. Our class must take a trip to the top of the Sears Tower.

_____

_____

2. Students should have the opportunity to visit a large city and see skyscrapers.

_____

_____

3. The best view of the city is from the sky deck.

_____

_____

4. The most important reason for visiting the Sears Tower is to learn more about urban architecture.

_____

_____

5. _____

_____

© Pearson Education, Inc., 4

Powerful Adjectives

Directions Write a word from the box to complete each sentence.

cautious	foolish	curious	odorous	amazing
dangerous	popular	primary	memorable	undisturbed

1. Yellowstone Park is one of the most _____ vacation spots in America.

2. The wildlife in Yellowstone is a _____ reason that many people visit the park.

3. You can see moose, elk, bison, bear, and an _____ number of other animals.

4. However, be _____ dealing with these animals.

5. Remember that they can be _____.

6. Respect their needs for _____ territory.

7. Never chase or try to pet animals, even if they seem _____ and approach you.

8. Never feed them, and store _____ items carefully in your campsite.

9. Remember that a _____ vacationer can get hurt.

10. Keep your distance, and bring your camera to record these _____ sights.

© Pearson Education, Inc., 4

Peer Teaching Conferencing Persuasive Essay

Directions Read your partner's essay. Refer to the Revising Checklist as you write your comments or questions. Offer compliments as well as revision suggestions. Then take turns talking about each other's draft. Give your partner your notes. After you and your teacher talk about your essay, add your teacher's comments to the notes.

Revising Checklist

Focus/Ideas

☐ Does the persuasive essay establish a position and then focus on the position?

☐ Is the position supported by enough details, reasons, facts, and examples?

Organization

☐ Is the position stated clearly in the introduction of the essay?

☐ Are the supporting details organized into paragraphs in the body?

☐ Does the essay end with a conclusion?

Voice

☐ Is the writer's voice confident and convincing?

Word Choice

☐ Are persuasive words and powerful adjectives used to make the position and supporting details clear and coherent?

Sentences

☐ Are sentences correct and written in a variety of types and lengths?

Things I Thought Were Good _____

_____

_____

Things I Thought Could Be Improved _____

_____

_____

Teacher's Comments _____

_____

© Pearson Education, Inc., 4

Cause and Effect

- A **cause** is why something happens. An **effect** is what happens.
- Clue words such as *because, so,* and *since* sometimes signal a cause-effect relationship.
- Sometimes one effect can become the cause of another effect, which causes another, and so on. This is called a chain of events.

Directions Read the following story. Then complete the diagram.

One day some time ago, a boy named Jack was doing homework. His mother began to examine Jack's textbook. A puzzled look clouded her face. She noticed that the book was worn and missing a dozen pages.

The next day, she told the school's principal that Jack deserved better materials. He agreed, but said that only schools in white districts got new texts.

Schools in African American areas got old, damaged books.

So Jack's mother met with a lawyer. They filed a legal case, claiming unequal and unfair treatment toward Jack. A judge decided that Jack's mother was right. The board of education agreed to revise the system for providing materials to schools in the district.

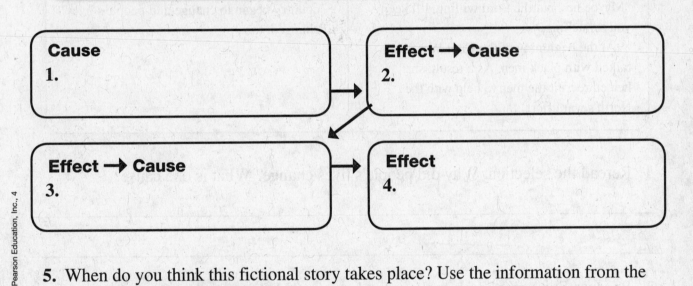

Cause 1.	Effect → Cause 2.
Effect → Cause 3.	Effect 4.

5. When do you think this fictional story takes place? Use the information from the text and your prior knowledge to answer the question.

_____

Home Activity Your child used a graphic organizer to determine causes and effects. Read a story together. Use a graphic organizer like the one above to map out the causes and effects in the story.

© Pearson Education, Inc., 4

Writing • Cause-and-Effect Essay

Key Features of Cause-and-Effect Essay
- describes events or outcomes
- includes details that explain why the events or outcomes happened
- uses words that signal cause-and effect relationships

Sojourner Truth

Sojourner Truth was born Isabella Baumfree. She was a slave in New York State around 1797. Later, after she gained her freedom, Isabella took the name of Sojourner Truth because it described her work as a preacher, traveling around the country making speeches about slavery. Throughout her life, due to Sojourner Truth's words, people's lives changed.

A white man once told her that her speeches were no more important than a fleabite. Consequently, she replied, "Maybe not, but the Lord willing, I'll keep you scratching."

At the beginning of the Civil War, Truth talked with black men. As a result, she helped recruit the men to help with the North's war effort.

In 1864, Truth used her words again to make a difference. She led a campaign, or group of activities, against the policy that did not allow blacks to sit with whites on trains.

After the Civil War, Truth spoke and worked with people to get jobs for blacks.

Because of Sojourner Truth's words and the words of others like her, slavery was abolished, unfair practices were made illegal, and many black people entered the work force. Little by little, our country began to change and people's lives changed, too.

1. Reread the selection. Why did people's lives change? What is one cause?

_____

_____

2. Because Sojourner Truth spoke, what happened? What was the effect over time?

_____

_____

_____

© Pearson Education, Inc., 4

Vocabulary

Directions Draw a line to connect each word on the left with its definition on the right.

1. avoided   very many

2. numerous   platform in a church from which the minister preaches

3. pulpit   protecting

4. minister   member of the clergy

5. shielding   kept away from

Directions Choose the word from the box that best matches each clue. Write the word on the line.

_____ 6. You probably tried to do this when you were about to run into something or someone.

_____ 7. This person works in a church.

_____ 8. Your great-great-grandparents are an example of these.

_____ 9. This describes a large number of something.

_____ 10. These are periods of about thirty years.

Check the Words You Know

___ancestors
___avoided
___generations
___minister
___numerous
___pulpit
___shielding

Write a Poem

Pretend you have just heard Dr. Martin Luther King Jr. speak at a civil rights meeting. Write a poem about the event. Use as many vocabulary words as you can.

© Pearson Education, Inc., 4

Home Activity Your child identified and used vocabulary words from *My Brother Martin*. Have your child draw pictures that represent the meanings of the words from the selection.

Conjunctions

Conjunctions are connecting words. The words *and, but,* and *or* are coordinating conjunctions. They can be used to join words, phrases, and sentences.

- Use *and* to add information or to join related ideas: Pam <u>and</u> Ann lived with them.
- Use *but* to join different ideas: He was gentle <u>but</u> strong-minded.
- Use *or* to suggest a choice: Sometimes you have to fight <u>or</u> give in.

Conjunctions also make compound subjects, compound predicates, and compound sentences. There is a comma before the conjunction in a compound sentence.

Compound Subject   Martin <u>and</u> his brother were younger than Christine.
Compound Predicate   They lived <u>and</u> played on Auburn Avenue.
Compound Sentence   Martin had many difficulties, <u>but</u> he worked to make his dream come true. (Note the comma.)

Directions Write the conjunction in each sentence.

1. White families and black families lived on Auburn Avenue.   _____

2. The kids were friendly with each other, but the grown-ups were not.   _____

3. Martin did not know whether he was more angry or sad.   _____

Directions Use the conjunction *and, but,* or *or* to join each pair of sentences. Write the new sentences. Remember to add a comma.

4. Martin could have lived a quiet life. He chose to take action.

_____

_____

5. He graduated from high school at 15. He got high grades in college.

_____

_____

Home Activity Your child learned about conjunctions. Ask your child to give you oral examples of how the conjunctions *and, but,* and *or* are used differently in sentences.

© Pearson Education, Inc., 4

Schwa

Spelling Words				
stomach	memory	Canada	element	mystery
science	remember	forget	suppose	iron
gravel	difficult	fortune	giant	architect
normal	notify	privilege	cement	yesterday

Antonyms Write the list word that has the opposite or almost the opposite meaning.

1. tomorrow _____   2. easy _____

3. remember _____   4. miniature _____

5. strange _____   6. forget _____

Synonyms Write a list word that has the same or almost the same meaning.

7. tummy _____   8. suspense _____

9. luck _____   10. designer _____

11. advantage _____ 12. remembrance _____

Missing Words Complete the sentence by writing a list word.

13. I _____ she will arrive on time.   13. _____

14. The new _____ sidewalk has no cracks.   14. _____

15. Walking barefoot on _____ is painful.   15. _____

16. Please _____ me when my package arrives.   16. _____

17. Montreal is a city in Quebec, _____.   17. _____

18. She is determined that people say she has a will of _____.   18. _____

19. His _____ experiment took 30 minutes.   19. _____

20. The _____ of surprise is important to a good story.   20. _____

© Pearson Education, Inc., 4

Home Activity Your child wrote words that have the schwa sound. Say the list words and have your child spell them.

Cause and Effect

Causes **Effects**

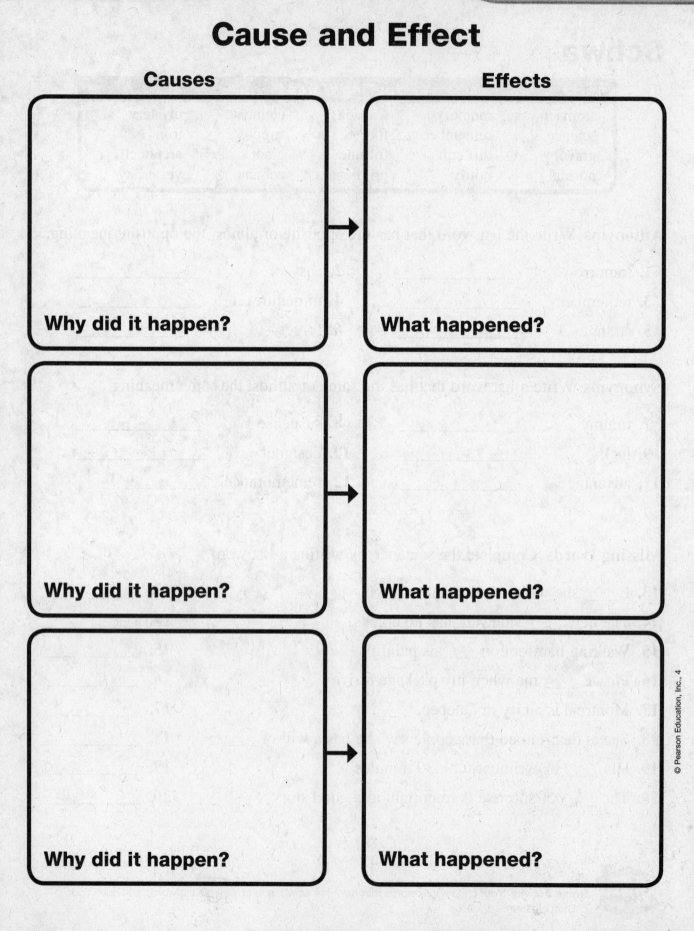

Why did it happen? What happened?

Why did it happen? What happened?

Why did it happen? What happened?

© Pearson Education, Inc., 4

Vocabulary • Root Words

- A **root word** is a word that other words are made from. Sometimes root words are also called base words.

- The root word for *shielding* is *shield*. The root word for *numerous* is *number*. The root word for *generations* is *generate (to begin)*. A *generation* includes all people born in the same period of time. The root word for *avoided* is *avoid (to stay away from)*.

Directions Read the following letter. Then answer the questions below.

Dear Dr. King,
I saw you speak today in front of numerous people. I could tell that you truly care about shielding people from danger today and making sure future generations are safe, as well. I know it must be hard to talk about equal rights when some people in this country are against it. You could have avoided the jail time you spent by just living out your days as a minister. However, you believed that change would not come that way. I admire your courage.

Sincerely,

Mrs. Roberta Watson

1. What do the words *avoid* and *avoided* mean? What is the difference between them?

_____

_____

2. What word in the passage has the same root as *number?* _____
How is that word's meaning related to the meaning of *number?*

_____

3. Think about a shield—a piece of armor used in battle. What does a shield do?

_____

What does *shielding* mean? _____

4. A generation includes all the people who are born at the same time. For example, all people born in the 1990s are from the same *generation*. What do you think *future generations* means?

_____

_____

© Pearson Education, Inc., 4

Home Activity Your child identified root words. Read a story together. Have your child show you how to identify root words in a sentence.

Take Notes/Paraphrase and Synthesize/ Record Findings

Taking notes and **recording findings** about key information in a text can help you understand and remember the text better. It can also help you organize information to study for a test or to include in a research paper. When you take notes, **paraphrase,** or put what you read into your own words. Try to **synthesize,** or combine, information as you take notes. This will allow you to include all of the author's ideas as well as important details. Use key words, phrases, or short sentences.

Directions Read the article below. Record notes on a separate sheet of paper. Then use them to answer the questions that follow.

Like Dr. Martin Luther King Jr., Cesar Chavez knew that equal rights were worth fighting for. He spent most of his adult life trying to do what he believed was right.

Chavez was born in 1927 in Arizona. When he was ten years old, his family lost its farm during the Great Depression. He and his family became migrant workers, moving from place to place in search of farm work. Later, Chavez joined the U.S. Navy, married, and settled down in California.

Chavez began working to improve social conditions when he became a member of the Community Service Organization. This group worked to fight discrimination against people of Hispanic background. Chavez spoke out against this discrimination, and he urged Latino citizens to use their power as voters. He believed that Latinos' votes could make the government take notice of needs in their community.

Chavez knew that one particular group of Latinos especially needed his help—the migrant workers. He started an organization to help farm workers receive the pay, benefits, and treatment they deserved.

He realized that the first challenge was getting the attention of people across the nation. He believed strongly in the idea of peaceful protest. Chavez helped convey the issues of farm work by staging strikes. Also, he urged consumers to stop buying products from companies that mistreated migrant farm workers. Another method of protesting was fasts. During a fast, a person does not eat food. Chavez once protested by fasting for thirty-six days.

Cesar Chavez never became a wealthy man. The purpose of his work was justice, not fame. He simply cared about helping others.

© Pearson Education, Inc., 4

1. How is this article organized?

_____

2. Paraphrase the first sentence in the article.

_____

Directions Refer to your notes to help you answer the questions below.

3. Why is it important to take note of the fact that Chavez was a migrant worker?

_____

_____

4. Is the detail about Chavez joining the U.S. Navy important enough to include in your notes? Why or why not?

_____

_____

5. What did Chavez do with the Community Service Organization?

_____

_____

6. What methods of peaceful protest did Chavez use?

_____

_____

7. Why is it important to write down only the most important ideas when note-taking?

_____

_____

8. When taking notes for a report, it is important to write down the title and author of the book or article you are reading. Why do you need to do this?

_____

_____

9. Descibe a graphic organizer you might use to organize your notes.

_____

_____

10. Copy a section of your notes from the article in the lines below.

_____

_____

© Pearson Education, Inc., 4

Home Activity Your child learned how to take notes and synthesize and paraphrase information. Read an article or story aloud to him or her. After each sentence, help your child to paraphrase it. See how many sentences he or she can paraphrase.

Schwa

Proofread a Report Circle six misspelled words in Alex's report. Write the words correctly. Find the sentence with capitalization errors and write it correctly.

Spelling Words

stomach
memory
Canada
element
mystery
science
remember
forget
suppose
iron

gravel
difficult
fortune
giant
architect
normal
notify
privilege
cement
yesterday

> Northern Lights
> The shimmering show of the Northern Lights used to be a mystary, but thanks to sciunce we now know the cause. Like iron to a magnet, particles in the sky are attracted to the Earth.
> The amazing sky show is best seen in places like Canida or Alaska, but it is diffacult to predict when a show will happen. Nature does not Notify Us in Advance. There is always an element of surprise. However, it is norml to see Northern Lights in August.
> Seeing a Northern Light show creates a beutaful memory. If you have the good fortune to see the wonderful sight, you will never forget it.

1. _____   2. _____

3. _____   4. _____

5. _____   6. _____

7. _____

Frequently Misspelled Words

first
beautiful

Proofread Words Cross out the misspelled list word in each phrase. Write the word correctly.

8. archatect designs a plan   8. _____

9. strong ciment sidewalks   9. _____

10. designs for ginat homes   10. _____

11. beautiful gravle walkways   11. _____

12. plans completed yesturday   12. _____

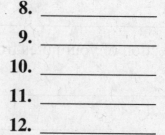

Home Activity Your child identified misspelled list words. Say each word in a sentence and have your child repeat the list word and write it.

© Pearson Education, Inc., 4

Name _____

Conjunctions

Directions Read the passage. Then read each question. Circle the letter of the correct answer.

Martin Luther King

(1) Martin Luther King Jr. fought for equality but justice. (2) He believed in action since not in violence. (3) Should people accept injustice to fight for their rights? (4) King dreamed of a better world, than he helped create one. (5) He was arrested nearly twenty times, but he kept on fighting. (6) People must take action but nothing will change.

1 What change, if any, should be made in sentence 1?

  A Change *but* to **not.**

  B Change *but* to **or.**

  C Change *but* to **and.**

  D Make no change.

2 What change, if any, should be made in sentence 2?

  A Change *since* to **but.**

  B Change *since* to **or.**

  C Change *since* to **as.**

  D Make no change.

3 What change, if any, should be made in sentence 3?

  A Change *to* to **so.**

  B Change *to* to **if.**

  C Change *to* to **or.**

  D Make no change.

4 What change, if any, should be made in sentence 4?

  A Change *than* to **and.**

  B Change *than* to **that.**

  C Change *than* to **after.**

  D Make no change.

5 What change, if any, should be made in sentence 6?

  A Change *but* to **than.**

  B Change *but* to **and.**

  C Change *but* to **or.**

  D Make no change.

© Pearson Education, Inc., 4

Home Activity Your child prepared for taking tests on conjunctions. Have your child make flash cards for the words *and, but,* and *or.* Take turns choosing a card and making up phrases that can be combined into sentences using these words.

Fact and Opinion

- A **fact** is a statement that can be proved true or false.
- An **opinion** is a statement that tells what someone thinks, feels, or believes.
- You can evaluate an opinion by asking yourself if the statement is valid or faulty.
- A single sentence might contain both a statement of fact and a statement of opinion.

Directions Read the following passage. Then complete the table below.

Jim Thorpe was once called the greatest athlete in the world. He excelled in many sports and won many awards and honors. For some, Jim Brown was the greatest athlete. One of the best football players, Brown was also an All-American lacrosse player. He excelled in baseball and could have been a professional boxer.

Wilt "The Stilt" Chamberlain was the most dominant basketball player ever. He once scored 100 points in a game! Chamberlain was also a track star. Although many have called Wilt the greatest college basketball player ever, no one knows who is really "The Greatest."

Statement	Can it be proved true or false?	Fact? Opinion? Both?
Jim Thorpe won many awards and honors.	1.	2.
Wilt "The Stilt" Chamberlain was the most dominant basketball player ever.	3.	4.
5.	The first part can be proved true or false, but not the second part.	Contains both fact and opinion

© Pearson Education, Inc., 4

Home Activity Your child identified statements of fact and opinion in a nonfiction passage. With your child, discuss people whose abilities are inspiring. As you talk, ask your child whether certain statements are facts or opinions.

Writing • Critical Review

Key Features of Critical Review

- tells what a book is about

- discusses the book's theme or message

- gives an opinion, or claim, about the book and develops an argument by using evidence and reasons to support the claim

Turn Your Life Around

In *Nothing but Trouble: The Story of Althea Gibson*, Sue Stauffacher writes about how a wild tomboy from the city became the greatest female tennis player in the world.

Growing up in Harlem, a poor neighborhood in New York City, Althea Gibson only cared about playing games like stickball, basketball, and paddle tennis. Because she didn't care what people thought and didn't like being told how to act, people often said that Althea was nothing but trouble.

When a play leader, Buddy Walker, discovered how well Althea played paddle tennis in the street, things began to change. Although he could barely afford it, Buddy bought Althea a used tennis racket. Then Buddy and a club member, Juan Serrell, made it possible for Althea to join a tennis club.

At the tennis club, a one-armed tennis pro, Fred Johnson, worked with Althea to improve her tennis game, and Mrs. Rhoda

Smith bought Althea her first tennis outfit. Still, Althea often lost her temper and showed poor sportsmanship on the court. People continued to say she was nothing but trouble. But again, with Buddy's help, Althea learned to stay calm and be polite. Soon she was winning major tennis tournaments. In time, Althea became the first African American, man or woman, to compete and win the Wimbledon Cup, one of the highest honors in tennis. Throughout her life, Althea never stopped thanking the people who helped her turn her life around.

I think the message that the author wants readers to know is that when people care enough to help us, we can change our lives and achieve our dreams. I enjoyed this book because it gave funny examples of why Althea was nothing but trouble. Also, it was interesting to learn how Althea completely changed from a wild tomboy to a polite, world-class athlete.

© Pearson Education, Inc., 4

1. Reread the book review. What is the title of the book? Who is the author?

_____

2. Does this book review make you want to read the book? Explain.

_____

_____

Vocabulary

Directions Choose the word from the box that best matches each definition. Write the word on the line.

_____ 1. the people of any particular time or place

_____ 2. a building with many rooms in which people sleep

_____ 3. power to withstand hard wear

_____ 4. done with the hands

_____ 5. land set aside by the government for a special purpose

Check the Words You Know

___ boarding

  school

___ dormitory

___ endurance

___ manual

___ reservation

___ society

Directions Choose the word from the box that best completes each sentence. Write the word on the line shown to the left.

_____ 6. Because I attended ___, I spent long stretches of time away from home.

_____ 7. Cars have either a ___ or an automatic transmission.

_____ 8. You have to have a lot of ___ to run marathons.

_____ 9. Years ago, the rules of ___ were very strict.

_____ 10. At college, Janet enjoyed living in a _____.

Write a Description

Write a description of how a boarding school might be different from your present school. Use as many vocabulary words as you can.

© Pearson Education, Inc., 4

Home Activity Your child identified and used vocabulary words from *Jim Thorpe's Bright Path*. Together, make up your own fill-in-the-blank sentences (like those that appear in the second activity), using the vocabulary words from the selection.

Name _____

Capitalization and Abbreviations

Here are some rules for **capitalizing** proper nouns.

- Capitalize the first word and every important word of a proper noun. Proper nouns name particular persons, places, or things. Names of magazines, newspapers, works of art, musical compositions, and organizations are proper nouns.

  Jim Thorpe   **Pro Football Hall of Fame**   *People Weekly*
  New York Times   the *Mona Lisa*   *Swan Lake*   **Sierra Club**

- Capitalize the first letter of an abbreviation. Capitalize both letters in a state postal abbreviation.

  227 Topeka **A**ve.   Fargo, **ND**

- Capitalize days of the week, months of the year, and holidays.

  Monday   **N**ovember   **M**emorial **D**ay

- Capitalize titles that are used before people's names.

  Coach and **M**rs. Warner asked us to come to their house.

- Capitalize the first word in a direct quotation.

  "**T**he football game was so exciting," she said.

Directions Rewrite each sentence. Use correct capitalization.

1. That letter goes to the united states indian industrial school in carlisle, pa.

   _____

   _____

2. He competed at the summer olympics in sweden.

   _____

   _____

Directions Write *C* if the group of words is capitalized correctly. If the group of words is capitalized incorrectly, rewrite it using correct capitalization.

3. Stockholm in sweden   _____

4. National Football league   _____

Home Activity Your child learned about capitalization. Write the addresses of three of your family's friends or relatives, leaving out all capital letters. Have your child rewrite the addresses and add the capital letters.

© Pearson Education, Inc., 4

Name _____

Prefixes *mis-*, *non-*, *re-*, *pre-*

Spelling Words				
misplace	nonsense	prepay	repack	misfortune
remove	precook	nonstop	recover	reseal
misbehavior	reunion	nonfiction	rebound	prejudge
readjust	misprint	nonprofit	nonstick	precaution

Missing Words Write the list word that best completes each sentence.

1. Textbooks and biographies are examples of ____ books.
1. _____

2. To avoid standing in line, we ____ for our movie tickets.
2. _____

3. My friends from kindergarten and I got together for a ____.
3. _____

4. My suitcase was too full to close so I had to ____ it.
4. _____

5. The forward got the ____ and made a basket.
5. _____

6. The trip from Atlanta to Seattle was a direct, ____ flight.
6. _____

7. The eye doctor had to ____ my glasses because they didn't fit.
7. _____

8. We ____ much of our food to save time.
8. _____

9. It is hard to make friends if you ____ people.
9. _____

10. A ____ pan is easy to clean.
10. _____

11. When boating, you should wear a life preserver as a ____.
11. _____

12. There was a ____ in last week's magazine.
12. _____

Antonyms Write the list word that has the opposite meaning.

13. find   13. _____

14. luck   14. _____

15. truth   15. _____

16. add   16. _____

17. relapse   17. _____

18. reopen   18. _____

19. obedience   19. _____

20. money-making 20. _____

Home Activity Your child wrote words with the prefixes *mis-*, *non-*, *re-* and *pre-*. Ask your child to explain how each prefix changes the base word's meaning.

© Pearson Education, Inc., 4

Four-Column Chart

© Pearson Education, Inc., 4

Name _____

Vocabulary • Multiple-Meaning Words

- **Multiple-meaning words** are words that have more than one meaning.
- Dictionaries provide alphabetical lists of words and their meanings. While reading, a reader may come across unfamiliar words, or familiar words used in unfamiliar ways. If this happens, use a dictionary or glossary to find the meaning.

Directions Read the following passage. Then answer the questions below, using a dictionary or glossary.

Since there was no school on Leslie's reservation, she attended a boarding school. Leslie was glad to go away to school, because otherwise she must get a job like her brothers. They earned their living doing manual labor, but Leslie was not particularly good with her hands.

At school every spring, Leslie played tennis. All year she looked forward to picking up a tennis racket. During bad weather, she even practiced hitting a ball against the walls of her small dormitory room. Leslie had big goals in life. She wanted to be a professional tennis player.

1. What is the meaning of *reservation* as it is used in the story?

_____

2. What is the meaning of *manual* as it is used in the passage? What is another meaning for this word?

_____

_____

3. What meaning of *goals* makes sense in this story?

_____

4. In this passage, what is the meaning of the word *racket*?

_____

5. Choose a word with multiple meanings from the story. Write a sentence using the word in a different way from the way it is used in the passage.

_____

Home Activity Your child identified the correct meaning of multiple-meaning words as they were used in a short passage. Write down a list of multiple-meaning words. Take turns acting out and guessing the different meanings of the words.

© Pearson Education, Inc., 4

Magazines/Periodicals

- A **periodical** is a publication printed at regular times, such as every week or every month. A **magazine** is a type of periodical. Magazines contain a variety of articles, including news stories, feature stories, editorials, and regular opinion columns, as well as advertisements.

- Most magazines organize articles by order of interest. They present important or high-interest stories first. A magazine's table of contents lists the various articles it contains.

- Most magazine articles follow the 5Ws and H format—that is, the reader learns the Who? What? When? Where? Why? and How? of a topic.

Directions Read the magazine article below. Then answer the questions on the next page.

INTERVIEWS

The Secret of Williamson's Success
by R. L. Dawson

Every time I sit down to write this monthly column, I find that I am pleasantly surprised by the character of the people in sports.

This month I had the chance to interview Bobby Edstrom, who plays for the Meadow College Tigers. Bobby is a football player who stands six feet five inches tall and weighs three hundred pounds. When you see him, you automatically think that if you offended him, he could stomp all over you in two seconds flat.

We sat down in his coach's office to talk. It was the beginning of training in the late days of summer. He was wearing a Tigers T-shirt and jeans. He looked very comfortable and welcoming. Suddenly I didn't feel so nervous anymore. I began by asking him about his background and how he got to be such a good football player. I was amazed at his answer.

You see, I thought Bobby was one of those "natural athletes"—the ones who are stars from their earliest days on the playground. That was not the case with Bobby. He struggled in high school. He almost did not make the team his sophomore year.

When I asked him how he got to where he is today, he said two words: "Coach Williamson." Bobby Edstrom's high school coach, Leonard Williamson, told him that practicing hard, even when you are struggling, can get you to where you want to be. This coach encouraged Bobby every step of the way. He never allowed Bobby to think that he could not achieve his goals. A tear came to Bobby's eye as he talked about his coach. I asked if Bobby had ever had a chance to thank his coach, and he said that he hadn't. Coach Williamson had moved away from town, and Bobby lost contact with him.

Well, Bobby, chances are that Coach Williamson will read this column. I think that you can consider this a sincere, if overdue, thank-you card to an important and inspiring teacher.

© Pearson Education, Inc., 4

1. What is the title or headline of this article?

_____

2. Who wrote this article?

_____

3. In what part or section of the magazine does this article appear?

_____

4. What kind of article is this selection? How do you know?

_____

_____

5. Who is the "who" in this article?

_____

6. What is the "what" in this article?

_____

7. In what kind of magazine might this article appear?

_____

8. How is this article different from an article reporting on recent football scores?

_____

_____

9. Do you think this interview would appear before or after news stories? Why?

_____

10. Why do you think the title of the article is "The Secret of Williamson's Success" even though the interview is with Bobby Edstrom?

_____

_____

© Pearson Education, Inc., 4

Home Activity Your child read and analyzed a magazine article. Together, examine the cover of a magazine. Invite your child to predict the content of the magazine's articles based on the information and graphics on the cover. Make another prediction based on the table of contents. Finally, browse through the magazine together to confirm predictions.

Name _____

Prefixes *mis-*, *non-*, *re-*, *pre-*

Proofread Rules All the rules, except the last rule, give bad advice and should not be followed! Circle six words that are misspelled. Write the words correctly. Write the sentence that has an incorrect pronoun correctly.

> Misplace your homework so you can't find it.
>
> Always prejuge people so they'll be mad at you.
>
> Talk non stop about something boring for hours.
>
> Open envelopes and then resel it.
>
> Tell everyone that you're having a reunion and don't go.
>
> Reajust the volume on the radio to wake everyone up.
>
> Beleve everything you see on television.
>
> Make sure you know that everything on this list is nosense.

Spelling Words
misplace
nonsense
prepay
repack
misfortune
remove
precook
nonstop
recover
reseal
misbehavior
reunion
nonfiction
rebound
prejudge
readjust
misprint
nonprofit
nonstick
precaution

1. _____   2. _____

3. _____   4. _____

5. _____   6. _____

7. _____

Frequently Misspelled Words
believe
watch

Proofread Words Circle the correct spelling. Write the correct word.

8. non profit   non-profet   nonprofit   8. _____

9. precook   pre-cook   pre cook   9. _____

10. misfortuun   misfortune   misfortoon   10. _____

11. rekover   recovar   recover   11. _____

12. precaution   pre caution   precation   12. _____

Home Activity Your child identified misspelled words with the prefixes *mis-*, *non-*, *re-*, and *pre-*. Say the base words of some of the list words. Have your child add the prefix and spell the list word.

© Pearson Education, Inc., 4

Capitalization and Abbreviations

Directions Read the passage. Then read each question. Circle the letter of the correct answer.

Jim Thorpe, Pennsylvania

(1) There is a town called jim thorpe, PA. (2) It is named in honor of the great athlete. (3) You can visit it and stay in Jim Thorpe's national register historic district. (4) There is an inn at 24 north broadway. (5) The "Greatest athlete in the world" is buried on the east side of town.

1 What change, if any, should be made in sentence 1?

  A Change *jim thorpe, PA* to **Jim Thorpe, PA.**

  B Change *jim thorpe, PA* to **Jim Thorpe, pa.**

  C Change *jim thorpe, PA* to **Jim Thorpe, pennsylvania.**

  D Make no change.

2 What change, if any, should be made in sentence 3?

  A Change *national register historic district* to **National Register historic district.**

  B Change *national register historic district* to **national register Historic District.**

  C Change *national register historic district* to **National Register Historic District.**

  D Make no change.

3 What change, if any, should be made in sentence 4?

  A Change *north broadway* to **North Broadway.**

  B Change *north broadway* to **n. Broadway.**

  C Change *north broadway* to **north Broadway.**

  D Make no change.

4 What change, if any, should be made in sentence 5?

  A Change *"Greatest athlete in the world"* to "greatest athlete in the world."

  B Change *"Greatest athlete in the world"* to "greatest Athlete in the World."

  C Change *"Greatest athlete in the world"* to "Greatest Athlete in the World."

  D Make no change.

© Pearson Education, Inc., 4

Home Activity Your child prepared for taking tests on capitalization. Have your child address an envelope to someone you know and check to see that he or she uses correct capitalization.

Sequence

- **Sequence** is the order in which events happen in a story. When you read, think about what comes first, next, and last.
- A story's plot has a sequence of main events.
- Sometimes main events are told out of sequence. An event that happened earlier may not be revealed until later.

Directions Read the following passage.

When Nana moved to her daughter's house, she was afraid that her old-fashioned ways might embarrass her granddaughter, Leah. First Nana changed her hairstyle to look like the ones in the magazines. Then she exchanged her dark dresses for colorful ones. She even tried to change the way she spoke.

One night, Nana struggled to cook food she thought her granddaughter would like.

Finally Leah told her "You know, Nana, I love you just the way you are. So don't change." With that, Nana went back to her comfortable dresses, the way she always spoke, and her beloved recipes. But she kept her new hairstyle!

Directions Answer the questions below.

1. What is the first main event of this story? _____

2. What does Nana do first to try and fit in? _____

3. What does she do next? What clue tells you this?

_____

4. In this passage, does the word *finally* signal the last event of the story? How do you know?

_____

5. Does Leah know all along that her grandmother was trying to change to please her? How do you know?

_____

Home Activity Your child read a short passage and answered questions about the sequence of events. After watching a movie or television show together, ask your child about the plot. What was the sequence of events? Were there any flashbacks?

© Pearson Education, Inc., 4

Writing • Skit

Key Features of a Skit

- a scene, usually comic, in which characters interact
- uses dialogue and stage directions
- has few characters and one setting
- written to be acted out, like a short play

Practice Makes Perfect

(Martin Luther King and Alfred Daniel King are in the living room of their house on a hot summer day. They are using screwdrivers to loosen the legs on a piano bench.)

MARTIN: I'm roasting! No way do I want to sit inside this stifling house playing the piano for an hour!

ALFRED: (rubbing his knuckles) I didn't practice at all this week. I can just feel the ruler crack when I can't play a tune.

MARTIN: Don't worry. Soon we'll be practicing baseball in the backyard, and then we'll be down at the firehouse practicing how to be firemen.

ALFRED: Hurry! I hear Mr. Mann. Put the bench back!

(Martin and Alfred put the bench upright and quickly hide the screwdrivers in their pockets. Mr. Mann enters the room holding sheet music and a ruler.)

Martin and **Alfred:** (holding back giggles) Good morning, Mr. Mann!

MR. MANN: (rapping the piano bench with the ruler) All right, boys. Who would like to play first? Come sit beside me on the bench.

(Mr. Mann sits on the bench and down he goes.)

MR. MANN: Whoa! You'll have to get this bench repaired.

MARTIN: So is our lesson for today cancelled?

MR. MANN: (standing up and smoothing his clothes) Yes, but next week we'll have a two hour lesson!

(Martin and Alfred exit shaking their heads.)

1. Why is it important to read the stage directions?

_____

2. Through his dialogue, how can you tell how Martin feels about piano lessons?

_____

© Pearson Education, Inc., 4

Vocabulary

Directions Draw a line to connect each word on the left with its definition on the right.

1. resemblance   moving about in a sly manner

2. affords   a military rank below general

3. glint   similar appearance; likeness

4. lurking   a gleam; flash

5. colonel   provides; yields

Check the Words You Know

___affords
___colonel
___glint
___lurking
___palettes
___quaint
___resemblance

Directions Choose the word from the box that matches each clue. Write the word on the line.

_____   6. An artist would use these.

_____   7. You might see this if you look at a mother and a daughter.

_____   8. A diamond might show this when it reflects light.

_____   9. An alligator watching its prey might be doing this.

_____   10. A tiny cottage built for dolls might be described this way.

Write a Conversation

Pretend a relative has just moved in with your family. Write a conversation you would have with this person. Use as many vocabulary words as you can.

© Pearson Education, Inc., 4

Home Activity Your child identified and used vocabulary words from *How Tía Lola Came to Stay*. Make up a story with your child about two people, an artist and a colonel, from different worlds. Use the vocabulary words from the selection.

Commas

Here are some rules for using **commas.**

- Use commas to separate items in a series.
  I enjoy football, baseball, and hockey.

- Use commas to set off the name of someone being spoken to. This is called *direct address*. Use commas when the name is at the beginning, in the middle, or at the end of a sentence.
  Dad, are you awake? Yes, Tony, I am. Then look at this replay, Dad.

- Use commas after introductory words and phrases in sentences.
  By the way, I never saw a play like that before. Boy, that was good!

- Use commas in dates and addresses.
  Between the day and the month: Friday, September 13
  Between the date and the year: The season starts on April 4, 2006.
  Between the city and the state: The World Series ended in St. Louis, Missouri.

- Use commas in direct quotations.

  "I went to the seventh game of the World Series," said Aunt Sue.

  Uncle Jake asked, "Who won that game?"

Directions Write *C* if commas are used correctly in the sentence. If commas are not used correctly, add them where they belong.

1. Grandpa did you ever see Juan Marichal pitch? _____

2. Yes, I saw his major-league debut on Thursday July 19, 1960. _____

3. "He was strong, fast, and unbeatable that day," Grandpa said. _____

Directions Write the sentence. Add commas as needed.

4. Juan Marichal played for the Giants the Red Sox and the Dodgers.

_____

_____

Home Activity Your child learned about commas. Ask your child to list objects in the room. Have him or her say the word *comma* after each item.

© Pearson Education, Inc., 4

Suffixes *-less, -ment, -ness*

Spelling Words				
countless	payment	goodness	fairness	hopeless
treatment	statement	breathless	restless	enjoyment
pavement	flawless	tireless	amazement	amusement
greatness	punishment	timeless	needless	painless

Synonyms Write the list word that has the same or nearly the same meaning.

1. roadway   1. _____

3. kindness   3. _____

5. penalty   5. _____

7. declaration   7. _____

2. eternal   2. _____

4. fidgety   4. _____

6. gasping   6. _____

8. pleasure   8. _____

Antonyms Write the list word that has the opposite or nearly the opposite meaning.

9. few   9. _____

10. injustice   10. _____

11. hopeful   11. _____

12. unimportance   12. _____

13. lazy   13. _____

14. imperfect   14. _____

15. essential   15. _____

Missing Words Complete the sentence by writing a list word.

16. Rest is one ___ for the flu.   16. _____

17. We went to an ___ park.   17. _____

18. Don't forget to make the monthly ___.   18. _____

19. The child looked at the magician with ___.   19. _____

20. The doctor said the exam would be ___.   20. _____

© Pearson Education, Inc., 4

Home Activity Your child wrote words with the suffixes *-less, -ment,* and *-ness*. Say a base word and have your child add a suffix to spell the list word.

Story Sequence B

```
┌─────────────────────────────────────────────┐
│                    Title                      │
│                                               │
│                                               │
└─────────────────────────────────────────────┘

┌─────────────────────────────────────────────┐
│                  Characters                   │
│                                               │
│                                               │
│                                               │
│                                               │
└─────────────────────────────────────────────┘

┌─────────────────────────────────────────────┐
│                   Setting                     │
│                                               │
│                                               │
│                                               │
└─────────────────────────────────────────────┘

┌─────────────────────────────────────────────┐
│                   Events                      │
│  _____  │
│  _____  │
│  _____  │
│  _____  │
│  _____  │
│  _____  │
│  _____  │
│  _____  │
│  _____  │
└─────────────────────────────────────────────┘
```

© Pearson Education, Inc., 4

Vocabulary • Unfamiliar Words

When you are reading and see an **unfamiliar word,** you can use context clues, or words around the unfamiliar word, to figure out its meaning.

Directions Read the following passage. Then answer the questions below.

All Amalia ever wanted to do was paint. One day, her aunt said she was looking for a nanny for her children. Amalia liked her little cousins so she asked her aunt if she could be the nanny. Being a nanny affords, or allows, Amalia plenty of time for painting.

Amalia and her cousins live in a quaint town with old-fashioned houses and cobblestone streets. One day, she caught the glint, or gleam, of light on a puddle. She was inspired by its resemblance, or likeness, to a mirror. When Amalia returned home, she mixed the paints on her palette to paint the light on the puddle.

1. What context clue helps you to figure out the meaning of *affords?*

_____

2. What context clues help you to figure out the meaning of *quaint?*

_____

_____

3. One context clue for *glint* is *gleam.* If you didn't know what *gleam* meant, how could you figure out the meaning from the context?

_____

_____

4. What context clue gives you the meaning of *palette?*

_____

5. Write your own sentence using a context clue for the word *resemblance.*

_____

_____

Home Activity Your child read a short passage and used context clues to identify the meanings of unfamiliar words. Read a challenging story together. When you find an unfamiliar word, have your child locate context clues. If they do not exist, help your child to paraphrase the information around the unfamiliar word.

© Pearson Education, Inc., 4

Dictionary and Glossary

A **dictionary** is a book of words and their meanings. A **glossary** is a short dictionary at the back of some books. It has definitions of words used in the book. Dictionaries and glossaries are organized in alphabetical order. **Entry words,** the words in dark type in both dictionaries and glossaries, might be broken into syllables. For each entry word, you might find a **pronunciation key,** the **part of speech,** the **definition,** a sentence, and how the spelling changes when endings are added. Glossaries might also have page references.

Directions Study the dictionary and glossary entries below. Then answer the questions that follow.

Dictionary Entries	Glossary Entries
cul-ture: (kul´chər), 1. *n.,* elegance; sophistication 2. *n.,* traditions and customs of a group of people; *The Italian culture is known for its food.* 3. *n.* developing land and crops; *v.* cul-tured, cul-tur-ing	**cul•ture** (kul´chər), noun, the customs of a group of people (p. 98)
	curb (kėrb), noun, a border of hard material, like stone or concrete, on the edge of a street (p. 53)
Cum-ber-land: (kum´bər lənd), *n.,* a river that flows in Kentucky and Tennessee; it connects to the Ohio River.	**de•cep•tive** (di sep´tiv), adjective, deceiving or misleading (p. 22)
cum-ber-some: (kum´bər sum), *adj.,* difficult to control; bulky; awkward; *adv.,* cum-ber-some-ly	**deep** (dep) adjective, difficult to understand (p. 40)

1. What is one difference between a dictionary and a glossary?

_____

_____

2. What is the entry word before *Cumberland*? Why does it come before?

_____

_____

© Pearson Education, Inc., 4

Directions Use dictionary and glossary entries to answer the following questions.

3. What is the pronunciation of *curb?* What tells you that this is the pronunciation?

_____

4. Where will you find out an entry word's part of speech? In a dictionary, how would you know if a word is a noun?

_____

_____

5. What part of speech is *cumbersomely?*

_____

6. In a glossary, what do the page numbers after the definitions mean?

_____

7. The dictionary shows several definitions for the word *culture.* Why do you think there is only one in the glossary?

_____

_____

_____

8. What do you think the words in a glossary have in common?

_____

_____

9. In the dictionary, what is the purpose of the sentences that are in *italics?* Write a sentence that could be added to the definition of *cumbersome* to show how it is used.

_____

_____

_____

10. Describe when you would use a glossary rather than a dictionary.

_____

_____

© Pearson Education, Inc., 4

Home Activity Your child learned how to use dictionary and glossary entries. Choose a word from a dictionary page. Memorize its definition, part of speech, etc. Give your child the dictionary opened to that page. Have your child ask you "yes" and "no" questions to try to figure out the word you chose. For example, "Is the word a noun?"

Name _____

Suffixes -*less*, -*ment*, -*ness*

Proofread an Essay Help Jake corect his essay for the school writing contest. Circle six misspelled words and one capitalization error. Write the words correctly.

> ### The Key to Success
>
> How does one reach grateness? Does it take countless hours of tireles work? Does it mean sticking with something even when things look hopeless? Does it mean pounding the paivment trying to convince others that you have a great idea? To be successful, you must do all these things, but you must also find enjoiment in your work. After all, the best payment is a job well done. Thomas a. Edison knew this. It tok over 10,000 experiments to invent the light bulb.

Spelling Words

countless
payment
goodness
fairness
hopeless
treatment
statement
breathless
restless
enjoyment

pavement
flawless
tireless
amazement
amusement
greatness
punishment
timeless
needless
painless

1. _____   2. _____

3. _____   4. _____

5. _____   6. _____

7. _____

Proofread Words Cross out the list words that are spelled incorrectly. Write the words correctly.

8. After running the 100-meter race, the runners were breatheless.

8. _____

9. No one liked the commissioner's statment about the new baseball rule.

9. _____

10. Pets must rely on the goddness of their owners.

10. _____

11. Celebrities always get special treatement at restaurants.

11. _____

12. Waiting always makes me resless.

12. _____

Frequently Misspelled Words

took
myself

School + Home **Home Activity** Your child identified misspelled words with the suffixes -*less*, -*ment*, and -*ness*. Say one of the suffixes and have your child find and spell all the list words that end with that suffix.

© Pearson Education, Inc., 4

Commas

Directions Read the passage. Then read each question. Circle the letter of the correct answer.

The Oldest Ballpark

(1) Fenway Park is located at 4 Yawkey Way Boston MA. (2) It's the smallest oldest, and strangest ballpark in the country. (3) Fenway Park opened on April 20 1912. (4) As a matter of fact the park is crammed full of history. (5) We have tickets to a ballgame there on Wednesday, June 4.

1 What change, if any, should be made in sentence 1?

A Change *4 Yawkey Way Boston MA* to **4 Yawkey Way, Boston MA.**

B Change *4 Yawkey Way Boston MA* to **4 Yawkey Way, Boston, MA.**

C Change *4 Yawkey Way Boston MA* to **4 Yawkey, Way Boston, MA.**

D Make no change.

2 What change, if any, should be made in sentence 2?

A Change *smallest oldest, and strangest* to **smallest oldest and strangest.**

B Change *smallest oldest, and strangest* to **smallest, oldest and strangest.**

C Change *smallest oldest, and strangest* to **smallest, oldest, and strangest.**

D Make no change.

3 What change, if any, should be made in sentence 3?

A Change *April 20 1912* to **April 20, 1912.**

B Change *April 20 1912* to **April, 20 1912.**

C Change *April 20 1912* to **April, 20, 1912,**

D Make no change.

4 What change, if any, should be made in sentence 4?

A Change *As a matter of fact the park* to **As a matter of fact, the park.**

B Change *As a matter of fact the park* to **As a matter, of fact, the park.**

C Change *As a matter of fact the park* to **As a matter, of fact the park.**

D Make no change.

© Pearson Education, Inc., 4

Home Activity Your child prepared for taking tests on commas. Help your child write a list, a date, and an address with no commas. Then ask your child to put in the correct commas.

Generalize

- A **generalization** is a broad statement or rule that applies to many examples.
- Clue words such as *all, most, always, usually,* or *generally* signal generalizations.
- A generalization is valid if it is supported by facts or details. It is faulty if it is not supported.

Directions Read the following passage.

Usually, Red Feather practiced lacrosse every day. It was a game he had learned from the village elders, who passed down the tradition from generation to generation. Like most Huron boys, he had been carrying around a lacrosse stick from the time he was old enough to walk.

When the Huron boys in Red Feather's village played against boys from other villages, Red Feather's team always won. It was as if the boys on his team were all born with a love for the game that the others could never equal. Lacrosse for boys in his village was more than just a game—it was a way of life.

Directions Complete the chart by writing generalizations and their clue words from the passage.

Generalization	Clue Word
Usually, Red Feather practiced lacrosse every day.	**1.**
2.	**3.**
4.	most
Huron boys were all born with a love for the game that others could never equal.	**5.**

Home Activity Your child identified generalizations and their clue words in a passage. Have your child make generalizations about events in his or her life. Challenge your child to use clue words from this passage.

© Pearson Education, Inc., 4

Writing • Play/Scene

Key Features of a Play

- a story with plot, setting, and theme written to be performed
- includes dialogue labeled using characters' names
- may be divided into acts and scenes

Davy Crockett's Biggest Boast

Characters: Davy Crockett, Annie Bates, Tom Ironsmith

Act I
(Setting: 1800s, a spot deep in the backwoods. Davy, Tom, and Annie are standing under a tree.)

TOM: Do you know what Davy bragged he could do? Davy said, "I can outgrin anything. I can grin a raccoon right out of a tree."
ANNIE: Let's see you do it, Davy!
DAVY: (pointing up high) I spy a raccoon on that high branch. Watch me grin him down.

(Davy looks up into the tree and starts grinning until his cheeks get tired.)

TOM: It looks like that raccoon is ready to sit in the tree all day.
DAVY: (angry) That critter won't get the best of me! I'll chop down the tree!

(Davy chops down the tree and it lands on the ground. Davy, Tom, and Annie rush to inspect it.)

ANNIE: You weren't looking at a raccoon. It's just a knot in the wood.
DAVY: (looks uncomfortable) That varmint was just a knothole?
TOM: Wait a minute. The bark around the knothole is gone. You grinned the bark right off the tree!
DAVY: (looks proud) I told you I could outgrin anything!

1. What is the setting of this play?

_____

2. What message about Davy Crockett does the author want readers to know?

_____

3. How does Davy feel when the raccoon doesn't come out of the tree?
How do you know?

_____

© Pearson Education, Inc., 4

Vocabulary

Directions Draw a line to connect the word on the left with its meaning on the right.

1. backdrop	a great plenty	
2. grazed	a long period of dry weather	
3. shock	to feed on grass	
4. abundance	something that suddenly upsets you	
5. drought	curtain at the back of a stage	

**Check the Words
You Know**

___ **abundance**
___ **backdrop**
___ **ceremonial**
___ **drought**
___ **grazed**
___ **shock**

Directions Choose the word from the box that best completes each sentence.

6. In the summer, the cattle _____ on grass all day long.

7. Due to the long _____, many crops wilted under the Texas sun.

8. The ranchers were in _____ at the thought of losing their herds.

9. Finally there was rain, and the harvest yielded an _____.

10. The villagers celebrated with a _____ dance.

Write a News Report

Imagine you are a reporter for a newspaper. On a separate sheet of paper, write a news report about a farm or ranching community that is struggling with a drought. Use as many of the vocabulary words as you can.

Home Activity Your child identified and used vocabulary words from *A Gift from the Heart*. With your child, write a story about a time of economic or agricultural hardship. Use vocabulary words from the story.

© Pearson Education, Inc., 4

Quotations and Quotation Marks

A speaker's exact words are called a quotation. When you write a quotation, use quotation marks (" ") at the beginning and end of the speaker's words. Begin the quotation with a capital letter. Use a comma in a direct quotation as follows:

- If the quotation comes last in a sentence, use a comma to separate it from the rest of the sentence: Wise Eagle said, "Mother Earth continued to sacrifice for us."

- If the quotation comes first, use a comma, question mark, or exclamation mark to separate the quotation from the rest of the sentence: "Who will make a sacrifice?" asked the Chanters.

- Place the end punctuation mark of a quotation before closing the quotation mark: Wise Eagle asked, "Who will help the Little One?"

Directions Underline the sentence in each pair in which quotation marks are used correctly.

1. "This doll is all I have left from my family," said Little One.

"This doll is all I have left from my family", said Little One.

2. "This is my favorite blanket!" Stargazer exclaimed.

"This is my favorite blanket," Stargazer exclaimed!

Directions Rewrite the sentence. Add quotation marks and other correct punctuation.

3. How will we play Great Spirit's favorite songs asked Bluebird.

_____

_____

Home Activity Your child learned about quotations and quotation marks. Ask your child to create a larger-than-life set of quotation marks using raisins, peanuts, or breath mints. Have him or her explain to you what the marks are used for. Have your child print lines of dialog and place the big quotation marks to demonstrate where they would go.

© Pearson Education, Inc., 4

Suffixes *-ful*, *-ly*, *-ion*

Spelling Words				
careful	tasteful	lonely	powerful	suggestion
peaceful	recently	extremely	certainly	wisely
harmful	monthly	yearly	successful	playful
thoughtful	actually	pollution	correction	eagerly

Rhymes Complete each sentence with a list word that rhymes with the underlined word.

1. When you have <u>only</u> one friend, sometimes you'll be ____.   1. _____

2. Recycling is one <u>solution</u> to the problem of ____.   2. _____

3. He spends other people's money ____ but his own <u>meagerly</u>.   3. _____

4. Reporters write <u>factually</u> but ____ make mistakes.   4. _____

5. I love my great aunt <u>dearly</u>, but I only see her ____.   5. _____

6. If you can handle times that are <u>stressful</u>, you will be ____.   6. _____

7. Toys by the <u>trayful</u> can make you feel ____.   7. _____

8. To my <u>recollection</u>, my homework required no ____.   8. _____

9. Our new puppy ____ started to behave <u>decently</u>.   9. _____

10. Thorns by the <u>armful</u> are bound to be ____.   10. _____

11. He asked me a <u>question</u> so I made a ____.   11. _____

12. Did you buy something ____, or were you just <u>wasteful</u>?   12. _____

Antonyms Write the list word that has the opposite meaning of the underlined word.

13. That was very <u>inconsiderate</u> of you.   13. _____

14. You must be <u>reckless</u> when hiking.   14. _____

15. Presidents are <u>helpless</u> leaders.   15. _____

16. The <u>warlike</u> koala is my favorite animal.   16. _____

17. He <u>foolishly</u> did not talk about others.   17. _____

18. I find my hobby <u>somewhat</u> interesting.   18. _____

19. <u>Failing</u> businesses have strong leadership.   19. _____

20. I <u>doubtfully</u> think I can go to the movies.   20. _____

© Pearson Education, Inc., 4

Home Activity Your child wrote words with suffixes *-ful*, *-ly*, and *-ion*. Take turns writing and saying the list words.

Story Sequence A

Title _____

Beginning

⬇

Middle

⬇

End

© Pearson Education, Inc., 4

Vocabulary: Context Clues

- When you read an unfamiliar word, look for **context clues.**
- The words and sentences around an unknown word can help you figure out a word's meaning.
- The author may include a definition, a synonym, or another clue to the word's meaning.

Directions Read the following passage about villagers experiencing a drought. Then answer the questions below. Look for context clues to help you figure out the meaning of any unfamiliar words.

> **Villager 1:** This is the worst drought I can remember. My well has gone dry.
> **Villager 2:** *(nodding)* The cattle have nothing to feed on. They grazed all they could.
> **Villager 1:** Have you been to the farmers' market in town? People walk around in shock, as if they didn't know what hit them.
>
> **Villager 2:** Can you blame them? Only six months ago, we had a time of abundance. The farmers had a plentiful harvest.
> **Villager 1:** Maybe it's time for us to leave the farming business altogether.
> **Villager 2:** *(shrugs)* I fear my cattle don't have that choice.

1. Is a *drought* a good or a bad thing? What clues from the story help answer this question?

_____

_____

2. What does the word *grazed* mean in this story? _____

_____

3. How does the context tell you what *abundance* means? _____

_____

4. Write a sentence that uses context clues to reveal the meaning of *shock.*

_____

_____

© Pearson Education, Inc., 4

Home Activity Your child used context clues to identify the meanings of unfamiliar words. Challenge your child to write a paragraph that includes context clues to reveal the meanings of difficult or unfamiliar words.

Online Manual

- A **manual** can be a book, or it can appear online. It contains instructions that tell how to do something. A manual usually has a table of contents, subject sections, photos or illustrations, a glossary, and an index.
- Online manuals are designed to help you locate information quickly, and they can be updated more often and more easily than manuals in book form.
- Manuals should be read carefully before attempting a procedure. They often have warnings about a procedure, explaining any danger involved.

Directions Study this page from an online manual.

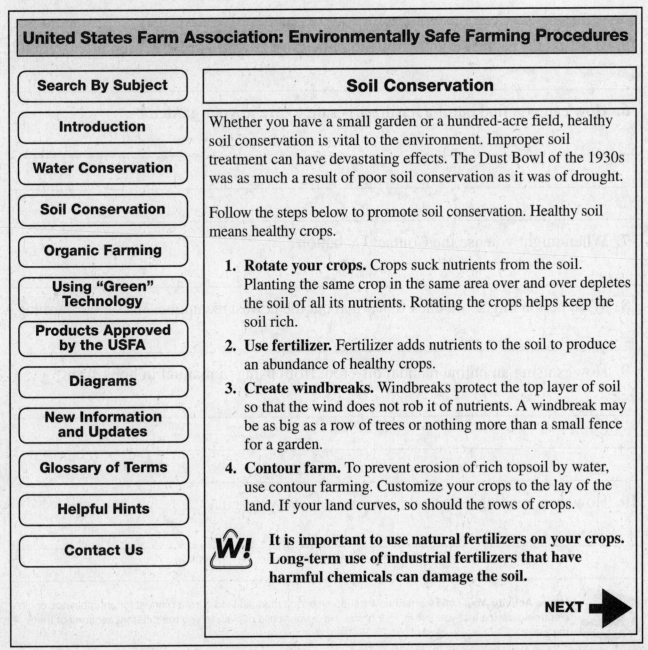

United States Farm Association: Environmentally Safe Farming Procedures

| Search By Subject |
| Introduction |
| Water Conservation |
| Soil Conservation |
| Organic Farming |
| Using "Green" Technology |
| Products Approved by the USFA |
| Diagrams |
| New Information and Updates |
| Glossary of Terms |
| Helpful Hints |
| Contact Us |

Soil Conservation

Whether you have a small garden or a hundred-acre field, healthy soil conservation is vital to the environment. Improper soil treatment can have devastating effects. The Dust Bowl of the 1930s was as much a result of poor soil conservation as it was of drought.

Follow the steps below to promote soil conservation. Healthy soil means healthy crops.

1. **Rotate your crops.** Crops suck nutrients from the soil. Planting the same crop in the same area over and over depletes the soil of all its nutrients. Rotating the crops helps keep the soil rich.
2. **Use fertilizer.** Fertilizer adds nutrients to the soil to produce an abundance of healthy crops.
3. **Create windbreaks.** Windbreaks protect the top layer of soil so that the wind does not rob it of nutrients. A windbreak may be as big as a row of trees or nothing more than a small fence for a garden.
4. **Contour farm.** To prevent erosion of rich topsoil by water, use contour farming. Customize your crops to the lay of the land. If your land curves, so should the rows of crops.

W! **It is important to use natural fertilizers on your crops. Long-term use of industrial fertilizers that have harmful chemicals can damage the soil.**

NEXT ➡

© Pearson Education, Inc., 4

Name _____

Directions Use the manual to answer the questions.

1. What is the manual for?

_____

2. Where could you click if you did not understand a word in the manual?

_____

3. Why would you use the Search By Subject button?

_____

4. What does the **W!** mean?

_____

5. What might happen if you grow the same crop in your garden season after season?

_____

6. How can you find out if a fertilizer is safe to use in your garden?

_____

_____

7. When might you use the Contact Us button?

_____

8. What button might you click to learn about the newest techniques in contour farming?

_____

9. How is using an online manual different from using a manual in book form?

_____

_____

10. How does reading a manual help you achieve your goal?

_____

_____

Home Activity Your child learned how to use an online manual. Find a print manual for an appliance or electronic device that you use in your home. Have your child explain to you the different sections of the manual.

© Pearson Education, Inc., 4

Suffixes *-ful*, *-ly*, *-ion*

Proofread an Article This short article needs to be corrected before it goes to the printer. Circle six misspelled words. Write the words correctly. Write the word with a capitalization error correctly.

© Pearson Education, Inc., 4

> A Healthy Vacation
>
> Have you ever considered going to a spa? Spas are especally common in europe. Spas are actually places to go to get healthier. People who go to them are extremly motivated to improve their health. Visitors begin by meeting with an expert for an exercise or diet suggestion. The experts wisly ask questions before making recommendations. The atmosphere in a spa is peacefull. The decorations are tastful. People learn to use their powerful self-discipline for exercise and diet. If the visit is succesful, they go home rested and relaxed and with the tools they need for a healthy, new lifestyle.

Spelling Words
careful
tasteful
lonely
powerful
suggestion
peaceful
recently
extremely
certainly
wisely
harmful
monthly
yearly
successful
playful
thoughtful
actually
pollution
correction
eagerly

1. _____   2. _____

3. _____   4. _____

5. _____   6. _____

7. _____

Proofread Words Circle the correct spelling. Write the correct list word on the line.

Frequently Misspelled Words
especially
really

8. egerly   eagerly   egerally   8. _____

9. suggestion   sugestion   suggesjun   9. _____

10. yerly   yearly   yearally   10. _____

11. sertinly   certinally   certainly   11. _____

12. playfull   playful   plaful   12. _____

Home Activity Your child identified misspelled words with the suffixes *-ful*, *-ly*, and *-ion*. Let your child dictate words for you to spell. Make some mistakes and let your child correct them.

Quotations and Quotation Marks

Directions Read the passage. Then read each question. Circle the letter of the correct answer.

The Sacrifice

(1) Little Buffalo said, It took me a long time to carve my drum." (2) "How will I defend our people? asked Shadow Hunter. (3) Who will make a sacrifice to the Great Spirit?" the Chanters asked. (4) Stargazer said This is my favorite blanket." (5) Hummingbird said, "Spirit gave us the gift of music." (6) "Should we toss our flutes in the fire?" asked Bluebird.

1 What change, if any, should be made in sentence 1?

   A Change *It* to **"It.**

   B Change *It* to **It's.**

   C Change *It* to **Little Buffalo.**

   D Make no change.

2 What change, if any, should be made in sentence 2?

   A Change *people?* to **people,"**

   B Change *people?* to **people."**

   C Change *people?* to **people?"**

   D Make no change.

3 What change, if any, should be made in sentence 3?

   A Change *Who* to **"who.**

   B Change *Who* to **"Who.**

   C Change *Who* to **Whom.**

   D Make no change.

4 What change, if any, should be made in sentence 4?

   A Change *said This* to **said, "This.**

   B Change *said This* to **said this,"**

   C Change *said This* to **said" this.**

   D Make no change.

5 What change, if any, should be made in sentence 6?

   A Change *fire?"* to **fire."**

   B Change *fire?"* to **fire"**

   C Change *fire?"* to **fire?**

   D Make no change.

© Pearson Education, Inc., 4

Home Activity Your child prepared for taking tests on quotations and quotation marks. Read your child a part of a story that includes dialog. Ask your child to tell you where the quotation marks should go.

Graphic Sources

- A **graphic source** of information is something that shows information visually.
- Looking at graphic sources before you read will help you see what the text is about. Looking at them again during reading will help you understand the text.

Directions Study the following graphic source. Then answer the questions below.

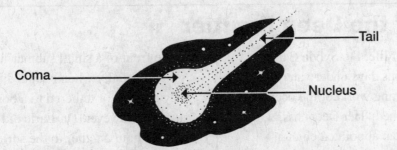

The Parts of a Comet

The comet is made up of three parts. Ice, gases, rocks, and dust form the *nucleus.* More dust and gases create the *coma,* or cloud, that surrounds the nucleus. The nucleus and the coma create the comet's head. Finally, the *tail* is the result of the dust and gases that are spread by solar winds.

1. What does this graphic source show you?

_____

2. What type of article might include this graphic source?

_____

_____

3. Which parts make up the head of the comet?

_____

4. Describe the coma of a comet.

_____

5. How does the diagram help you to understand the information in the caption?

_____

Home Activity Your child used a graphic source to answer questions about a text. Find an article that contains a graphic source in a newspaper or magazine. Have your child look at the graphic source before and during reading. Together, talk about how the graphic source makes the text more understandable.

© Pearson Education, Inc., 4

Writing • Narrative Nonfiction

Key Features of Narrative Nonfiction

- tells about a true event
- includes important details
- is often told in the order in which events occurred

Queen of the Deep Frontier

Throughout her life, Dr. Sylvia Earle spent numerous days underwater exploring the exciting world of the oceans. Dr. Earle, nicknamed "Her Deepness," was the first woman appointed chief at the National Oceanic and Atmospheric Administration of the United States. However, Dr. Earle is probably best known for the record she set on the day she stood alone on the floor of the Pacific Ocean.

Dr. Earle's most famous dive took place in 1979 off the coast of the Hawaii. Before she entered the water, Dr. Earle had to get into a protective diving suit called a Jim Suit. Like the suits astronauts wear, the Jim Suit protected Dr. Earle and provided air and normal temperature. Dr. Earle made her voyage to the bottom strapped to the front of a small submarine named *Star II*. Usually when people dive deep, they are tied or tethered to a boat on the surface. However, Dr. Earle did her deep dive without a tether to the surface. This made the dive even more dangerous than others. When she finally reached the bottom, she had only a short tether to *Star II*. Dr. Earle spent the next 2½ hours walking along the ocean floor gazing at amazing sea creatures such as flashing fish and glowing coral. At last, it was time to return to the surface. The *Star II* lifted Dr. Earle from the ocean floor, where she had set the record for the deepest dive (1,250 feet, or 381 meters) without a tether to the surface. The record she set still stands today.

Reread the selection. Answer the questions with important details from the text.

1. Who is this narrative nonfiction account about?

_____

2. What was the real event described in this account?

_____

3. Where did the event happen?

_____

4. When did the event happen? _____

© Pearson Education, Inc., 4

Vocabulary

Directions Choose the word from the box that best matches each definition. Write the word on the line.

_____ 1. the line where the Earth and sky seem to meet

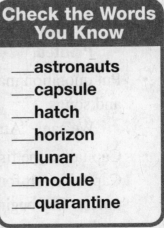

Check the Words You Know

___astronauts
___capsule
___hatch
___horizon
___lunar
___module
___quarantine

_____ 2. a self-contained unit within a larger system

_____ 3. the enclosed front section of a rocket

_____ 4. of, like, or about the moon

_____ 5. isolation to prevent the spread of an infectious disease

Directions Circle the word or words that have the same or nearly the same meaning as the first word in each group.

6. **horizon**	skyline	sunset	sphere
7. **capsule**	train	ship	pod
8. **astronauts**	waiters	teachers	space crew
9. **quarantine**	freedom	isolation	disease
10. **hatch**	trapdoor	closet	cabinet

Write a Story

On a separate sheet of paper, write a story about traveling in space. Describe what you see and do during the journey. Include as many vocabulary words as you can.

Home Activity Your child identified and used vocabulary words from *The Man Who Went to the Far Side of the Moon*. With your child, read an article about space or space exploration. Discuss the article, using the vocabulary words from this selection.

© Pearson Education, Inc., 4

Titles

> - In your writing, underline the **titles** of books, magazines, and newspapers. When these titles appear in printed material, they are set in italic type.
>   **Handwritten**   <u>New York Times</u>, <u>Time</u>, <u>Stuart Little</u>
>   **Printed**   *New York Times, Time, Stuart Little*
> - Put quotation marks around the titles of stories, poems, magazine articles, and songs.
>   We sang "America," and Ms. Collins recited "If."
> - Capitalize the first word, the last word, and other important words in titles. Capitalize all forms of the verb *be*. Do not capitalize the following short words unless they begin or end a title: the articles *a, an,* and *the;* the conjunctions *and, but,* and *or;* and prepositions with fewer than five letters, such as *to, for, in, of, on, at,* or *with.*
>   "I Was with Washington at Valley Forge"   *Toronto Globe and Mail*

Directions Write the title in each sentence.

1. Our class is making a book called *Getting Creative.*

_____

2. Tori contributed a poem called "Total Eclipse."

_____

Directions Correct any mistake in capitalization in the title. Write *Correct* if the title has no errors.

3. *The Lord of the Rings*

_____

4. *When we were Very Young*

_____

Home Activity Your child learned about titles. Look at titles of books, magazines, or newspaper articles in your house. Ask your child to explain why some words begin with capital letters and some don't.

© Pearson Education, Inc., 4

Silent Consonants

Spelling Words				
island	column	knee	often	known
castle	thumb	half	wring	whistle
autumn	knuckles	numb	Illinois	rhyme
climber	limb	plumbing	unwritten	clothes

Missing Words Write a list word to complete each familiar saying.

1. "To go out on a _____" means to take a chance.

2. "A rule of _____" is something that is generally true.

3. To "wet your _____" means to take a drink.

4. "A _____ jerk reaction" is a gut reaction or feeling.

5. "There's no _____ or reason" means it doesn't make sense.

6. If your "glass is _____ full" you always look on the bright side.

1. _____

2. _____

3. _____

4. _____

5. _____

6. _____

Complete Write a list word to complete each sentence.

7. The author's book is still _____.

8. We built a sand _____ at the beach.

9. I like to buy new _____.

10. Abraham Lincoln spent much of his life in Springfield, _____.

11. George Washington was _____ as a person who didn't lie.

12. Something you do all the time is an activity you do _____.

13. Without gloves, my fingers became _____ from the cold.

14. Apple harvests and colorful leaves are the nice things about ___.

15. Your _____ are the joints in your fingers.

16. Dip the sponge in water and _____ it dry.

17. When the pipes squeak, it may be time to get some new ___.

18. Hawaii is an _____ state.

19. The mountain _____ is very skilled.

20. The teacher wrote a long _____ of numbers for us to add.

7. _____

8. _____

9. _____

10. _____

11. _____

12. _____

13. _____

14. _____

15. _____

16. _____

17. _____

18. _____

19. _____

20. _____

Home Activity Your child wrote words that have silent consonants. Pronounce each list word incorrectly, saying the silent consonant as in *iz-land*. Have your child correct your pronunciation and spell the word.

© Pearson Education, Inc., 4

Scoring Rubric: Narrative Nonfiction

	4	3	2	1
Focus/Ideas	Clear narrative nonfiction account of a true event; includes important details	Mostly clear narrative nonfiction account of a true event; a few important details	Unfocused narrative nonfiction account; details are unimportant	Confusing and undeveloped narrative nonfiction account; no details
Organization	Events clearly described in time-order sequence	Organized in a mostly time-order sequence	Sequence isn't always clear	Lacks any logical order; events confused and jumbled
Voice	Writer is clearly involved; informative and entertaining	Writer makes a good effort to be informative	Writer not very involved with topic	Writer totally uninterested
Word Choice	Specific language; brings events to life	Words specific and occasionally colorful	Ordinary; sometimes vague word choice	Incorrect or confusing word choice
Sentences	Varied sentences; short, related sentences are combined	Some variety in sentences; few short, related sentences	Little variety in sentences; too many short, related sentences	Fragments or run-on sentences
Conventions	Accurate, no mistakes; correct use of commas; correctly written titles	Few mistakes; mostly correct use of commas; no errors in titles	A lot of mistakes; some errors in use of commas and in titles	Frequent mistakes that take away from understanding; too many errors

© Pearson Education, Inc., 4

Vocabulary • Multiple-Meaning Words

- **Multiple-meaning words** are words that are spelled the same but have different meanings.
- When you are reading you may run across words whose meanings you know, but whose meanings do not make sense in the sentence.

Directions Read the following passage. Then answer the questions below.

> Sandy Robinson, an astronaut, slipped through the hatch and into the capsule. She was ready for her mission—researching rocks on the moon. Two years ago, Sandy orbited the moon in a single-person module while other crew members walked on the moon's surface. Some people said it wasn't fair. This time,
>
> though, Sandy would walk on the moon herself.
>
> Sandy made sure she was ready. Then she lowered the landing gear safely on the surface of the moon. Sandy made sure her spacesuit was fitted properly. She could hardly bear the nervous feeling in her stomach. Then the door opened.

1. In this passage, what is the meaning of the multiple-meaning word *hatch?* How do you know? _____

_____

2. How do you know *fair* does not mean "a gathering of buyers and sellers"?

_____

3. What context clues help you understand the meaning of the word *spacesuit*?

_____

_____

4. Are the words *two, to,* and *too* multiple-meaning words? Why or why not?

_____

5. Explain why you believe that the word *bear* is—or is not—a multiple-meaning word. How could you learn if it is or not?

_____

_____

© Pearson Education, Inc., 4

Home Activity Your child used context clues to identify multiple-meaning words. Together, choose a handful of multiple-meaning words. Then write a poem that uses all the meanings of the multiple-meaning words.

Encyclopedia

An **encyclopedia** gives general information about many different subjects. The information in an encyclopedia is organized alphabetically by topic in a set of volumes, or books. An **entry** is the information on a particular topic. An entry begins with an **entry word** that names the topic. If you can't find an entry for a particular topic in an encyclopedia, you may need to think of another **key word** to help you locate the information.

Directions Read the encyclopedia entries below. Then answer the questions on the next page.

Entry 1

CONSTELLATION
A cluster of stars that seem to form a visual pattern in the sky. Many constellations were named long ago. Their names come from ancient myths. For example, the constellations Perseus and Orion were named for important people in myths, and other constellations were named for mythical animals like Cygnus the Swan and Leo the Lion. There are eighty-eight named constellations.

Some of the most famous star formations are part of larger star groups. For example, the Big Dipper is part of the larger constellation Ursa Major. Similarly, the Little Dipper is part of the constellation Ursa Minor.

See also entries for the following constellations: *Andromeda; Cygnus the Swan; Draco the Dragon; Hercules; Leo the Lion; Libra the Balance.*

Entry 2

MARS
A planet in our solar system. In terms of distance from the sun, Mars is the fourth planet. Mars is red, and at times appears to be very bright. The diameter of Mars is about half the size of the diameter of Earth. The atmosphere on Mars is made of carbon dioxide, argon, and nitrogen gases. The temperatures on the surface of the planet range from around 80 degrees Fahrenheit during the day to about –100 degrees Fahrenheit at night.

The surface of Mars looks like a desert, yet there are also craters, canyons, and volcanoes on it. The planet seems to experience a change of seasons. Scientists hold this view based on the fact that polar caps—made of ice or possibly dry ice— seem to shrink during certain times of the year. Scientists have not discovered any living things on Mars.

See also entries for *planet, solar system,* and *space.*

© Pearson Education, Inc., 4

Name _____

1. What is the entry word for Entry 1?

_____

2. If this encyclopedia contains twenty-six volumes (one volume for each letter of the alphabet), in which volume would you find Entry 1? Entry 2?

_____

3. How many constellations have been named?

_____

4. What color is Mars?

_____

5. Where do the names of the constellations come from?

_____

_____

6. If you wished to look at a chart comparing Mars to other planets, where might you look in this encyclopedia?

_____

_____

7. What are some of the physical features of Mars?

_____

8. In which larger star groups can you find the Big Dipper and the Little Dipper?

_____

9. Why does Entry 1 end with a suggestion to look also at six other entries?

_____

_____

10. Do you think it is important to use an encyclopedia with a recent date of publication? Why or why not?

_____

_____

Home Activity Your child used encyclopedia entries to answer questions. Look up an unfamiliar subject in a volume of an encyclopedia. After your child finds the entry word, have him or her read and summarize the entry for you.

© Pearson Education, Inc., 4

Silent Consonants

Proofread a Poster As a joke, Jack's pals made up this poster.
Circle seven words that are spelled incorrectly. Write the words
correctly. Circle a verb that does not agree with its subject, and
write the correct form of the verb.

Have you seen Illinoi Jack?

His sleeves covers his nuckles, and he always
has some chocolate in his pocket.

His cloths are full of patches, and he is as
pale as a gost.

Jack is known for his ability to rhyme and whisle.

He will fix your plumming when he is not
writing poems.

Jack is offen seen with his pet calf, Nellie.

1. _____   2. _____
3. _____   4. _____
5. _____   6. _____
7. _____   8. _____

Spelling Words
island
column
knee
often
known
castle
thumb
half
wring
whistle
autumn
knuckles
numb
Illinois
rhyme
climber
limb
plumbing
unwritten
clothes

Complete the Word Each word below has a missing letter.
Write the complete word on the line.

9. autum _____   10. iland _____
11. haf _____   12. casle _____
13. colum _____   14. num _____
15. thum _____   16. lim _____
17. climer _____   18. nee _____
19. nown _____   20. Chrismas _____

**Frequently
Misspelled
Words**

Christmas
chocolate
would

Home Activity Your child identified misspelled words with silent consonants. Have your child find three
words with silent *k* and make up a rule about when *k* is silent.

© Pearson Education, Inc., 4

Titles

Directions Read the passage. Then read each question. Circle the letter of the correct answer.

Reading Matters

(1) My dad's favorite book is news of the century. (2) I used to get a magazine called <u>Highlights for Children</u>. (3) One article called you can be a writer was interesting. (4) It also had a poem I learned called sunrise and sunset. (5) Sometimes it has the words to songs such as my darlin' clementine.

1 What change, if any, should be made in sentence 1?

  A Change *news of the century* to <u>**News of the Century**</u>.

  B Change *news of the century* to "**News of the Century.**"

  C Change *news of the century* to <u>**News of the century**</u>.

  D Make no change.

2 What change, if any, should be made in sentence 3?

  A Change *you can be a writer* to "**You Can Be a Writer.**"

  B Change *you can be a writer* to "**You Can be a Writer.**"

  C Change *you can be a writer* to <u>**You Can be a Writer**</u>.

  D Make no change.

3 What change, if any, should be made in sentence 4?

  A Change *sunrise and sunset* to "**Sunrise and Sunset.**"

  B Change *sunrise and sunset* to <u>**Sunrise and sunset**</u>.

  C Change *sunrise and sunset* to <u>**Sunrise and Sunset**</u>.

  D Make no change.

4 What change, if any, should be made in sentence 5?

  A Change *my darlin' clementine* to "**My Darlin' Clementine.**"

  B Change *my darlin' clementine* to "**My Darling Clementine.**"

  C Change *my darlin' clementine* to <u>**My Darlin' Clementine**</u>.

  D Make no change.

© Pearson Education, Inc., 4

Home Activity Your child prepared for taking tests on titles, using correct capitalization, and underlining or using quotation marks. Read your child a list of book titles, magazine titles, articles, and song titles. Have your child explain which titles should be underlined, which are to be in quotation marks, and what is the proper capitalization for each.

Schwa

Spelling Words				
stomach	memory	Canada	element	mystery
science	remember	forget	suppose	iron
gravel	difficult	fortune	giant	architect
normal	notify	privilege	cement	yesterday

Words in Context Write a list word to complete each sentence.

1. Voting is an American's basic _____.
2. Grandpa's _____ of World War II is clear.
3. The _____ of this building did a great job.
4. What happened to the Roanoke colony is a _____.
5. It is difficult to walk on a _____ road barefoot.
6. The post office will _____ you when the package comes.
7. She made a _____ by starting an Internet company.
8. My _____ pumpkin won first prize at the county fair.
9. It is warmer today than it was _____.
10. _____ lies on the northern border of the United States.

1. _____
2. _____
3. _____
4. _____
5. _____
6. _____
7. _____
8. _____
9. _____
10. _____

Word Meanings Write the list word beside its definition.

11. pouch in digestive system for receiving food
12. a substance made up of atoms that are alike
13. to bring back to mind
14. to imagine, think, or guess
15. a metallic element used to make steel
16. to fail to remember
17. hard to do or understand
18. a substance used to make concrete
19. average; agreeing with the usual standard
20. knowledge gained by observation and experiment

11. _____
12. _____
13. _____
14. _____
15. _____
16. _____
17. _____
18. _____
19. _____
20. _____

© Pearson Education, Inc., 4

 Home Activity Your child learned words that contain the schwa sound. Write each word, leaving a blank for the letter with the schwa sound. Have your child complete each word.

Conjunctions

Directions Circle the coordinating conjunction in each sentence.

1. People from Europe and Africa settled in North America.

2. Most Europeans were free, but most Africans arrived in chains.

3. White people farmed and traded freely.

4. Africans were enslaved workers on farms and in cities.

5. Many people protested this injustice, but change was slow to come.

6. Would America take the path of freedom or of slavery?

Directions Use the coordinating conjunction *and, but,* or *or* to join each pair of sentences. Write the new sentences. Remember to add a comma.

7. The Civil War ended slavery. African Americans were set free.

_____

_____

8. It seemed that society had changed. New laws soon oppressed the freed slaves.

_____

_____

9. African Americans were free. They were still treated like slaves.

_____

_____

10. They must accept these cruel laws. They would suffer harsh punishment.

_____

_____

© Pearson Education, Inc., 4

Prefixes *mis-, non-, re-, pre-*

Spelling Words				
misplace	nonsense	prepay	repack	misfortune
remove	precook	nonstop	recover	reseal
misbehavior	reunion	nonfiction	rebound	prejudge
readjust	misprint	nonprofit	nonstick	precaution

Word Meanings Write the list word beside its meaning.

1. bad luck

2. to arrange again to make fit

3. gathering of people who have been apart

4. silliness; gibberish

5. bad conduct

6. to take away

7. to prepare food in advance

8. to bounce back

9. to judge too early

10. to get back after losing

1. _____

2. _____

3. _____

4. _____

5. _____

6. _____

7. _____

8. _____

9. _____

10. _____

Analogies Write the list word that best completes the sentence.

11. Praise is to criticize as find is to _____.

12. Haiku is to poetry as biography is to _____.

13. View is to preview as pay is to _____.

14. Plan is to preplan as caution is to _____.

15. Jet is to airplane as direct is to _____.

16. Corporate is to profit as volunteer is to _____.

17. Fact checker is to error as proofreader is to _____.

18. Pavement is to road as _____ is to pots and pans.

19. Open is to close as unwrap is to _____.

20. Load is to unload as unpack is to _____.

11. _____

12. _____

13. _____

14. _____

15. _____

16. _____

17. _____

18. _____

19. _____

20. _____

© Pearson Education, Inc., 4

Home Activity Your child learned words with the prefixes *mis-, non-, re-* and *pre-*. Write each list word without its prefix. Write the prefixes in bold on sticky notes. Have your child add prefixes to spell each list word.

Capitalization and Abbreviations

Direction Rewrite each sentence using correct capitalization.

1. Both london and new york city wanted to host the 2012 olympics.

_____

_____

2. find out more from different united states olympic organizations.

_____

_____

3. andy warner and i went to a training center for olympic athletes.

_____

_____

4. andy's father, mr. warner, drove us there one saturday last august.

_____

_____

5. The center's address is 1 olympic place, colorado springs, colorado.

_____

_____

Directions Write *C* if the group of words is capitalized correctly. If the group of words is capitalized incorrectly, rewrite it using correct capitalization.

6. *Sports illustrated* _____

7. august 17, 2012 _____

8. coach Mario Tartini _____

9. *San francisco Chronicle* _____

10. mayor Michael r. Bloomberg _____

11. a young man from Idaho _____

12. New York, Ny _____

© Pearson Education, Inc., 4

Suffixes *-less*, *-ment*, *-ness*

Spelling Words				
countless	payment	goodness	fairness	hopeless
treatment	statement	breathless	restless	enjoyment
pavement	flawless	tireless	amazement	amusement
greatness	punishment	timeless	needless	painless

Word Search Circle the list words in the puzzle.

```
P  A  Y  M  E  N  T  Y  B  T  W  P  C
G  A  M  A  Z  E  M  E  N  T  F  S  O
O  E  O  E  I  U  A  E  B  E  A  S  U
O  S  T  A  T  E  M  E  N  T  I  E  N
D  I  A  B  C  H  U  X  Z  E  R  N  T
N  K  L  B  S  X  S  J  M  H  N  T  L
E  C  A  I  O  R  E  R  D  O  E  A  E
S  R  N  F  V  P  M  A  L  P  S  E  S
S  U  R  H  O  P  E  L  E  S  S  R  S
P  B  W  E  D  Q  N  T  C  L  H  G  H
H  A  K  R  V  R  T  C  A  E  L  E  N
```

payment
statement
goodness
punishment
countless
amazement
amusement
hopeless
fairness
greatness

Words in Context Write a list word to complete each sentence.

1. The dress has a _____ quality. It won't go out of style.
2. The workers put new _____ on the road.
3. Running the long race made me tired and _____.
4. I love good books and often read for _____.
5. The doctor prescribed a _____ for my ear infection.
6. Teeth cleaning is _____. It doesn't hurt at all!
7. The firefighters were _____. They did not rest.
8. I was _____ and could barely sleep. I was too excited!
9. The perfect diamond in Lucy's wedding ring was _____.
10. It's _____ to wash the floor again. Dad did it yesterday.

1. _____
2. _____
3. _____
4. _____
5. _____
6. _____
7. _____
8. _____
9. _____
10. _____

School + Home **Home Activity** Your child learned words with the suffixes *-less*, *-ment*, and *-ness*. Read a magazine article with your child and locate more words with these suffixes.

© Pearson Education, Inc., 4

Commas

Directions Write *C* if commas are used correctly in the sentence. If commas are not used correctly, add them where they belong.

1. Our team has a game on Friday May 2. _____

2. We play in Columbus, Ohio. _____

3. The Tigers, the Spartans and the Browns are also in our league. _____

4. I'll be playing shortstop first base, or third base. _____

5. The address is Seymour Drive Columbus, Ohio 43235. _____

6. Well I sure hope you can make it. _____

Directions Write the sentences. Add commas as needed.

7. Jim's uncle lived on Torrance Avenue in Brooklyn New York.

_____

_____

8. Jim's tenth birthday was Tuesday April 23 2005.

_____

_____

9. He arrived at his uncle's house feeling happy excited and curious.

_____

_____

10. His uncle said "Jim I've got tickets for the Yankees game."

_____

_____

© Pearson Education, Inc., 4

Suffixes *-ful*, *-ly*, *-ion*

Spelling Words				
careful	tasteful	lonely	powerful	suggestion
peaceful	recently	extremely	certainly	wisely
harmful	monthly	yearly	successful	playful
thoughtful	actually	pollution	correction	eagerly

Synonyms Write the list word that has the same, or nearly the same, meaning as the word.

1. cautious _____
2. calm _____
3. light-hearted _____
4. strong _____
5. damaging _____
6. deserted _____
7. sensibly _____
8. really _____

Words in Context Write a list word from the box to complete each sentence.

9. We waited _____ for summer vacation to begin.
10. A _____ person considers the feelings of others.
11. A _____ note to the winner shows good sportsmanship.
12. I have a _____ for how to improve crowding in schools.
13. Most families pay their bills _____.
14. Prices have gone up a lot _____.
15. Mom was _____ angry when we lied about our grades.
16. An egg dropped seven stories will _____ break.
17. If you ask politely, you are more likely to be _____.
18. The Nobel Prizes are awarded _____ in the fall.
19. _____ poisons our air and water.
20. The teacher pointed out a _____ that was needed.

9. _____
10. _____
11. _____
12. _____
13. _____
14. _____
15. _____
16. _____
17. _____
18. _____
19. _____
20. _____

© Pearson Education, Inc., 4

 School + Home **Home Activity** Your child learned words with the suffixes *-ful*, *-ly*, and *-ion*. Have your child pick ten list words. Together write a story about your family using the words.

Quotations and Quotation Marks

Directions Underline the sentence in each pair in which quotation marks are used correctly.

1. The Chanters asked, "Great Spirit! Why do you ignore our calls for help?"

   The Chanters asked, Great Spirit! "Why do you ignore our calls for help?"

2. Three times the Chanters asked, Who will make a sacrifice to the Great Spirit?"

   Three times the Chanters asked, "Who will make a sacrifice to the Great Spirit?"

3. "Without water, nothing will grow," Little One told her doll.

   "Without water, nothing will grow, Little One," told her doll.

4. "Wise Eagle heard Great Spirit's words, you took many gifts from Mother Earth.

   Wise Eagle heard Great Spirit's words, "You took many gifts from Mother Earth."

5. "The blue flowers are a special gift from the Great Spirit," said Wise Eagle.

   The blue flowers are a special gift from the Great Spirit, said Wise Eagle.

Directions Rewrite each sentence. Add quotation marks and other correct punctuation.

6. The Earth is alive again the narrator exclaimed

   _____

   _____

7. Wise Eagle said we'll call the new flowers bluebonnets

   _____

   _____

8. Little One, I saw the sacrifice you made said Wise Eagle

   _____

   _____

© Pearson Education, Inc., 4

Silent Consonants

Spelling Words

island	column	knee	often	known
castle	thumb	half	wring	whistle
autumn	knuckles	numb	Illinois	rhyme
climber	limb	plumbing	unwritten	clothes

Classifying Write the list word that fits each group.

1. princess, knight, dragon, _____   1. _____
2. hip, ankle, wrist, _____   2. _____
3. Ohio, Iowa, Nebraska, _____   3. _____
4. twist, squeeze, mangle, _____   4. _____
5. winter, spring, summer, _____   5. _____
6. pinky, toe, index, _____   6. _____
7. sing, hum, warble, _____   7. _____
8. trunk, roots, leaves, _____   8. _____
9. rhythm, metaphor, alliteration, _____   9. _____
10. coats, blouses, pants, _____   10. _____

Word Scramble Unscramble the list words and write the letters on the lines.

11. dinlas   _____   16. snukklec   _____
12. monclu   _____   17. bmnu   _____
13. fonet   _____   18. crimelb   _____
14. wonnk   _____   19. blingmup   _____
15. flah   _____   20. twinnerut   _____

 School + Home

Home Activity Your child learned words with silent consonants. Say each word and have your child name its silent letter.

© Pearson Education, Inc., 4

Titles

Directions Put a check mark by the sentence in each pair that has the title written correctly.

1. _____ My grandmother used to sing a song called "Catch a Falling Star."

   _____ My grandmother used to sing a song called *Catch a Falling Star*.

2. _____ My aunt subscribes to "Better Homes and Gardens" magazine.

   _____ My aunt subscribes to *Better Homes and Gardens* magazine.

3. _____ We bought a book called *Teaching Your Puppy to Behave*.

   _____ We bought a book called "Teaching Your Puppy to Behave."

4. _____ "Things That go Bump In the Night" is a funny poem.

   _____ "Things That Go Bump in the Night" is a funny poem.

5. _____ *The Springfield Argus And courier*, our local newspaper, published my story.

   _____ *The Springfield Argus and Courier*, our local newspaper, published my story.

Directions Write the following titles correctly. The words in ( ) tell you what they are.

6. boston herald (newspaper)

   _____

7. my bonny lies over the ocean (song)

   _____

8. where the wild things are (book)

   _____

9. healthy eating and living (magazine)

   _____

10. the best computer games of the year (article)

    _____

© Pearson Education, Inc., 4

KWL Chart

Directions Fill out this KWL chart to help you organize your ideas.

Topic _____

What I **K**now	What I **W**ant to Know	What I **L**earned

Controlling Question _____

_____

© Pearson Education, Inc., 4

Topic and Detail Sentences

Directions Decide how you will organize your paragraphs. Then write a topic sentence and supporting details for each paragraph.

Paragraph 1
Topic Sentence _____

_____

Detail Sentences _____

_____

_____

Paragraph 2
Topic Sentence _____

_____

Detail Sentences _____

_____

_____

_____

Paragraph 3
Topic Sentence _____

_____

Detail Sentences _____

_____

_____

_____

Paragraph 4
Topic Sentence _____

_____

Detail Sentences _____

_____

_____

_____

© Pearson Education, Inc., 4

Combining Sentences

When you write, you can combine short, choppy sentences into one longer sentence. You can make compound sentences by joining sentences with the conjunctions *and, but,* and *or.* You can make complex sentences by joining sentences with words such as *when, because,* and *if.*

Directions Use the words in ( ) to combine the sentences. Remember to capitalize the first word of each new sentence and replace the first period with a comma.

1. (because) Dolphins are intelligent. They learn quickly.

_____

_____

2. (and) They do tricks. They entertain audiences.

_____

_____

3. (but) Dolphins can hear well. They have no sense of smell.

_____

_____

4. (when) Dolphins communicate. They use a sonar system.

_____

_____

5. (or) See them at the aquarium. You can read about them at the library.

_____

_____

© Pearson Education, Inc., 4

Editing 3

Directions Edit this paragraph. Look for errors in spelling, grammar, and mechanics. Use proofreading marks to show the corrections.

Proofreading Marks	
Delete (Take out)	⸺ꝗ
Add	∧
Spelling	◯
Uppercase letter	≡
Lowercase letter	/

The South China tiger is in trouble. It is listed as one of the most endanjered

species in the world. Some of the reasons for this is pollution, lack of food and

destruction of forests hunters are also a problem. In 1977, china past a law making

it a crime to hunt or kill these animals. However hunting continued, since many

people beleived that the tigers were dangerous. Today their are about 60 south

China tigers in zoos, and no one have seen these tigers in the wild for more then

30 years. According to BBC News, a farmer claim to have seen one of the tigers

on October, 3 2007. He had pictures but they were proven to be fakes.

Now you'll edit the draft of your research report. Then you'll use your revised and
edited draft to make a final copy of your report. Finally, you'll share your written work
with your audience.

© Pearson Education, Inc., 4